WHAT PEOPLE ARE SAYING ABOUT
THE JESUS-HEARTED WOMAN

· · · · · · · · · · ·

"If you want to live for something that will outlast your life, *The Jesus-Hearted Woman* is for you! Jodi Detrick skillfully weaves biblical truth, real-time examples, and coaching principles throughout every chapter in a way that challenges the mind and heart of the reader to make intentional choices that produce mature Christian leaders. Whether you are a seasoned ministry leader or a new Christian who longs to make a difference, this book is for you. Buy one copy for yourself and another for the woman you are mentoring."

—CAROL KENT
Speaker and Author
Becoming a Woman of Influence (NavPress)
www.SpeakUpConference.com

"Jodi's easy-reading style of writing makes this book a pleasure to read, yet the depth of the content will challenge the most seasoned leader. She skillfully encourages women in ministry leadership to grow in ten qualities—like authenticity, resilience, courage, and self-care. Each chapter is full of practical, biblical advice. Jodi's 'gracious confidence' shines through every chapter, absolutely inspiring us to be true Jesus-hearted women! I love this book and its author!"

—KERRY CLARENSAU
Director of National Women's Ministries, Assemblies of God, author *Secrets: Finding Love and Happiness in Your Marriage* and *Love Revealed*

"The skillful unpacking of life-transforming leadership principles in *The Jesus-Hearted Woman* will infuse you with creative energy, as well as strength to lead and last! Jodi's compelling approach is personal and flows from a depth of wisdom. A fresh new vision will bubble up as you encounter God's blueprint for leadership in this work of art. *The Jesus-Hearted Woman* is a must-read for any twenty-first century female who desires to excel as an authentic, confident, and powerful leader. I guarantee your life will be radically transformed!"

—DR. AVA OLESON
Doctor of Ministry Program Coordinator, Adjunct Professor,
Assemblies of God Theological Seminary

"*The Jesus-Hearted Woman* is a fresh, insightful word about leaders and leadership that raises the bar while it offers practical and reasonable steps to forward movement! Jodi walks us into the realities and reasons for leadership, and keeps the mandates of Christ before us all. The powerful coaching questions are insightful and meaningful tools to those struggling with or in leadership. This book is written for women, but it's a powerful word for us all! Keep writing Jodi!"

—EDWARD HAMMETT, PCC
Church and Clergy Coach, Author of
Reaching People Under 40 While Keeping People Over 60

"It is encouraging to see women begin to regain their collective voice in the twenty-first century church. *The Jesus-Hearted Woman* is a significant contribution to that end. Jodi Detrick is a skilled and transparently engaging writer who lives deeply, takes leadership risks, and gives her life to forming other women into

Jesus-like leaders. This book is the overflow. It is an honor to recommend this highly significant work to you."

—DR. JAMES BRADFORD
General Secretary,
The General Council of the Assemblies of God

"Jodi brings a unique perspective to women's leadership after many years of ministry. She captures the biblical basis for women to lead themselves and others. Jodi's coaching background also adds a dimension that provides tools to mine the incredible influence all women have in their homes, communities, churches, and workplaces."

—FRAN LAMATTINA
Leadership Coach, Strategies for Greatness,
Former Director of Women's Community Groups at
North Point Community Church, Alpharetta, Georgia

"In *The Jesus-Hearted Woman,* Jodi Detrick paints a picture of a woman who influences all those around her for the Kingdom of God. Jodi's clear message, writing style, and transparency will convince you that you, too, can be that woman! Enjoy this book for yourself and give it to those you influence!"

—PHYLLIS H. HENDRY
President and Chief Executive Officer, Lead Like Jesus

"*The Jesus-Hearted Woman* is a refreshing, rare resource for women in leadership who hunger to lead like Jesus in our complex twenty-first century world. Jodi Detrick is a gifted and engaging writer who grapples honestly with the spiritual and practical challenges women leaders face—both internally and externally. Integrating rich biblical truth, diverse resources, and everyday life stories, Detrick inspires, stirs our souls, makes us wince, and spurs us on to Jesus-hearted leadership with hope and delightful humor. What a great resource in leadership development for individual women leaders, small groups, and coaching for women ministers!"

—DR. BETH GRANT
Co-founder and Co-director of Project Rescue,
Missionary, Educator

"Jodi Detrick has the gift for creating an elegant tapestry with her writing. A lilting style graced by personal experience leads us to biblical truth and leadership principles that are inviting, convicting, and doable. *The Jesus-Hearted Woman* is a mirror image of the author. Women will read it, and men should read it."

—DR. DAVID MCKENNA
Author and former President of Spring Arbor University,
Seattle Pacific University, and Asbury Theological Seminary

The Jesus-Hearted Woman: 10 Leadership Qualities for Enduring & Endearing Influence is now on my highly-recommended list of leadership books for both experienced and emerging leaders. A gifted and skilled writer, Jodi Detrick masterfully weaves great literature, personal and biblical narratives, and insights drawn from her reflections on some of the best writing blended with her own unexpected journey in leadership. Her concluding coaching questions, scriptural passages, and little lessons for new leaders at the end of each chapter provide a great opportunity to pause and reflect on how to embody each of the ten leadership qualities she presents. This is a great book for both men and women!

—CAROL A. TAYLOR, PHD
President of Vanguard University

THE JESUS-HEARTED WOMAN

10 LEADERSHIP QUALITIES FOR
ENDURING & ENDEARING INFLUENCE

· · · · · · · · · · ·

Jodi Detrick

Foreword by Joanna Weaver

Published by Influence Resources
1445 North Boonville Avenue
Springfield, Missouri 65802

Published in association with The Quadrivium Group—Orlando, Florida
info@TheQuadriviumGroup.com

Cover design by Keith Locke (www.KeithLocke.com)
Interior design by Prodigy Pixel (www.ProdigyPixel.com)

Unless otherwise specified, Scripture quotations used in this book are from The Holy Bible, New International Version®. NIV®. Copyright © 1973, 1978, 1984 by the International Bible Society. Used by permission of Zondervan Publishing House.
Scripture quotations marked (MSG) are taken from The Message, copyright © by Eugene H. Peterson 1993, 1994, 1995, 1996, 2000, 2001, 2002. Used by permission of NavPress Publishing Group.
Scripture quotations marked (NLT) are taken from the Holy Bible, New Living Translation, copyright © 1996, 2004, 2007 by Tyndale House Foundation. Used by permission of Tyndale House Publishers, Inc., Carol Stream, Illinois 60188. All rights reserved.
Scripture quotations marked (NKJV) are taken from The New King James version®.
© 1982 by Thomas Nelson, Inc. Used by permission. All rights reserved.
Scripture quotations marked (KJV) are taken from the King James Version of the Bible.
Scripture quotations marked (ESV) are taken from the english standard version.
© 2001 by Crossway Bibles, a division of Good News Publishers.

ISBN: 978-1-93783-055-7
Printed in the United States of America
17 16 15 14 ● 3 4 5 6

．　．　．　．　．　．　．　．　．　．　．

This book is dedicated to my kind, courageous, and adventuresome mother, Louise Lankford Dunlap, the first Jesus-hearted woman in my life and still one of the most remarkable. Thanks for your life-long example of "doing what you can where you are" and for passing on the writing bug to your baby girl!

It is also dedicated to my amazing, wise, and loving husband, Don, who has never stopped encouraging me to fulfill the extraordinary dreams Jesus put in this ordinary heart. Each season with you is the best. Yours is truly the most enduring, and endearing, influence in my life.

And finally it is dedicated to my precious offspring, Kristi, Mark, and Jana, who (along with their wonderful spouses and precious kids) have been my most constant supporters on this long journey. You top the list of reasons why I want to be a Jesus-hearted woman.

．　．　．　．　．　．　．　．　．　．　．

CONTENTS

. . . .

1   Foreword

5   Acknowledgements

11   Introduction

15   CHAPTER ONE
These Shoes Are Too Big!
Leadership Quality: Confidence

39   CHAPTER TWO
Plastic Lipstick
Leadership Quality: Authenticity

61   CHAPTER THREE
Floor Exercise
Leadership Quality: Humility

91   CHAPTER FOUR
Take the Stairs
Leadership Quality: Stamina

121   CHAPTER FIVE
The Cringe Factor
Leadership Quality: Resilience

159   CHAPTER SIX
Pocketbook Punches
Leadership Quality: Courage

193   CHAPTER SEVEN
Terra-Cotta Warriors
Leadership Quality: Self-Awareness

215   CHAPTER EIGHT
First-Clappers
Leadership Quality: Kindness

243   CHAPTER NINE
The Green Room
Leadership Quality: Soul-Care

285   CHAPTER TEN
Dancing on Prayers
Leadership Quality: Vision

307   Epilogue

311   Endnotes

315   About the Author

FOREWORD

. . . .

I remember how nervous I felt. New to ministry and just a few years into my twenties, I had a passion to minister to women that just wouldn't go away. Sometimes in church, as I listened to sermons or sat in Bible studies, I felt as if I would burst with the "fire shut up in my bones" (Jer. 20:9). But God didn't open doors for that kind of ministry, and He wouldn't allow me to pursue opportunities on my own. For the most part, I was okay with that. But at the same time, I felt desperate for a mentor . . . someone to help me along the way.

Finally, between sessions at a women's conference I was attending, I worked up courage to approach the director. I don't know if it was a lack of time or perhaps the desperation that probably marked my face, but her eyes seemed to glaze over a bit as I stumbled through an explanation of what God was stirring in my heart.

"Just pray, honey," she said patting my hand before turning to talk to someone else. I still remember how my heart sank as I walked away.

I had so hoped that she might be able to help me understand the longing, the stirring, the burning in my heart. I wasn't interested in *making* anything happen ministry-wise. I just wanted to know what to do in the meantime—what I should do to prepare my heart and my life for whatever God might have ahead for me.

When I received my copy of *The Jesus-Hearted Woman: 10 Qualities of Enduring & Endearing Influence*, I'd read only two chapters before I realized that this was the mentor I'd been looking for back in my early twenties. This was the companion I'd needed when we took our first pastorate in my early thirties. And that afternoon as I hungrily read each page, I found the practical advice I needed to navigate the busy ministry I currently find myself in. The very type of ministry I'd dreamed about so long ago.

In a sense, I wasn't surprised. I've had the incredible privilege of being Jodi Detrick's friend for over eight years. I've watched her life up close, and I am constantly astounded by the wisdom and the winsome beauty of her love for Jesus. She doesn't just talk about being a fully devoted follower of Jesus Christ. She lives it every day. She doesn't push and shove to get farther in ministry. She simply follows Jesus, and Jesus makes the way.

Jodi has the rare combination of gentle humility and bold confidence that I long for. But she also has an incredible gift of communicating truth that somehow disarms the flesh as it enables the spirit. Emboldening as it corrects. Comforting as it challenges.

You'll find practical advice in this book but so much more. I believe you're going to find yourself falling more in love with Jesus as you discover what it means to belong to Him. Drawn so close into His arms that you catch His heartbeat. Held so near that your heart begins to beat in time with His.

For you, my friend, were meant to be a Jesus-hearted woman: a humble, bold, and lovely woman who brings the love and life of the Lord to a broken-hearted world.

If you long to do something significant for God, this is the book that you've been looking for. This is the book that you and I need.

Because of Him,

JOANNA WEAVER

Bestselling author, *Having a Mary Heart in a Martha World: Finding Intimacy with God in the Busyness of Life*

ACKNOWLEDGEMENTS

. . . .

I used to think that to write a book you went into a room, shut the door behind you, and prayerfully wrestled with thoughts and ideas until enough words and sentences took form to create something worth showing to the world. That's a piece of it, yes—especially if you repeat that first part many times over.

But now that this process is behind me, I realize writing is more of a team sport than one would think. There are so many people who contributed significantly, in big and small ways, to this book starting its literary race and then crossing the finish line to publication. And though there are many more names (probably enough for another small book!) that I could include, I especially owe a huge, heartfelt debt of gratitude to:

- My wonderful husband, best-friend, and love of my life, Dr. Don Detrick. This guy has one of the most brilliant minds, and biggest hearts, you will ever meet. He believed in me as a writer, as a leader, and as a woman in ministry long before I ever aspired to be any of those. Without his patience, prodding, and constant encouragement—not to mention helping with practical things like laundry, cooking, and housework (yes, real men *do* vacuum!)—this book would never have been written. And without his almost four-decades of love, I would not be who I am today: a joyful wife married to my incredible partner in life and ministry.

- My parents, Hershel and Louise Dunlap. Although my daddy has been with Jesus for a few years now, I want to express how valuable it was to grow up with parents who loved me, were proud of me, and expressed that in so many ways. I know their prayers, along with their example in ministry, helped shape my heart to love Jesus and others.

- My dearly-loved children, Kristina Hinds (and her husband, Jesse), Mark Detrick, and Jana Judd (and her husband, Chris). A mother's heart holds things for her children that simply cannot be expressed in words, but I am beyond grateful for each of these amazing, compassionate people. They care about things that matter in our broken world—and they still care about their mother and her crazy dreams to write a book! Each time they asked how it was going or said "You can do it!," it was like a fresh gust of wind in my writing sails. And my three precious grandgirls, Lilia, Liberty, and Mira, provide galaxies of inspiration and oceans of joy every time I look into their sweet faces.

- My fabulous friends who have supported me in ways too numerous to mention—there are many of you but I especially want to acknowledge the following special women:

  Vicki Judd has been my best friend, comrade in ministry, study buddy (as we went through seminary together), traveling companion, prayer partner, sharer of sorrows, and lifter of spirits since I met her in 1991. Who knew back then that we would also become family in an even deeper way when her son, Chris, married our daughter Jana! I can't imagine doing life without her, and I'm not sure this book would have been written if I had not had this sister-friend to keep cheering me on.

Cheryl Werth is my "ministry midwife." She is not only a dear lifelong friend (as is her husband, Ted) but someone I can call for a prayer SOS—and someone whose quiet, consistent belief in me called out the writer who was hiding inside.

Every writer should be so blessed to have a mentor-friend and kindred spirit like my dear Joanna Weaver! She came alongside me over and over, offering wisdom from her vast experience as a best-selling author, and spiritual CPR when I felt like I was drowning in the enormity of it all. She has prayed with me, talked me off more than a few ledges, and celebrated wildly at every new stage of progress. I owe her so much.

Some people just bring beauty to the world and to the lives of those around them. That's the kind of person my sweet friend, Elaine Tolson, is. She and her husband, Ben, became such close friends when they served on our church staff in Chehalis,

Washington, and remain so today. Thank you, Ben and Elaine, for allowing me to use your beautiful mountain cabin as a writer's retreat. The solitude was just what I needed—and those trays of gourmet meals hand-delivered to my door by Chef Elaine . . . spectacular!

Speaking of writer's retreats—I want to thank my good friends Dr. Brian and Amy Roberts for the use of their gorgeous cabin, as well. Your generosity in allowing me several days in that lovely, quiet setting was a crucial part of this book becoming a reality!

I also want to mention dear friends like Stephanie Nance (my incredible assistant at the Network for Women in Ministry), Kerri Chittim, Kerry Clarensau, Dr. Ava Oleson, Dr. Cheryl Taylor, Dr. Lois Olena, Dr. Byron Klaus, Dr. Beth Grant, Dr. Debbie Gill, Dr. Carolyn Tennant, Dr. Melody Palm—(I love *all* my AGTS professors, faculty, and fellow-cohort *anam charas!*), Beth Backes, Darice Welk, and Debbie Cole (my sweet and amazing fellow executives' wives at the Northwest Ministry Network), Connie Taylor, Jeannie Collins, Angela Craig, and Gail Johnsen. I could write pages about each of you and how you have contributed so significantly to my life and to the things written in this book. You are all Jesus-hearted women who have shown me another facet of who He is.

I want to say one more big thank you to the courageous women who allowed me to share pieces of their moving stories in these chapters. I know their vulnerability will bring hope to hearts—it has to mine.

- The wonderful publishing team at Influence Resources. I'm so grateful to Steve and Susan Blount for believing in me, having great patience when this project was delayed due the medical crisis with our daughter, and for offering just the right words of encouragement along the way. And I think God must have hand-picked my wonderful editor at IR, Terri Gibbs! Terri, your deft hand at steering this project in a slightly different direction and excellent editing skills have made this a much better book. I am so thankful for your help and so proud to be a part of the Influence Resources family!

- And finally, but always foremost . . . my Hero, my Hope, my Jesus. I fully agree with Peter's words in John 6:67–68 (MSG): "Master, to whom would we go? You have the words of real life, eternal life. We have already committed ourselves, confident that you are the Holy One of God."

INTRODUCTION

. . . .

I t's happening everywhere. Women are looking for ways to grow and use their God-given leadership gifts—with or without an official title or position. And despite the obstacles, opportunities abound. Yes, I know about the struggles and inequities. But many of us inhale the freest air women have ever breathed in the history of this planet, and we want to make every lung-full count. We also watch in amazement when our sisters around the globe, even those still under the gloom of oppression, courageously step up as godly influencers in their homes, communities, churches, and nations.

When the hip young college student sits across the table from me at Starbucks, I see it in her eyes, backlit with passion, as she describes the outreach she wants to organize for prostitutes working in her city. I hear it in the longing-soaked words of singles and moms with young children in their twenties and thirties, career women in their forties and fifties, and the still-energetic-but-experienced retirees in their sixties and seventies (and yes, even eighties). They know the needs around them are daunting, and they want to offer the best of what they've learned from life to make a difference. They yearn to translate the renovating love God has poured out on them into transforming influence on others. These women want to be Jesus-hearted leaders!

But what does that look like in the real world? As a leader with decades of experience, I know this: the things that impassion and energize us in leadership can be the same things that eventually drain and defeat us. (Like, "I would be a great leader if

I didn't have to work with people" or "I could teach a great class on time management if I could ever finish my to-do list.")

And let's be honest. Leadership for women comes with its own unique set of challenges and struggles. There are potholes, dead-ends, and dangerous curves galore on this journey. I've seen too many women who had the potential to be great leaders turn back in discouragement or defeat, leaving others without the light of their influence. That doesn't need to happen.

More than ever, I'm convinced our broken-hearted world needs women who are Jesus-hearted leaders. And I'm pretty sure you are one of them, or long to be, if you've picked up this book. Perhaps you're a veteran leader, or maybe you don't have a clue about where to begin. No worries—wherever you are in your leadership journey, I think you'll find something to relate to, and encouragement to move you forward, in the pages ahead.

When I sat with that young woman at Starbucks, sipping our steaming lattes and talking about her ministry vision, I found myself wishing we had weeks and months together to explore what it means to lead with love in a Jesus-hearted way. To lead in a way that maximizes influence and minimizes the hazards. And I've wished it again as I've traveled the country, talking to women with all kinds of gifts and passions who, just like you, know it's time to step up and make a difference.

Since I can't have weeks and months with each of you over unlimited lattes (not until eternity anyway—*surely* there will be coffee in heaven!), the Lord nudged me, and friends and family encouraged me to write this book. The ten qualities of Jesus-hearted leadership in the chapters ahead are exactly what I would talk about with you if we could meet in person—and I think you'll love the real-life, where-the-sandals-meet-the-sidewalk stories of people whose experiences make us wiser. I will also share frankly from my own leadership stumbles (gulp!) and strides.

But best of all, we will learn from Jesus, Himself, through His Word, about the surprising differences between *His* kind of leadership and what the world models to us. Because, here's the thing when it comes to leadership . . . if you develop the qualities—if you have the *heart*—you can learn the skills.

That face you see every day in the mirror? Yeah, it's yours. But that stirring in your chest to use your gifts and abilities? That urgency to do something about the broken lives around you? Those dreams of how things could be different and what it might take to make them so? That's the heart of Jesus beating in you.

Take a deep breath of that free air and let's dive in. After all, a Jesus-heart inside means a God-adventure ahead!

(Learn more about being a Jesus-hearted woman at www. jesusheartedwoman.com.)

chapter one

THESE SHOES ARE TOO BIG!

LEADERSHIP QUALITY: CONFIDENCE

• • • • • • • • • • •

"On what are you basing this confidence of yours?"
—SENNACHERIB, KING OF ASSYRIA

I put the phone down, still shaking my head in disbelief. *What were they thinking?* Swiveling the chair around, I faced my husband, Don, who had just walked into the room.

"You'll never guess who that was." I said. "And if you do, you'll never believe what he wanted." Don waited for me to fill him in.

With a dazed look on my face, I explained that one of the leaders from our denomination had called. He wanted to let me know that the woman who had served as Women's Ministries Director for our network of churches, about 330 in Washington and northern Idaho, had recently resigned. They were looking for someone to oversee that department and fill her position on the Northwest Ministry Network (NWMN) Leadership Team. What did I think about having my name included with those who were being considered for this role?

Yikes! This would mean following a wonderful, well-respected leader who had served successfully in that position for more than thirteen years. It would mean taking on a long list of responsibilities in areas of leadership that were new to me: planning and putting on conferences and large regional events for women, working with an executive team of female leaders from two states, interacting with other District Directors on a national level, taking on hefty missions and charitable giving projects, handling departmental budgets (since I've never been a math kind of girl, this one *really* freaked me out), creating leadership training opportunities for women, developing promo videos and Web site material, and launching a leadership e-group, just to name a few. And one more thing . . . I would be serving as the only female voice at the top-tier leadership table for our Network with several men, all respected regionally and nationally as cream-of-the-crop, forward-thinking ministry leaders.

I GRAPPLED WITH ALL THE REASONS I WASN'T UP FOR THIS ASSIGNMENT.

It was an easy decision—in fact the word *no* popped into my mind automatically while I was still on the phone, and I had to swallow it down several times in the course of the conversation. But since it was such an honor to even be considered for this position, and it was presented so graciously by Steve, who had called, I politely promised to talk with Don and to pray about it over the weekend before I gave an answer. *That,* I soon discovered, was my first mistake if I wanted to maintain a comfortable status quo and stay off the path to growing as a Jesus-hearted leader.

Since I had committed to do so on the phone, I prayed a lot that weekend (and even fasted—not my most, shall we say, "routinely-used" spiritual discipline). Instead of sensing the resounding confirmation I had expected, *that's right, Jodi . . . this is not for you . . . just say no and be done with it,* other thoughts kept rising to the surface:

> *What if this is one of the things God put me on earth to do? If I say no, will it be because I'm living a fear-based, instead of a faith-based life? Is dread of failure bigger to me than wanting to do God's will? Do I really believe God can do amazing things through ordinary people who love and trust Him? Do I really love and trust Him enough to say yes if I believe this is what He wants for me? Am I ready to put forth the effort and stretch to grow in the areas this position will require?*

These were not lightly asked or easily answered questions. Throughout that weekend, especially during the night hours, I grappled with all the reasons I wasn't up for this assignment.

Inexperience. Yes, it was true that I had more than gotten my feet wet, when it came to ministry. It was more like I had been drenched in it all my life. Born into a third-generation pastor's family, I grew up actively participating in church life and working with people in a variety of settings even when I was very young. Then, in high school, I had fallen still more passionately in love with Jesus and was one of those radical Jesus-freaks of the 1970s. I wasn't shy about passing on the good news of God's love to my fellow students, teachers, and even an occasional stranger. At that time, I also began to develop and use some basic leadership skills at school and in our local congregation. But that was in a little town (we are talking less than 2,000 residents and not quite 35 students in my graduating class) and in a very small church setting. Did that count?

Lack of higher education. I'd met Don while we were still in high school and was so impressed with this guy from a neighboring city who was as passionate about serving Jesus as I was. I'll admit, I also thought he was cute, smart, and funny— truly a young gentleman and he treated me like a queen from the start. (Like the time he took me shopping and bought me six pairs of shoes. *Sigh!*) We began dating during the height of the Jesus Movement, zipping off to Andraé Crouch or *Love Song* concerts and Jesus Marches in his shiny little, canary-yellow Vega. *Good times!* By the time Don graduated and went off to college to prepare to be a pastor, we were engaged.

During those days, we were just sure Jesus was coming back any minute—not a bad way to live, by the way—and we couldn't wait to get married, do ministry together, and turn the world upside-down. (Okay, so we were slightly over-the-top optimists.) Instead of both of us going to college as newlyweds (later, one of our big "should haves"), I worked as a dental assistant to help pay the bills while Don finished up his degree.

Before long, we were up to our eyebrows in family and ministry life. Don was glad to be fulfilling his calling by serving as a pastor in a small town on the Oregon coast. I was happy in my role as pastor's wife and, eventually, new mommy to three beautiful children. In the course of the next several years, Don would be the lead pastor to three different churches in the Pacific

Northwest. I loved serving alongside him, and I loved the great people in those congregations.

Highly engaged in ministry life, Don often referred to me as his unofficial (and unpaid) associate staffer. I know many pastors' wives and women in ministry would chafe at that description these days—there are certainly understandable reasons why—but I thrived on doing life and ministry in partnership with him and didn't really feel the need to have a title or a paycheck for validation. Besides, I'd always felt my most important ministry in that season was with my kids, and my plate was more than full with all the joys, struggles, blessings, and complications that come with parenting. (*That's* another book!)

So it didn't seem to matter much, especially in those early years, that I hadn't been able to earn a college degree. After all, I had taken a few night classes now and then along the way. I was also an avid reader and loved to learn on my own. Don and I attended many seminars and conferences together, and I was a sponge when it came to soaking up knowledge. I even discovered I had a gift for instructing others and spent years developing and teaching Bible studies for women in the congregations where we served.

Eventually, I began to accept occasional invitations to speak to groups of women from various denominations at retreats and conferences, something I enjoyed immensely. During those years, I had also begun to write and was overjoyed when some of my articles were included in a number of different publications. By the time I got Steve's call on behalf of the NWMN, Don had been pastoring a wonderful congregation of several hundred people in western Washington for more than a decade, and I was a seasoned pastor's wife whose youngest child would be heading off to college in the fall. I assumed I would keep doing what I had been doing for most of my adult life . . . maybe have a little more time for writing, now that our baby birdies had grown up and flown from the nest.

Then came that perplexing phone call! As I lay on my bed that Saturday night considering what answer I would give on Monday morning, (and trying vainly not to keep Don awake with all my tossing and turning), I thought about my history up to this point. I didn't regret for one moment the life that God had given me, but all my prior leadership experiences seemed pretty insignificant. Bottom line . . . I was essentially a small-town girl. I had little know-how in the scope of responsibilities required by this position. And I had no academic degree or formal training that would give me a leg up, much less the credibility, to assume this level of leadership. *What were they thinking? These shoes are too big!*

• GOD USES RELUCTANT LEADERS •

Astute thinker that you are, you may have jumped ahead and guessed the outcome of my inner wrestling that weekend. With Don and my family cheering me on, and with the encouragement of a few key, trusted friends, I came to a conclusion.

Despite my sense of inadequacy when it came to this new position, I would keep walking through any doors God opened along the way. I knew I would have to go through several steps including an interview process so I was pretty sure, and half hoping, that once they knew my lack of qualifications, the doors would shut. That would be the end of it, and I could just go on with things as they were. Instead, the doors kept opening. And on the other side of that final one was a b-i-g pair of shoes for my little leadership feet to grow into.

> **GOD CHOOSES AND USES RELUCTANT LEADERS — A REASSURING FACT.**

God chooses and uses reluctant leaders—a reassuring fact. If that describes you, too, we're in pretty good company. It's not hard to think of biblical characters like Moses, Gideon, Jeremiah, and of course, the lovely Queen Esther, who fit that billing. From the perspective of more than a decade later, I smile to think that God heard my high-pitched, tearful whisper into my pillow . . . *yes, Lord* . . . and sent me off, wobbly-kneed, down the path to growing as a leader. I wouldn't trade this grand adventure, the unforeseen twists and turns it's taken me on, or the amazing people I've met along the way for anything.

There's a phrase in one line of Robert Frost's poem "The Road Not Taken" that grabs me: "Yet knowing how way leads on to way I doubted if I should ever come back."[1] *Way leads on to way.* When we take one way, it leads us on to another way and another and another . . . places we could never foresee when we're standing at the fork deciding whether to take the safe, predictable path or the less-traveled one that requires risk and trust.

When I gingerly put on those too-big shoes, there were so many things I couldn't see and didn't know. I had yet to learn how fulfilling it could be to work with so many amazing women in our Network as we tackled everything from giving projects to leadership training to inspirational events (and a lot more in-between) together. I didn't know how much I would love watching women grow as leaders and what a deep joy it would be to invest in their development.

I had no idea how much I would learn from the gifted, gracious men I worked closely with every week as we attempted to strategically strengthen and develop empowered leaders and churches. Those guys respected my voice at the leadership table and we became not only ministry colleagues but good friends. (And I have to tell you . . . there was a distinct advantage to being the only female on the team. I never had to wait in line at the bathroom when we took a break from our meetings!)

During that weekend when I was struggling with what to tell Steve, I had no clue that, as part of an organization that valued lifelong learning, I would be able to go on an academic journey where I would eventually earn a master's degree (graduating, to my utter amazement, summa cum laude—*thank you, Jesus!)* from a wonderful seminary. The study bug has bitten hard and now I've just finished a doctoral program, something I never dreamed was remotely possible a few years back.

· · · · · · · · ·

I'VE OFTEN FELT LIKE A LITTLE GIRL, CLOMPING AWKWARDLY ALONG IN HER MOMMY'S HEELS.

· · · · · · · · ·

I didn't know about the incredible women from other parts of the country I would meet as we served together on national committees, leaders who would be iron-sharpening-iron influences in my life. Or that at a national seminar for Women's Ministries Directors (thank you, dear Arlene Allen!) I would be introduced to the concept of life-coaching and would become so passionate about it that I would pursue training to become a coach, myself. I wouldn't have guessed that someday I would have the privilege of coaching leaders both here in the United States and in other countries (thanks to Skype).

There was no way to know, back then, that the girl from a tiny church in a small town with only a high school diploma would someday be asked to be a guest speaker for university classes and chapels, or that she and her husband would be invited to deliver the baccalaureate message together when their daughter graduated from college.

And seriously, you could have knocked me over with a feather duster if you had told me that this mainly-a-mom/ordinary pastor's wife would one day be writing a religion column for *The Seattle Times*, the Pacific Northwest's Pulitzer prize-winning daily newspaper with 1.8 million readers. I couldn't have imagined having that kind of voice for faith in Jesus to one of the most unchurched, skeptical-toward-organized-religion-and-Christianity parts of the country. But from this vantage point, a little farther down that risky path, I now know that all those things have been a part of this journey.

• WAY LEADS ON TO WAY •

I'm convinced that none of these adventures in leadership growth would have happened if I had followed my fears and pushed those too-big shoes back across the counter of divine invitation with a polite *um, no thank you.* I don't think God would have been mad at me or that my life would have been meaningless, but . . . oh, how much I would have missed! And because of what the Bible has to say about stewardship (see Matt. 25:15–29 for a refresher on this principle), I believe that good things have come from my life that others would have missed as well.

If I'm giving the impression, however, that stepping into those too-big shoes was a sunny stroll on the beach, let me set the record straight. There have been many times in this past decade when my "What were they thinking?" has turned to "What was I thinking?" I've often felt like a little girl, clomping awkwardly along in her mommy's heels.

I remember the sting of embarrassment when a man I respected stood in the back of the room and laughed at me as I struggled with one of my first PowerPoint presentations in front of a large group. Whoever said there are no dumb questions has never heard some of the ones I've asked in our Leadership Team meetings. And don't even get me started about my frustration (to the point of tears) with financial spread sheets and budget reports.

I could tell you about hotels that forgot to inform me they were under new management and could no longer honor the room reservations I had made (months in advance, by the way) one week before a big conference event. We could have a frank discussion about what it's like to deal with conflict on a team and hurt feelings between those who *(sound of gritting teeth)* serve together. I could fill you in on to-do lists that seem endless and obstacles that seem insurmountable. We could talk about big plans that fizzled and times when I let others, and myself, down. The shoes of leadership have many ways to pinch and blister the feet of those who walk in them.

But here's the thing, when we *do* walk in them despite the difficulties and challenges, our gait gradually changes from an ungainly, self-conscious toddle to a poised, purposeful stride that inspires trust in those who follow. Contrary to what some may think, insecurity is not humility. Quite the opposite, it's *me*-focused and is more concerned with self-protection than risking rejection or pain for the benefit of others. True story . . . I've been there.

Knowing my inclination toward personal insecurity, I've learned to pray this prayer and I do so often: "God, please give me the gracious confidence required to lead in this setting."

• GRACIOUS CONFIDENCE •

Here's the thing . . . I'm pretty sure that, once you've donned those too-big shoes, having confidence as your inner attitude and outer demeanor is the best way to grow into them. It's a little hard to define, but those who have it put those they serve with—and those they lead—at ease. A person with gracious confidence:

- Is comfortable in her own skin and doesn't try to mimic the styles or gifts of others; she doesn't yearn for someone else's shoes.
- Can lead and follow at the same time.
- Isn't afraid of the spotlight but doesn't seek it, either; she is quick to shine it on others when she has a chance.
- Presents her thoughts and ideas without having to have the last word.
- Accepts both praise and criticism without setting her heart too completely on either.
- Is satisfied to give her best for the benefit of others and has a quick word of encouragement when she sees someone else doing the same.
- Realizes that she will likely still have butterflies before she steps behind a podium, may still feel intimidated around certain other leaders, and may

second-guess her decisions, but doesn't let those feelings affect her actions and reactions.

- Rests easy after she's done her best (even if it's not perfect), knowing that outcomes are up to God and the free-will responses of others.
- Knows she will have "off days," so cuts herself the same slack she would cut others.
- Laughs at herself and learns from her mistakes.

I think that much-analyzed, virtuous woman of Proverbs 31 displayed gracious confidence when she "perceived that her merchandise was good" (verse 18) . . . good enough to bring out of her private spaces and offer up to the scrutiny of others. (Perhaps her merchandise included the fine linen garments and sashes she sold to the merchants mentioned in verse 24.) The choice of whether or not to buy what she was selling was theirs, but she knew she had brought *good* stuff.

Are you making the connection? At some point along the way, we have to summon the courage to pull out the "good merchandise" we've been working on and put it out there for others to see and use, if they choose.

The same thread runs through Matthew 5:14–16 when Jesus tells us we are the light of the world and to "let our lights so shine before others that they would see our good works and glorify the Father in heaven." Sure sounds like gracious confidence to me! It means we're willing to actually "shine" (instead of shrink back) "before others" (not just privately to God) and let them "see our good works"—the things that we can do well, and do for the sake of others, in order to bring glory to God.

Just a quick disclaimer, though: having gracious confidence does not mean following some positive therapy mantra that claims "I can be, and do, anything and everything I ever dream." I could dream all I want to (not that I want to) of being a successful accountant (my friends are all laughing now . . . stop it, you guys!) or a long-distance runner or a portrait artist, and it would never happen. Those are *not* the gifts God has put in me. I have to learn to discern whether or not I at least have the latent, perhaps underdeveloped but God-given, capacity to do the thing I'm considering before I jump into it with both feet. Presumption is not the same as confidence.

I would hate being an accountant, but I would love to be a portrait artist. The running thing? Not so much. There are some things I never *should* do as a vocation—the things I'm not suited for—and a good clue is that I will find them unappealing, unsatisfying, and relentlessly stressful. On the other hand, there are some things I never can do because I don't have the aptitude or intrinsic gifting for them, even though they seem appealing. And there are lots of things between those two. But there are a few things that are truly my sweet spot—things that I can learn to do well, that also make me come alive inside.

PRESUMPTION IS NOT THE SAME AS CONFIDENCE.

Sometimes it takes a little exploring to discover our sweet spot. I well remember my drive into Seattle on a lovely spring day a few years back. (Yes, we do have warm, rain-free days in Seattle, despite what you have heard.) Pulling into the parking lot across the street from the venerable old *Seattle Times* building, I concluded the forty-minute prayer time I had enjoyed on my drive from the nearby town of North Bend, where I live. "Jesus, only let me do this if I *can* do this," I said as I pushed my van's door shut with a clunk. It was an odd prayer, to be sure, but I was certain the Lord knew what I meant.

I was going in for an interview with the newspaper's executive editor, as well as several departmental editors, and would also get to sit in on a news reporters' meeting. The outcome of this day would determine whether or not I would be added as a regular columnist for the weekly *Faith & Values* feature, writing in rotation with four others, which included a Jewish rabbi, a Catholic priest, and a Muslim gentleman.

At that point in my life, I knew God had given me writing gifts, but I had no idea whether or not those could be developed into being a full-fledged columnist for a secular newspaper. Having already stepped into one pair of too-big shoes, however, gave me the confidence to at least try on another. But the *last* thing I wanted to do was to take on something I couldn't even hope to grow into doing well. The idea of possibly dishonoring or misrepresenting Christ (or my fellow Christians) with a shabby effort, especially in such a public setting, was unthinkable. Hence, my prayer: "Jesus, only let me do this if I can do this. Don't let me waste your resources and my time trying to pursue what looks so good when someone else does it, if it's not what you have equipped *me* to do."

> **GRACIOUS CONFIDENCE MEANS I TAKE THE GIFTS GOD HAS PLACED IN ME AND DEVELOP THEM AS FULLY AS I CAN, IN EVERY WAY I CAN.**

After my interview, I was asked to write a few sample columns for the editorial staff to read. They had several more potential columnists to interview, they told me, but would let me know the outcome in a few weeks. Truthfully, I wasn't too hopeful that I would actually get to wear those big shoes, though trying them on had been pretty remarkable. "Oh well! It was a great learning experience, and I got to see a real newsroom," I told myself.

To say I was stunned and amazed when I got the call saying that I had been chosen to be their new columnist would be *waaaay* beyond an understatement. And it's been an extreme privilege to write for *The Seattle Times* for several years now, especially when some reader feedback lets me know that God has used my written words to pry open a once-closed heart just enough for His love and truth to begin to shine through.

• CONFIDENCE BASED ON GOD •

This is what I'm learning as I keep putting one foot in front of the other on this path. Gracious confidence means I take the gifts God has placed in me and develop them as fully as I can, in every way I can. It means doing my best as I offer those gifts back to God in service to others as He gives me opportunity, trusting Him with the outcome. It's leading with a blend of strength and humility, of will and flexibility, of serious-headedness and light-heartedness. Gracious confidence will help my feet to grow into those too-big shoes.

However, while confidence is a necessary element of healthy ministry and leadership, it should never be misplaced. Even though it was asked by an arrogant bully, the question Sennacherib, the king of Assyria, put to King Hezekiah in 2 Kings 18:19 is a good one and worth pondering: "On what are you basing this confidence of yours?"

This pagan king, who had Jerusalem surrounded by his massive army, tried to undermine any and every source of confidence the godly king of Judah might have. He also assumed, wrongfully, that Hezekiah would be leaning on Egypt, whom he referred to as a "splintered staff," for military assistance.

As I continue to grow more comfortable in my leadership roles, occasionally I need to ask myself the same question (minus the mocking undertone and intimidating taunts, of course) . . . *on what am I basing this confidence of mine?* Every day comes with new challenges that seem to get more complex with time, not less so. I need confidence if I'm going to fight and win my daily battles.

I can get in big trouble at lightning speed, however, if I begin to base my core confidence on any of my own "splintered staffs": natural abilities, cleverness, charm, appearance, history of success, titles and positions, academic accomplishments, affiliations with the powerful and privileged, or human acclaim. These things can be helpful, for sure—even God-sent to propel us on our way. But, like me, you've probably seen the sad results when ministry leaders have made some twisted combination of these the basis of their confidence. They leaned heavily on an attractive but unreliable "splintered staff" only to have it break beneath the weight of reality.

I love the rest of the story of Hezekiah's conflict with Sennacherib, how he took his aggressor's threatening letter and spread it out before the Lord. His response to an overwhelming leadership challenge was not to buck up and soldier on in his own strength and resources but to place his confidence fully in the Lord.

Years ago, when I was that young, Jesus-freakin' teen-age girl with the waist-length, parted-down-the-middle hair and a One Way sticker (index finger pointed skyward—ultimate Christian coolness back in the day!) on her Bible, Hebrews 10:35 became one of my life verses: "So do not throw away your confidence; it will be richly rewarded."

I wish that girl had learned sooner not to despise small beginnings or underestimate the experiences God was giving her along the way. If only she had known that to do so is to throw away the confidence He is building, layer by layer, through the years. I wish she had grasped what Corrie ten Boom meant when she said, "Every experience God gives us, every person He puts into our life, is the perfect preparation for the future that only He can see."[2]

• GOD GROWS US INTO HIS CALLING •

These days, my hair is considerably shorter (much to my husband's chagrin) and considerably redder (at least this month), thanks to my hairdresser and good friend, Marge. And, finally, I've come to understand that I'm not a better leader because I've been given bigger responsibilities and a few outstanding opportunities. I'm a better leader because I stepped forward (albeit with fear and trembling) into the next thing God called me to, stuffing the toes of those too-big shoes with tissues of trust that He would grow me into His calling.

Thankfully, that can happen anywhere, whatever the setting and without acquiring a new position or role. Some of the most amazing, fully-developed leaders I know serve quietly, but powerfully, in what others would see as relative obscurity. But being the graciously confident people they are, they don't let the size of their setting, the scope of their authority, or the span of their acclaim—large or small—define them or keep them from making a deep, eternal impact on lives.

In fact, oddly enough, sometimes our next big step forward as a leader is to step *down* from a position, to push away from a table where we have had authority and influence. That has been true in my life. After almost nine years in my leadership role with the Northwest Ministry Network, that became my challenge. I began to sense that God's "next" for my life was to pull back from the more organizationally-oriented leadership position in which I had been serving so that I could give greater focus to my growing passions for writing, life-coaching, and speaking.

If I had learned anything from the wisdom of my friends around that long conference room table, it was that you should pay close attention to the passions God is stirring in your heart. But I had grown to dearly love those I worked with and, to be honest, quite pleased with the status of being part of such a wonderful, well-respected team. Those shoes were now a comfy fit. Once again, it seemed risky to lay aside what I knew and had grown accustomed to for something still pretty vague. What would it look like for me to give myself fully to writing, life-coaching, and speaking? I wasn't so sure.

My mind went back to that long-ago weekend of decision when a position with the NWMN was beginning to become a possibility for me. The more I thought about it, I realized it all boiled down to the same basic issues, though presented in a different set of circumstances: did I trust God enough to step out of the shoes that now fit, lovely shoes with a shiny title and the cushion of a regular salary? Could I now risk stepping into another set of too-big shoes: the self-leadership footwear required to be a serious writer, skilled coach, and graciously confident speaker?

After some more wrestling (this time it took several months instead of a weekend), I was ready for my next set of too-big shoes. And once again, I feel a little awkward and ungainly as I step forward. It was bitter-sweet when I packed up my office at the NWMN campus and said good-bye to the people who had become like a second family in many ways. (Thankfully, we still have many close connections and can stay in touch!)

But the fact that you're holding this book in your hand, reading these words I've labored over into the wee hours of many mornings (I have a real affinity with Louisa May Alcott who did all her writing at night) is one sure sign that once again, my feet are beginning to grow.

How about it, girlfriend . . . are you ready for a new pair of shoes?

• JODI'S COACHING QUESTIONS •

- What life experiences and parts of your personal history have you minimized when it comes to your development as a leader? How can you use experiences from where you've been to prepare for where you're going?

- Who are some people you know who lead with gracious confidence?

- Which of their qualities and characteristics stand out most to you?

- What are some of the too-big shoes you've stepped into? How did you grow into them?

- What might be your next pair of too-big shoes? How will you know if God wants you to put them on? What steps will you take to try them on?

• A LITTLE LESSON FOR NEW LEADERS •

Sometimes the best way to grow as a leader is not to take a position but to take a class. It may not mean leading a team but joining someone else's team. I grew so much as a leader by learning from others, and by serving under those who were good at what they did. It's not where you start, but where you're willing to go, that matters.

• HEART-DEEP IN THE WORD •

Psalm 118:8 (NKJV) says, "It is better to trust in the LORD than to put confidence in man." Read the story of Asa in 2 Chronicles 16:1–10 and describe how and why he put confidence in people instead of God. What was the outcome?

_____

_____

_____

_____

Read Jeremiah 17:5–10. Considering the strong cautions expressed in those verses, what does it look like today when we place our confidence in others or ourselves instead of God?

_____

_____

_____

_____

While trusting solely in ourselves is arrogant and a big mistake, there's a gracious confidence that's biblical, healthy, and necessary for good leadership. Read the following passages and describe how the truths in each section contribute to gracious confidence:

- Genesis 1:27
- Joshua 1:9
- Psalm 139:13–14, 16–18

- Isaiah 64:8
- Jeremiah 29:11
- 2 Corinthians 3:5
- Ephesians 2:10

_____

_____

_____

_____

_____

_____

Read the description of the virtuous woman in Proverbs 31:1–31. How did she display gracious confidence?

_____

_____

_____

_____

_____

_____

_____

chapter two

PLASTIC LIPSTICK

LEADERSHIP QUALITY: AUTHENTICITY

· · · · · · · · · · ·

The most exhausting thing in life is being insincere.
—ANNE MORROW LINDBERGH

I t was hard for me to believe this was the same person I had just seen on stage. In the illumination of the spotlight, her performance had been brilliant. And I don't just mean the beautiful vocals. She also seemed to display a warm, loving heart as she interacted with the crowd and engaged in friendly banter with her band members between songs. The key word, however, was *seemed*. Out in the hallway not a half hour later, her stage persona melted (along with my illusion and admiration) from the heat of her anger at some underling's lack of aptitude in catering to her prima donna wishes. The shrillness of her voice as she berated him with stinging, acidic words made me forget about the loveliness of her earlier songs.

That scene took me back to another encounter . . . different, but with the same toxic root. My husband and I sat in silence at the crowded table, a setting that should have been conducive for great conversation. Oh, there was conversation, alright—just not with us. As a young couple who had only recently begun life in the pastorate, we were thrilled to be at this conference and to glean from other leaders who had a storehouse of experience and wisdom to offer.

When we were randomly seated for dinner with experienced ministry couples from some of the larger churches in our region, we were excited about the opportunity to ask a few questions. What a terrific chance to get to know these people we had admired from a distance! It wasn't long, however, before their dismissive looks and clipped answers (sometimes not in any way related to the question we had just asked or a comment we had made) told us we weren't in their league and should just mutely bask in their glory. In the meantime, though, they had a wonderful time chatting with each other. But not one question or meaningful comment was ever directed our way. It was a long dinner.

IF I THOUGHT NO ONE ELSE WOULD EVER SEE OR KNOW . . . HOW WOULD I REACT?

I have to be honest . . . the next few times I saw some of our tablemates showcasing their gifts publicly at regional church gatherings, I remembered what it was like to feel invisible in their presence. I wrote in my journal at that young age: "Note to self: if, by God's grace on my life, I am ever in a position of leadership or influence where others might want to be in my presence (which seems like a stretch these days!), I will treat everyone the same. I will ask personal questions and be interested in the lives of those within my proximity, knowing that no one is unimportant . . . that every person is of value and can teach me something."

Awhile back, ABC ran a TV news-reality show (along the lines of *Dateline* or *20/20*) called, *What Would You Do?* In the show, people were filmed by hidden cameras in various situations where they had the chance to step up—to be heroic, decent, and honest—or to cop out as deceitful, heartless cowards.[3]

The show explored many social dilemmas such as how people might react to someone weaker being bullied—if they thought no one was watching. Would people speak up when others refused service to someone because of race or picked on someone because of obesity—if they thought no one was watching? How would they react if they saw an obviously sick woman unable to pay for her prescription at the pharmacy counter—if they thought no one was watching? What would happen if they witnessed a hazing or caught a thief in the act? If they saw a stranger trying to lure away an unattended child on a playground, would they intervene—if they thought no one was watching?

At times it was heartening to view an average Joe or Jane rise to the occasion and do the right thing, even when that person thought no one else could see. Too often, though, it was disappointing to observe people who had the power to make a difference turn away in self-protectionism or even join sides with the wrong-doer.

I had a bigger question when I watched this program. What would *I* do in those circumstances? If I thought no one else would ever see or know . . . how would I react? Jesus addressed the same issue in Luke 12:1–3 (NLT, emphasis mine):

Meanwhile, the crowds grew until thousands were milling about and crushing each other. Jesus turned first to his disciples and warned them, "Beware of the yeast of the Pharisees—beware of their hypocrisy. The time is coming when everything will be revealed; *all that is secret will be made public.* Whatever you have said in the dark will be heard in the light, and what you have whispered behind closed doors will be shouted from the housetops for all to hear!"

This is a fascinating scenario. A massive crowd had gathered, yet Jesus seemed more concerned about communicating with His disciples than taking advantage of this day in the spotlight. In this teachable moment, Jesus knew His team could easily be swept up by the glory of attracting such a throng. "Watch out," Jesus warned as He issued the disciples a strong hypocrisy alert.

• CROWDS CAN MAKE US DUPLICITOUS •

Many eyes on us can tempt us to put on an affect that's less than genuine. We can suddenly become all-wise, super-spiritual, and sweet as a powdered-sugar-dusted honeycomb when we're "on stage" before an adoring crowd. And not all stages occur in large, public gatherings. We can develop a "stage presence" around friends we want to impress, leaders we want to sway, even strangers we want to outdo. I've sat in meetings where it was obvious that someone was playing only to the team leader—no one else's opinion mattered. And (ahem . . . gulp, swallow), there have been times that person was me. In the setting of a crowd, often it's not the crowd that needs controlling . . . it's me.

Jesus took this occasion to warn the disciples about pharisaical hypocrisy, the root of which is *being different in secret than you are in public. Integrity* means being whole or undivided . . . the same all the way through. He had strong words for leaders who tried to look good to others but were something altogether different on the inside: "Woe to you, because you are like unmarked graves, which men walk over without knowing it" (Luke 11:44). Everything looked grassy and beautiful on the surface, but underneath was hidden decay.

If you're starting to squirm because there are situations where you know you act differently depending on the setting or who you're with, you're not alone. Not that it's any real consolation, but even some of the great New Testament leaders had the same problem. In fact, no one less than the apostle Peter, himself—the one who had spent years traveling with Jesus, the one whose bold preaching to crowds in Jerusalem helped usher in the birth of the Church—even *he* got caught up in duplicity.

• DUPLICITY IS A MATTER OF THE HEART •

In Galatians 2:11–16, Paul tells about having to confront Peter for his hypocrisy. Peter had been in the habit of dining with Gentile believers . . . that is, until some influential (and legalistic) Jews arrived. At that point, he became a separatist and wouldn't even share a meal with his non-Jewish friends anymore. Take a look at these verses: (Gal. 2:12–13, emphasis mine)

> Before certain men came from James, he used to eat with the Gentiles. But when they arrived, he began to draw back and separate himself from the Gentiles

because he was afraid of those who belonged to the circumcision group. The other Jews joined him in his hypocrisy, so that by their hypocrisy even Barnabas was led astray.

Peter "was afraid." When we get at the heart of the matter, duplicity is really a matter of the heart. We play to the crowd because we have fearful hearts. So we take on almost any role and change colors to blend in with our surroundings in order to avoid rejection by those we deem most powerful or favorable.

In his book, *The Painful Side of Leadership: Moving Forward Even When It Hurts,* Jeff Iorg unearths one tendril of hypocrisy's ugly root. He writes, "Jesus recognized an important reality: People are often controlled by false sources of security. Security is such a strong need, a compelling drive, a powerful thirst, that whoever or whatever satisfies the need will be obeyed. Leaders who draw security from God through Jesus are free to obey God. Leaders who long for security through affirmation from their followers will do whatever is necessary to obtain it."[4] And apparently that includes being phonies, if a large number of headlines about religious leaders from the last three decades are any indication.

The sad thing is, this kind of hypocrisy is contagious. In the biblical story above, the double-standard virus infected Peter's Jewish friends until even Barnabas, who was known for being an encourager, a good man full of faith and the Holy Spirit (Acts 11:22–24), came down with a bad case of insincerity. Duplicitous leaders endanger those they lead. It's not unlikely or uncommon for a whole group, be it a church or an organization or a business, to take on the same air of pretension as the one in charge.

We all need a good friend like Paul to whop us upside the head with a good, hard "brick" of candor now and then. "When I saw that they were not acting in line with the truth of the gospel, I said to Peter in front of them all, 'You are a Jew, yet you live like a Gentile and not like a Jew. How is it, then, that you force Gentiles to follow Jewish customs?'" (Gal. 2:14). *Ouch!*

It takes staring honestly at our unvarnished selves in the mirror of God's Word to bring us back to reality and to get the crowd-pleasing part of our hearts under control again. I love what the great preacher, Haddon Robinson, used to say whenever he got up to speak: "Lord, if these people knew what you know about me, they wouldn't listen to a word I say." Now *that's* great crowd control!

One of my seminary professors, a clinical psychologist, used a phrase I try to remember whenever I'm tempted to cater to a crowd, be it large or small. One of Dr. Melody Palm's maxims for a healthy approach to life is: "Nothing to prove, nothing to lose." I love that! This is no longer a fearful heart, trying to prove its worth to those in power. And it's no longer intimidated into believing that being "the real me" will result in loss . . . at least not the kind of loss that counts.

WHEN WE GET AT THE HEART OF THE MATTER, DUPLICITY IS REALLY A MATTER OF THE HEART.

Authority and influence that has its basis in duplicity is a weight too heavy for anyone to carry for long. Trying to keep up with being who you think the next person wants you to be (which is something altogether different from what the last person wanted you to be) will wear you out. I began this chapter with one of my favorite quotes by Anne Morrow Lindbergh: "The most exhausting thing in life, I have discovered, is being insincere."[5] *Nothing to prove; nothing to lose.*

One of the things I love most about Jesus in the Gospels is that He never pandered to the powerful or catered to the crowd. Never. The "I Am that I Am"? Well, He was who He was . . . always. With everyone. Period. When He needed to give a rebuke, it was without consideration of someone's rank or power. And when He offered compassion and kindness, it was without taking into account someone's lack of status or being perceived as an outcast. Of all the things that draw me to Jesus, His authenticity is high on the list. His other attributes would be tarnished if He weren't for real. But His is *real* love, *real* compassion, *real* power, *real* grace. Real.

Nothing is more disheartening than finding out someone you've loved, trusted, and believed in, is not who you think they are. My own heart hurt when I read the account of just such a double life in the Saturday, July 24, 2010 edition of *The Seattle Times.*

Kateen Fenter thought her husband of twenty-five years was a good man. In her eyes, thirty-nine-year-old Michael was a law-abiding farmer and father to their three children. Why, a few years back he had even moved the whole family to Colorado to help build a new Foursquare church. Michael, who had gone to school for marine carpentry, had the reputation of being a hard worker in his job as a boat builder. But he had a lighter side, too, and frequently broke into song.

Eventually, the couple was able to fulfill a long-held dream. With the help of Kateen's parents, they bought forty acres and started up Compass Rose Farms in the beautiful little town of Port Townsend, Washington. It was a lot of work, to be sure, and start-up farming is not very profitable at first. But by living simply and without credit card debt, they were making it, and life was good. Michael was a good man.

Duplicity is a fragile mask, one which often grows even more brittle, more likely to break, over time. A phone call from the FBI saying her husband was in jail shattered Michael's mask of respectability and pierced Kateen Fenter's life with the shards of his deception. In the following days she would learn that the man she thought she knew so well—the good man, the clean-living farmer with no criminal history—was actually robbing banks. He had stolen thousands of dollars, using bomb threats and carrying a gun.

Kateen could hardly take it in, but the surveillance photos were indisputable. *The Seattle Times* article captures her reaction:

> "My life just came to a screeching halt," she said. "Here was this load of information you have to assimilate into a way of life that makes no sense to you at all. What are you going to do? What are you going to believe?" She said the Michael she knew would never rob, never threaten. . . . For months Kateen said she did little more than lay on the floor, in shock. "How did I miss this?" she wondered.[6]

Not all stories of being inauthentic are as dramatic as Michael Fenter's, but they all diminish the brightness of our lives, disappoint others, and damage our ability to lead for the long-haul. Years ago, I heard that when bank tellers learn to tell the difference between real and counterfeit currency, they focus on knowing the real deal instead of trying to learn everything about the "funny money." Because they become so familiar with what is authentic, it becomes easier to spot the phony stuff.

• WHAT AUTHENTICITY LOOKS LIKE •

What does authenticity look like in the life of a Jesus-hearted woman? Let's get familiar with three components (though there are more) of being the real deal as Christ-following leaders. An authentic Jesus-hearted woman:

Tells the Truth About the Messy Parts of Her Life

I love the definition of authenticity by author and coach, Tony Stoltzfus: "the appropriate amount of transparency for the occasion without thought of how it makes me appear to others."[7]

Sometimes we have to get comfortable being *un*comfortable with some things about ourselves, our performance, our limitations. It's easy to become addicted to feeling good about ourselves. And while we do need a certain sense of accomplishment about who we are and what we do, we can and must learn to live with the tension of being a mixed bag—greatness and grime.

But how can we tell what the appropriate amount of transparency is for any given situation? I mean, how much of the "real me" can people stand when I get pretty sick of myself at times? There's an art, a cost, and a high return to being genuine.

While there's no hard and fast rule for when to talk honestly and openly about your failures, struggles, and sins, these are some guidelines I've found helpful. I'll expose the messy parts of my story: (1) when I think it will benefit others who are struggling in the same areas; or (2) when my vulnerability paves the way for others to relate to a bigger message God wants to speak through me; or (3) when I need help and am pretty certain those who are listening to my "muddy side" are spiritually-healthy people who can handle my struggles with godly care and confidentiality.

On the other hand, those who are in the habit of venting (I might call it "verbally vomiting" but that would be gross) any time, any place, to anyone without concern for the effect on others, are not being authentic—

> **WE CAN AND MUST LEARN TO LIVE WITH THE TENSION OF BEING A MIXED BAG—GREATNESS AND GRIME.**

they're being selfish. They may feel better after a cathartic airing of their dirty laundry, but those around them are reeling. At times I've winced as a leader chattered, almost gleefully, about her past illegal or immoral antics, or inappropriate "escapades"— or perhaps about an ugly conflict with a parishioner, or another leader—while new believers or young children listened, wide-eyed and dismayed. Not wise.

For others, their "back story" (as a victim, or an addict, or . . . fill in the blanks) can become their primary identity in a way that's not healthy or doesn't allow them to become the person God wants them to be. We've all heard commercials on the radio or TV repeated so often we get sick of them to the point that we determine *not* to buy the product, even if it's a good one! That can happen with people, too.

Today there's a focus on telling our stories in the Christ-following community, and I love it! In fact, I wrote a workshop that's become one of my favorites to teach. It's called *The Power of Your Story*. But, guess what? You are more than your story, if by that you mean the overarching history of your past and how God worked there, as great as that may be.

That is you, yes. But you are also the way you spoke to the clerk in the grocery store (who overcharged you for the bananas) and the attitude you had toward your husband when he forgot to pick up the dry cleaning . . . again. You are the fresh throbbing of faith beating in your heart from the insights you gained as you spent time in the Word this morning. You are the over-comer who squelched the desire to gossip when you had a juicy piece of news and an overwhelming desire to tell it. You are the attentive disciple of Jesus who stopped for a divine-appointment conversation with your neighbor on a busy Tuesday earlier this week.

I'm not saying we should ever stop telling our "big story," the most outstanding testimony of divine deliverance in our lives. But that shouldn't be the only story we tell. The God-work of grace is current. It's as much about what happened this afternoon, and what will happen tomorrow morning, as it is that "big sin" God saved you from, or that tragic experience He brought you through. Tell your *now* story, too. It might not be as dramatic, but it will help you to live in authenticity about your walk with God today instead of just relying on a canned version of yesterday's experience.

What I'm saying is, please don't be like the engaging speaker who moves everyone to tears by her story, but moves those closest to her to tears by the way she treats them. Got it? Good.

Is More "Colorful"

As a little girl, I was both tomboy and girlie-girl. I loved making forts and climbing trees. I also relished playing dress-up and walking around in high heels. At the local dime store, I would beg my mother to buy me those little packages of pretend cosmetics. They contained a mirror (of sorts, which was usually just shiny foil, not real glass), a small brush and comb, a bottle of "nail polish" (which only held air), and a tube of hard plastic lipstick.

I *loved* that lipstick! It was usually a daring shade of bright pink or red, and I dreamed it would make me look glamorous, like a movie star! But no matter how often and how hard I rubbed it over my little lips, they stayed the same.

Here's the thing. Authenticity is sometimes a bit untidy and unpredictable, but it colors everything. Phoniness in leadership is a little like using plastic lipstick. You can apply it all you want but since it's not real, nothing changes.

I love leaders who are willing to try something off-the-map even if it flops because they're desperate to see life-change in those they serve. These leaders are willing to exchange the appearance of perpetual success (because they keep doing the same thing forever) for the possibility of making a bigger impact down the road.

My young friend, Tiffany, is not a plastic-lipstick leader. Today, as I write this, is her twenty-fifth birthday and already she has slashed away at hell's future population. When I served as Women's Ministries Director for the Northwest Ministry Network, a well-respected pastor from one of the great churches in our state called my office. He wanted to know if I had any recommendations for a new pastoral staff position at his church. He said they especially wanted a woman for this role (God bless him!) and would love someone who was willing to think outside the box. (Double bless him—that's what *he* was doing!)

I gave him several names of outstanding women leaders and then, towards the end of our conversation, one more name popped into my head. (I'm pretty sure I know who put it there.) "Pastor, this is kind of a wild card, but I want to mention one other person to you. She's very young and she hasn't gone through all the traditional channels of preparation you might require for this role, but I'm going to throw her name into the mix."

To my surprise, the more I told him about Tiffany, how passionate and articulate she was, how she had spent a couple of years working with the destitute and broken on the streets of London, how she was willing to do whatever it took to reach people for Jesus, the more intrigued he became. Soon he connected with Tiffany and decided she was the person for the job!

And that's how Tiffany Bluhm came to serve as the Pastor of Influence and Outreach at an outstanding church in Washington. When you talk with Tiffany, her beautiful eyes shimmer with passion and she identifies herself as a social entrepreneur. That means she's always coming up with new ways to make a difference in the darkness around her. Tiffany is a colorful, Jesus-hearted leader.

After Tiffany started serving on this church staff, she and some other young women (including my daughter, Jana), began to feel deeply heart-broken over the women working in the sex industry in the greater Seattle-Tacoma region. So prayerfully and boldly, they started an outreach called Esteem.

Here is how Esteem works: once a month, these courageous young women go to many of the strip clubs in the area, along the I-5 corridor. When they get to a club, three of them go in and take gifts to the girls who work as strippers there while the rest stay in the van with their male driver and pray. They rotate who stays in the van and who goes inside as the night progresses.

The gift bags contain sweet little things that any girl would appreciate, as well as a small touch card with a Web site on it. When the young women from the clubs go on the Web site (which they often do because of the kindness of the Esteem women and the relationships that form), they find the personal stories of others who have left the sex industry and have found hope and a new chance at life through a relationship with Jesus. Additionally, the Web site has information about how to find a mentor, how to write a job resume, as well as links to other important resources for those who might be considering going in a new direction.

When I Skyped with Tiffany recently, she told me that as a result of this ministry, and others that have sprung from it, more than 500 young women have left their jobs as strippers and have started new lives! Tiffany has formed a partnership with local law enforcement in dealing with the problem of prostitution and is also working on housing for a number of the young women who find themselves homeless while trying to find a new means of support.

This work, and Tiffany's approach to leadership, has not been tidy and predictable; it's not always been safe or easy. But the bright colors of grace are now splashed over the lives of many formerly dark, broken souls. Tiffany is an authentic Jesus-hearted woman, and her leadership is vibrant. She considers me a coach/mentor/friend, but I want to be more like Tiffany.

Is Approachable and Relatable

Is it just me, or are there some people who put on such a "spiritual air" that they make the rest of us feel like a lower caste, simply because we're human? They are the ones who *tsk, tsk* at humor and laughter, especially in a holy setting. They have a spiritual application for every possible situation. ("You had a flat tire on the way to church? I think the Lord might be telling you to pump up your personal Bible study habits, my dear!") And God forbid you should reveal an area of personal struggle in your marriage or your health or your kids' lives—or even that you have trouble staying on top of the piles of laundry in any given week! If you do, be ready for "the look" and a quick-fix formula to set you straight. *Sigh.*

On the other hand, authentic Jesus-hearted women can laugh at themselves and their foibles. They can admit to days when they eat too much chocolate and put on mismatched shoes in the early morning hours or forget to pack underwear when they're flying off to an important week of meetings. (Don't even ask where I came up with these examples!)

You want to know one thing that keeps women apart, that keeps us from connecting on a heart level? The wrong assumption that she (whoever "she" is) has it all together and I don't. The not-so-funny thing is that *she* is probably thinking the same thing about *you!*

Many years ago, my friend Jeannie Collins and I were on our way to a big Christmas gift show event. As we neared the destination, a large coliseum, I turned on my blinkers and tried to merge into the crowded turn lane. About that time, we were parallel to a beautiful, super-expensive foreign sports car driven by an elegant, lavishly dressed woman.

Since we were all creeping along super slowly, we had time to take in this woman's expression as she looked over at us in our not-so-new, mom-style minivan. She took her time in scrutinizing us, then literally turned up her nose with a look of disdain and pulled ahead without allowing us to merge. Honestly, her expression was so obvious and exaggerated that Jeannie and I looked at each other in disbelief. *Wow, really?!!* Thankfully the next driver was a bit more gracious so we pulled in, right behind Sports Car Lady.

As we merged, Jeannie and I couldn't keep from bursting out in laughter when we read Sports Car Lady's bumper sticker: UPPITY WOMEN UNITE! It gets even

AUTHENTIC JESUS-HEARTED WOMEN CAN LAUGH AT THEMSELVES AND THEIR FOIBLES.

better. Guess who we found ourselves next to among the crowds streaming through the doors as we waited to buy our entrance tickets for the event? *Yep!* Sports Car Lady! Trying to be frugal, Jeannie and I had both brought coupons that allowed us a discounted price for our tickets . . . and I had an extra. I couldn't resist. Turning to Sports Car Lady, I offered, "I have an extra discount coupon. Would you like to use it?" She stammered her thanks, took the coupon (and used it!), and we all went in together.

Jeannie and I have had many chuckles together about that experience. But here's the sad thing: uppity women *can't* unite. It's only when we come down off our high horses and allow ourselves, and others, the room to be imperfectly human, that we can come together and help each other become a little more godly. A Jesus-hearted woman is real, down-to-earth, and approachable. She'll be the same person in any setting and really tries to show kindness to everyone, no matter their social status, wealth, credentials, or role in life.

While I can remember the sting of being treated rudely or ignored by a few people in positions of leadership through the years, I have many more memories of those who, though they outranked me on so many levels (renown, talent, wealth, beauty, intelligence, credentials, and authority—to name a few), were genuinely kind, approachable, and down to earth. When we spoke, they looked into my eyes and asked me a personal question or two. Their verbal responses showed they were paying attention to my inquiries, not just trying to brush me off. Some of them made an extra effort to remember my name or to follow up in some way that exceeded my expectation. Even though we would never become best friends (not something I was seeking anyway), they showed me I mattered as a person.

Here's the thing, and it's especially important for those of us in ministry leadership to remember: God really does have a *"What Would You Do?"* camera rolling. Live your life as if there were no secrets, because some day that will be true! And if we've lived a life of secret integrity and authenticity, we'll have cause for open celebration for all those hidden moments when our actions revealed a Jesus-heart that beat for God's glory!

• JODI'S COACHING QUESTIONS •

- As a leader, how do you treat people around you who seemingly have nothing to add to your life or are there to serve you in some way? When was the last time you were intentionally kind to a waitress or a member of a hotel's housekeeping staff?

- What would it look like to take off one layer of insincerity? Where would you start? Who should you talk to about this?

- Think of yourself in the spotlight of the crowd. What is your demeanor? How do you attempt to come across? Now think of yourself with those closest to you, especially co-workers and family members. Is there a difference between your demeanor and tone of voice before the crowd and in the presence of your family? If so why? How can you build integrity into your life by being the same person in every setting?

- What simple questions can you ask at the next opportunity to show interest in others, even casual acquaintances or strangers?

• A LITTLE LESSON FOR NEW LEADERS •

Rather than allowing yourself to be intimidated by more seasoned (but perhaps self-absorbed) leaders, use any negative experiences with them to propel you to decide ahead of time what kind of leader you want to be, and how you want to treat others if you should ever be the person in charge or the one being admired by a crowd. Write down the qualities you want to have at your core as a leader and how you want to affect those who relate to you, in public or in private.

• HEART-DEEP IN THE WORD •

Duplicity began in the Garden of Eden with the fall of humanity. Read the account from Genesis 3:1–19 and notice how Adam and Eve moved from authenticity and openness to deceit and cover-up. How does that parallel with the progression towards inauthenticity in people's lives today?

_____

_____

_____

_____

Jesus warned His disciples against hypocrisy both publicly and privately. Many of these cautions relate to some of our basic spiritual practices today. Read the verses below that correspond with the spiritual discipline listed. Then describe ways that these good things can become tainted by phoniness, and note how to prevent hypocrisy in each area:

- Prayer (Matt. 6:5–6)
- Giving (Matt. 6:2–4)
- Fasting (Matt. 6:16–18)
- Getting rid of sinful behavior (Matt. 7:1–5)
- Making a convert or a disciple (Matt. 23:15)
- Praising God (Mark 7:6–8)

_____

_____

_____

_____

Sincerity is another word for authenticity; it's used in various Bible translations and paraphrased versions. Psalm 15 describes the characteristics of a sincere person. Read that chapter and write down, or discuss, all the marks of sincerity described there.

_____

_____

_____

Romans 12:9 says "Love must be sincere." How can you identify sincere love in yourself and in others?

_____

_____

_____

_____

_____

chapter three

FLOOR EXERCISE

LEADERSHIP QUALITY: HUMILITY

. . . .

Life is a long lesson in humility.
—JAMES MATTHEW BARRIE
(NOVELIST AND CREATOR OF PETER PAN)

I love gymnastics. I should say I love to *watch* gymnastics since I couldn't even do a simple cartwheel if my life depended on it. But when the summer Olympics roll around every four years, that's the sport I'm glued to, given the chance.

One of my favorite gymnastic events is the floor exercise. It amazes me how gymnasts (especially the women, I think) can be so graceful and agile as they go through those jaw-dropping routines. It's astounding to watch their lithe, flexible bodies twisting, flipping, and bending through the various moves, all in perfect time to a musical score, no less! My back aches just thinking about it.

There's something utterly compelling about a leader who has mastered the "floor exercise" of humility. It's akin to that *gracious confidence* quality I talked about in the first chapter. This trait of a Jesus-hearted woman allows her to move through life gracefully, flexibly, in cadence to the God-music she hears in her heart—her spirit dances but her feet touch the ground. She may even fly through the air now and then, but she always comes back to earth. Like a skilled gymnast, she turns the floor—a lowly place—into a canvas where beauty happens.

Some leaders prefer the high-wire over the floor. Like a circus performer, they want to do all their moves far above an awestruck crowd. On the other hand, for those who do the floor exercise, the crowd is always above them. They shine from below. Hmmm . . . is this beginning to sound familiar?

> **HUMILITY . . . IS LESS ABOUT WHAT YOU DO TO YOURSELF AND MORE ABOUT HOW YOU VIEW AND TREAT THOSE AROUND YOU.**

There's a lot you can learn on the floor. In the last chapter, we looked at authenticity, an invaluable quality for Jesus-hearted women who want to be enduring (and endearing) leaders. Now, our focus goes to authenticity's twin sister, *humility.* I purposely put them in this order because it's pretty hard to be truly humble if you're not authentic first . . . if you can't be honest and real about both your strengths and weaknesses.

The Bible has so much to say about humility (especially when you look at the examples of those who did and did not display it); it's almost daunting to know where to begin. It even mentions false humility, so perhaps that's a good place to start.

We've all heard lines like, "once you finally think you're humble, it's proof you're not" or "he was so proud of being such a humble guy." In his novel *David Copperfield,* Charles Dickens created an interesting, annoying, and completely unlikable character named Uriah Heep who fit that description. He never passed up a chance to tell people how "'umble" he was![8]

Colossians 2:18 talks about a whole group of Uriah Heeps. These people delighted in *appearing* humble, but it was a false humility. From the context of the entire chapter, we see that these folks combined legalistic rules with severe, self-imposed bodily discipline and threw in esoteric visions with the worship of angels for good measure . . . all to show how humble they were (in a spiritually-superior way, of course). The kicker comes in verse 23, however: "Such regulations indeed have an *appearance* of wisdom, with their self-imposed worship, their *false humility* and their harsh treatment of the body, *but they lack any value in restraining sensual indulgence"* (emphasis mine).

What I gather from this is that humility has to start on the inside. And it's less about what you do to yourself and more about how you view and treat those around you. Titus 3:2 makes that plain when it says we're to show true humility *to* everyone. Humility is a "to" thing. And it's to *everyone,* not just a privileged few.

Are people confused about what humility (or meekness, a biblical synonym) means these days? I think so. Some think that to be humble I have to wear frumpy, plain clothes (no bright colors, for heaven's sake!), stay away from anything pleasurable, never really have an opinion, use a wimpy voice, and look at the floor when I'm talking to anyone. But like Colossians 2:23 explains, none of that changes the human heart in a way that makes us truly humble. In fact, we can do all those and still be screaming on the inside, "Hey, notice me!" or "If you only knew . . . I'm really better than you."

So, can a boisterous personality, someone who is outgoing and confident, still be humble? Absolutely, and she had better be if she wants to be an honest-to-goodness, Jesus-hearted leader! Being humble is not based on your personality type. It's far deeper than that. It's a spiritual posture—an internal bending of the knee, the heart bowing in honor and service, both to God and others. It's the willingness to exercise our gifts at floor level, if that's where we're needed and where we can make a difference. *Floor exercise.*

• LEADERSHIP TRAPS •

In Matthew 23, Jesus warned about another set of twin traits, dangerous ones: *hypocrisy* and *pride.* They go together in the same way that their opposites, authenticity and humility, do. In fact, that whole chapter of Matthew 23 makes a great study in how to avoid specific ministry leadership traps. The traps are:

- **Preaching over practice** (3b) "they do not practice what they preach."
- **Showmanship over substance** (5a) "Everything they do is for show."
- **Prominence over preferring others** (6a) "And how they love to sit at the head table at banquets and in the most prominent seats in the synagogue!"
- **Star syndrome over servanthood** (7a) "They enjoy the attention they get on the streets"

- **Title over task** (7b) "and they enjoy being called 'Rabbi.'"

So how do we avoid those leadership traps? I've got three suggestions.

Don't Go for the Title—Go for Ministry

Jesus told how the scribes and Pharisees (who wanted the acclaim of religious titles) put burdens on others but were not willing to lift a finger to help (v. 3 and 4). They cared more about position than exertion—actually doing the work! Have you ever known anyone like that in leadership? It's not pretty for those around her.

So that raises a query: are all titles wrong? That's a good question for those of us in leadership who often end up with a label attached to our name. What about being called reverend, doctor, pastor, professor, or some other title? I think Jesus was aiming at the danger of being enamored with rank and status more than a blanket condemnation of all titles. Sometimes Jesus allowed himself to be called Rabbi (or Teacher), Lord, and Master—all titles. And later Paul called himself an apostle. But more often they both self-identified as "servant." Don't let titles trump the task of serving from the heart.

Here it is in black and white (verse 11): "The greatest among you must be a servant." We just talked about task over title, but *this* is where *that* springs from. This verse doesn't just say "serve"—something you *do*. It says *"be* a servant"—something you *are*, which in turn produces service, the things you do.

No matter what title anyone else calls you, be a servant and then do what a servant does . . . from your heart. That's where humility starts.

Walk on Level Ground as Family

You're no better or worse, above or beneath, anyone else. That's the freeing piece of humility that we sometimes overlook. I love verse 8b: Jesus said, "and all of you are on the same level as brothers and sisters." There's something leveling about family; even when you've achieved great success, at home everyone knows you, warts, bad hair days, and all! And when you've face-planted in the dirt due to some disastrous failure, they still know and love you there. That leveling "family factor" helps you pick yourself up and try again.

> YOU'RE NO BETTER OR WORSE, ABOVE OR BENEATH, ANYONE ELSE.

Shoot for the Rug

Want to escape some of the most dangerous and destructive ministry and leadership traps? Aim downward. "The greatest among you will be your servant" (v. 11). Since we're all family anyway, there's nothing degrading or demeaning about going to the floor for the sake of your brother or sister. Jesus asks them to do the same for you.

This is opposite of what we hear in the world, and even in the church, where we're told to "go higher" and "shoot for the stars." Now in the best sense, those can be good challenges—we need to dream and have the faith to attempt big things for God. We should stretch towards the high calling of God for our lives, absolutely.

Still, Jesus said exaltation finds its candidates on the floor, picking up the debris left by the prideful . . . bending down to wash a sister's feet . . . kneeling in awe of God's greatness. "But those who exalt themselves will be humbled, and those who humble themselves will be exalted" (v. 12).

TEN REASONS TO MASTER THE "FLOOR EXERCISE"

Honestly, I wish this book were equipped with a megaphone right now because I really want you to get how *huge* the humility issue is if you're serious about being a Jesus-hearted leader. Pride can disqualify us from long-term, effective ministry quicker, and more permanently, than just about anything. And our only immunization from it (or antidote, once it has taken hold) is humility.

But why? Really, what's the big deal with this whole "be humble" thing, anyway? I mean, if we're hard workers, have good intentions, are gifted, and can do the job, what does it matter? Here are ten reasons why Jesus-hearted women need to master this kind of "floor exercise."

1. Humility Is a Quality God Loves and Is Looking For

When I read the account of Mary's place in God's plan to bring His Son into the world, I'm struck by the emphasis upon her humility and its contrast to the prideful. In her song-prayer of praise, which has come to be known as the *Magnificat,* she says this (Luke 1:46–52, selected verses, emphasis mine): "My soul glorifies the LORD and my spirit rejoices in God my Savior, for he has been mindful of *the humble state of his servant. . . .* He has performed mighty deeds with his arm; he has *scattered those who are proud* in their inmost thoughts. He has *brought down rulers* from their thrones but has *lifted up the humble.*"

Want to know what God comes looking for when He wants to use someone greatly in this world? Apparently the lowly-hearted are standouts. Isaiah 66:2 makes this clear: "This is the one I esteem: he who is humble and contrite in spirit, and trembles at my word."

The humble make God's short list because humility prepares us to handle promotion and human admiration in a God-honoring way. And, by the way, it keeps us from turning into jerks toward others when we finally have some clout. First Peter 3:8 points this out: "Finally, all of you, live in harmony with one another; be sympathetic, love as brothers, be compassionate and humble."

We see this played out in the lives of many leaders in the Bible: Moses, David, Gideon, Esther, Deborah, and Jeremiah, to name a few. As you read their stories, you find they all have the common denominator of being humble people, though they were also bold, courageous leaders.

2. Humility Puts Others at Ease

In one of His most beloved invitations, Jesus says, "Come to me, all you who are weary and burdened, and I will give you rest. Take my yoke upon you and learn from me, for I am *gentle and humble in heart,* and you will find *rest for your souls*" (Matt. 11:28–29, emphasis mine).

Did you catch that? He ties His humility to our rest! Why is that? Think for a minute what it's like to be around a prideful person. I know how it makes me feel: tense, on edge, like I need to make a good impression, to measure up somehow. I leave worrying that I might have said the wrong thing. I feel anxious, maybe even a little disgusted by the whole encounter, and disappointed that I let it get to me.

On the other hand, when I'm in the presence of a humble person, I relax. We talk about things that matter without the worry of one-upmanship or competition. I'm encouraged to be myself by her demeanor and authenticity. I usually learn something because I know I won't be scoffed at for asking questions. My spirit breathes a big sigh of relief, and I go away refreshed and, yes, somehow rested.

That's how I want to affect people, and it will only happen if I'm a person of humility.

3. Humility Makes Us More Like Jesus

As I grew up in the church, I heard repeatedly how we should try to be like Jesus. That could mean many things: to love deeply, sacrifice, have more power, or be holy. However, we wouldn't even know about those things, or know about *Him,* if He hadn't humbled Himself and come down to us first.

Philippians 2:3–8 says it so well: "Do nothing out of selfish ambition or vain conceit, but in *humility consider others better than yourselves.* Each of you should look not only to your own interests, but also to the interests of others. *Your attitude should be the same as that of Christ Jesus:* Who, being in very nature God, did not consider equality with God something to be grasped, but *made himself nothing*, taking the very nature of a servant, being made in human likeness. And being found in appearance as a man, *he humbled himself* and became obedient to death—even death on a cross!" (emphasis mine)

What are you grasping that could be laid aside for the sake of "coming down" to others? We often say, "Wow, that person really made something of herself!" But this verse says that Jesus made Himself *nothing*. That's a depth of humility we find hard to imagine! So, do you *still* want to be more like Jesus?

4. Humility Lets You Be Part of the Secret Service

Okay, so this might need a bit of explanation. No, you don't get to wear those cool, dark sunglasses, carry a pistol inside your black suit jacket, and follow the president around, just by being humble. But humility will put you in an elite group: those who look for ways to give and serve in secret and are happy about it!

Again, Jesus was such a good example of this. Centuries earlier the prophet Isaiah wrote this prophetic description of Him, "He will not shout or cry out, or raise his voice in the streets" (Isa. 42:2). Jesus was not on earth to seek fame or popularity or to make a name for Himself. He didn't put up big signs, send out a press release, and say "Here I am!" In fact, very often when He healed someone, He asked that person to tell no one. That seems odd to us today, unless you factor in humility.

Interestingly, even His own brothers urged Him to make a big splash with His miracles. Look at their words in John 7:3–5: "Jesus' brothers said to him, 'You ought to leave here and go to Judea, so that your disciples may see the miracles you do. *No one who wants to become a public figure acts in secret*. Since you are doing these things, show yourself to the world.' For even his own brothers did not believe in him" (emphasis mine). It was not about faith to them; it was about "becoming a public figure," being popular. Jesus resisted their urging and explained that it was not "His time."

The last verse in the Gospel of John says that "Jesus did so many other things while He was on earth that if they were all written down, the whole world couldn't contain the books" (John 21:25). So when we read about the good works that were recorded in Scripture—His kindness, His healings, His grace to sinners, His generosity in helping the poor and hurting—we're only scratching the surface. My guess is that many (perhaps most?) of those other unrecorded deeds were done in secret, only to be revealed in eternity when all good works will be on display to glorify God! Then it really will be "His time!"

What about us? Jesus invites us to join His "secret service" when He tells us to do our giving, fasting, and praying in secret. (See Matt. 6:4, 6, and 18.) Can I be transparent here? Boy, this is a tough one for me. Full disclosure . . . if I've done something good for someone, especially if it's extra generous or anywhere near the "above and beyond" category, I love to casually weave that into later conversations—in a very humble *(ahem!)* manner, of course. I wonder how many times I've been booted out of God's Secret Service without even knowing it. Unlike Jesus, who was willing to wait for His good deeds to be exposed at the right time, I want others to know what I did *now*—I'm so quick to trade the approval of God for the praise of people.

But God is working in me to make me His Jesus-hearted woman. So I'm learning more and more the joy that comes from giving and serving in secret. I just can't tell you about it right now—that would spoil the secret!

5. Humility Allows Us to Repair Broken Relationships

It took one glance at her face to see something was wrong. This was a friend who had also been a colleague in ministry for several years, and I could tell I had offended her somehow. I knew what I needed to do next, though I dreaded it. I would need to find a quiet, private place. I would need to ask how I had hurt her; then I would need to own my part, apologize sincerely, and make things right. It was time for another floor exercise in humility—the kind that stretches us and brings a lot of discomfort!

Ever been there? I'm sure you've figured this out by now, but even people who sincerely love Jesus and love each other—even seasoned leaders—can and do bring pain into one another's lives. Sometimes we don't mean to . . . and other times? Well . . .

IT TAKES HUMILITY ON BOTH ENDS TO MAKE THINGS WORK AND TO HEAL THE BROKEN BONDS OF FRIENDSHIP.

Jesus knew we would need a way to heal the breaks that happen in relationships among His followers. Matthew 18:15–35 spells out the approach for dealing with offenses and ends with a big emphasis on forgiveness.

Because I've had plenty of practice both in apologizing and forgiving, I can say this with certainty: it takes humility on both ends to make things work and to heal the broken bonds of friendship. To say, "I'm really sorry—will you forgive me?" and "Yes, I forgive you—and I still love you" requires humility to travel from the heart to the tongue. Often the mind and the will, fortified by pride, set up a blockade along that path. *Why should* I *be the one to apologize? She's just as wrong as I am . . . I'm just not ready to forgive him again. I don't think he's really sorry at all!*

But when I take my pride to the floor and exercise humility in these matters, there is healing and grace. First Peter 5:5 says, "All of you, clothe yourselves with humility toward one another, because, 'God opposes the proud but gives grace to the humble.'"

I've faced different kinds of opposition in my life, but I really don't want *God* to oppose me! I need all the grace I can get!!

So I met with that friend. We talked it out. It was humbling and painful to apologize. We cried together, we hugged, and then we healed. I learned again the truth of Isaiah 57:15: "The high and lofty one who inhabits eternity, the Holy One, says this: 'I live in that high and holy place with those whose spirits are contrite and humble. I refresh the humble and give new courage to those with repentant hearts.'"

6. Humility Allows Us to Ask for Help

I have a favorite Goethe quote given to me by my dear friend Dr. Ava Oleson. Done in a lovely calligraphy and beautifully framed, it hangs in my home where I see it literally every day. It says:

> "The moment one definitely commits oneself, then Providence moves too. . . . Whatever you can do or dream you can do, begin it. Boldness has genius, power, and magic in it. Begin it now."

Those words always inspire me to take that first step—to just begin and see what happens. Interestingly, I learned recently that Goethe liked to say that only about 2 percent of his thought was original. In my mind, that makes him brilliant *and* humble, which makes me like that calligraphy quote even better!

Wayne Booth writes, "We, if we're authentic, will expose the fact that we rely heavily on so many people for our best efforts, ideas, and accomplishments."[9] Here then, is a huge upside to humility. You realize that you can't accomplish all you want, or even all God wants to do through you, by yourself. The truly Jesus-hearted woman leaves behind her inner two-year-old who shouts, "I do it myself!" and humbly asks for help.

Sometimes we tend to think a good leader should never admit a deficiency but should always present herself as totally capable and sufficient. That's a mistake. Former US Supreme Court Justice Sandra Day O'Connor has said, "We don't accomplish anything in this world alone. Whatever happens is the result of the whole tapestry of one's life—all the weavings of individual threads from one to another that create something."[10]

Even Jesus asked for help—not because He was incapable, but to model humility and to let others be part of His good works. Think about it for a moment: did Jesus *really* need the servants to fill the water pots in order to make wine—after all, if He could make the wine, couldn't He also put the water in the pots? Couldn't He have fed the five thousand without the boy's loaves and fishes—and without the disciples' help to organize and distribute the meal?

When it was time to pay their taxes, did He really need Peter to catch the fish with the money in its mouth? And when He asked the woman at the well for a drink, don't you think that

He, the Water of Life—the One who spoke to wind and waves and made them behave, the One who *walked* on water—could have quenched His own thirst without her help? But Jesus made a point to ask for help, even when He was entirely capable.

Strong, Jesus-hearted women in leadership are also humble enough to ask for help. But it's because we really *do* need it! There've been so many times on my own leadership journey when I've had to ask for roadside assistance. One episode quickly comes to mind. I think I may have mentioned my . . . shall we say . . . exceptional lack of math-whiz skills in the first chapter of this book? Dealing with numbers and budgets almost always leaves me perplexed and trying to rub the tension headache away with my fingers (which impedes me from counting on them!).

So many times during my tenure at the Northwest Ministry Network, I had to humble myself and go to our amazing bookkeeper, Barbara Williams, for help. Barb is one of the sweetest, most accommodating women you'll ever meet—not to mention exceptionally smart with math and accounting! Over and over she helped me make

> STRONG, JESUS-HEARTED WOMEN IN LEADERSHIP ARE ALSO HUMBLE ENOUGH TO ASK FOR HELP.

sense of the numbers without once making me feel dumb or a bother. People like Barb make all the difference for people like me. They're God's gifts to our lives if we're humble enough to admit our need and ask for their help.

If you read business leadership books, you know about the role of mentors and sponsors. Mentors pour into us from their own experiences and acquired wisdom. Sponsors go one step further. They do that, but they also take an active role in helping us reach our goals.

In a great book about women and leadership in the business world, *How Remarkable Women Lead: The Breakthrough Model for Work & Life,* Joanna Barsh writes, "Your sponsor believes in you and so is willing to stick his or her neck out to create opportunities and to protect you when the chips are down."[11]

It's true! Having a sponsor is a great gift. He or she may write a letter of recommendation or pass along your name to someone who wants to fill a position that might fit your gifting. A sponsor goes to bat for you and opens doors that might have remained closed.

Barnabas did that for Saul in Acts 9:26–27 when the believers in Jerusalem were afraid of him. Paul frequently forwarded that gift to others in his letters as he sponsored those in ministry leadership (including several women) through favorable commendations. Listen to what he wrote about Phoebe in Romans 16:1–2: "I commend to you our sister Phoebe, a servant of the church in Cenchrea. I ask you to receive her in the LORD in a way worthy of the saints and to give her any help she may need from you, for she has been a great help to many people, including me." Wow, how would you like to have a sponsor like that?

I've had many sponsors throughout my life, and without them I would never have had so many opportunities for leadership and ministry. But my best sponsor is the man I live with every day. Forgive me for getting a little bit sappy here (and I may need to grab a tissue as I write this), but you wouldn't be reading this book without Don's sponsorship in my life.

Throughout our marriage, he has recognized and called out gifts in me long before I, or others, could see them. He has often commended me to others for leadership and cheered me on as I tried my wings. That's especially true in the area of writing.

When I first began writing for *The Seattle Times* back in 2007, without my request or knowledge (I promise!), Don sent e-mails with my column to several people. Honestly, I was a little embarrassed by that at first, but it was so sweet of him and the responses we got back were encouraging—so the list grew and more people asked to be included.

I know Don has taken a little ribbing for being so proud of me. He's not only a great leader but a man of humility who's been willing to love and serve his wife as Christ loved and served the church—which was also in a pretty public manner! At any rate, because of Don's sponsorship, many more people have read the things I've written than would have otherwise. And that's opened numerous doors for speaking, writing, and leadership opportunities, which, I'm quite sure, led to this book being written and published.

So there you have it! The very words you're reading now are a direct product of someone helping me in ways that I couldn't help myself. (Thank you, Don, my love!) Like Saul turned Paul, it's a gift I'll be sure to keep passing along for the rest of my life.

7. Humility Is a Package Deal

I ask the Lord for certain things almost every day. One of those is wisdom. Another is to have good, healthy relationships. When I read the Scriptures, I see that these things are linked to humility . . . they're a package deal. "When pride comes, then comes disgrace, *but with humility comes wisdom*" (Prov. 11:2, emphasis mine). Apparently you can be successful and arrogant.

You can be rich and arrogant. You can even be smart and arrogant. But you cannot be wise and arrogant. True wisdom is interwoven with humility—they cannot be separated.

As for good relationships? It's hard to overestimate the importance humility plays in those, whether with a spouse or family, our co-workers, friends and neighbors, or even strangers who cross our paths. Notice how central humility is in these verses that talk about how we're to treat each other: *"Be completely humble and gentle;* be patient, bearing with one another in love. Make every effort to keep the unity of the Spirit through the bond of peace" (Eph. 4:2–3, emphasis mine). "Finally, all of you, live in harmony with one another; be sympathetic, love as brothers, *be compassionate and humble"* (1 Pet. 3:8, emphasis mine). Humility is one of the prerequisites to healthy relationships—don't leave home (or stay home!) without it.

> **HUMILITY IS ONE OF THE PREREQUISITES TO HEALTHY RELATIONSHIPS—DON'T LEAVE HOME (OR STAY HOME!) WITHOUT IT.**

There's another counterpart to humility—one that seems surprising at first glance: *honor.* After all, isn't humility about being willing to go lower? Yes, but that isn't the whole story. Look at these verses: "The fear of the LORD teaches a man wisdom, and *humility comes before honor"* (Prov. 15:33). "Before his downfall a man's heart is proud, *but humility comes before honor"* (Prov. 18:12, emphasis mine).

Sometimes we think God doesn't want us to experience honor. Nothing could be farther from the truth. If that were the case, we wouldn't be told that humility comes before honor.

Notice that the verse doesn't say humility comes *instead of* honor, but *before* it. And we wouldn't be instructed to honor one another or to show honor to our leaders and those in authority. In fact, much of the time when we act in humility, it's to express honor to others.

We're told to honor our parents (Eph. 6:2), our spouses (1 Pet. 3:7; Eph. 5:33), and those who lead well as they labor for Christ among us (1 Thess. 5:12). In Philippians 2:29 (speaking of Epaphroditus) Paul says to "give him the honor that people like him deserve" (NLT).

God delights in you and wants you to know the joy of both giving and receiving honor. He may take you from the floor to the podium when He knows you're ready to stand up there clothed in humility. In the book of James, we're told: "Humble yourselves before the LORD, and *he will lift you up*" (James 4:10, emphasis mine). Notice who is doing the "lifting up" in that verse—the Lord, *not* you.

Often the honor part of this duo is just a matter of timing, as it was with Joseph in Egypt. "Humble yourselves, therefore, under God's mighty hand, that he may lift you up *in due time*" (1 Pet. 5:6, emphasis mine). Sometimes we think we've put in enough floor time and are ready for the platform. Joseph thought so when he interpreted the dreams of his fellow-prisoners and asked to be remembered to Pharaoh. But more years passed before the dreamer's dreams came true.

It would be nice to peek into God's calendar and see our "due time" so we could shine our shoes and get our nails done, but that's not how it works. We can trust Him with the timing of being "lifted up," and even with what that will look like when it happens. Our part is to be humble. Here's the thing to remember:

humility and honor are traveling companions, but humility always walks in first.

8. Humility Gives Us a New Perspective

Psalm 25:9 says, "He guides the humble in what is right and teaches them his way." When it comes to the need for humility, that one verse would pretty much nail it for me. I want to know what's right in a world where that's often unclear. And I long for God to teach me "His way" when there are so many paths I could take . . . and so many different ways of doing things.

One of my seminary professors and a wise mentor-from-afar, Dr. Carolyn Tennant, told our class about a time when she faced a dilemma that involved tough professional decisions as well as some sticky relational quandaries. She spent much time and emotional energy trying to find the best answer but kept coming up short.

Should she solve this by going around, through, or over the challenge? She weighed all her options. Then she sensed God speaking these powerful words to her spirit: *you could always go lower.* With that, she came upon a solution she hadn't considered before, but one that would require humility. Being the godly woman she is, this strong, confident leader took the path of meekness and found it was the right one.

How that statement has stayed with me! *You could always go lower.* It reminds me of one of Jesus' most profound lessons about humility. It's captured in all three gospels of Matthew, Mark, and Luke. Here is Matthew's version (18:1–4, emphasis mine): "At that time the disciples came to Jesus and asked, "Who is the greatest in the kingdom of heaven?" He called a little child and had him stand among them. And he said: "I tell you the truth, unless you change and *become like little children,* you will never enter the kingdom of heaven. Therefore, whoever *humbles himself like this child* is the greatest in the kingdom of heaven."

This is a classic case that's still being repeated today—in families, on ministry teams, church staffs, and academic faculties . . . in business, politics, and entertainment—you name it. The question, even if unspoken, still hangs heavy in the air: *Who is the greatest?* And like He did with the disciples, Jesus still points to a child and says, "There . . . greatness starts there, with the humility of a child. Get that perspective if you want to understand kingdom-of-heaven greatness."

I don't know how long it's been since you were a child, but for me . . . well, let's just say it's been awhile. But I've received an enchanting refresher course in Kid Perspectives 101 these past few years. It's called grandparenting.

What a gift it is to be with the little people who spring from your offspring—and it's quite a classroom, too! A while back our then six-year-old grandgirl, Libby, stayed with us a few days after her baby sister was born. When she was at our house, I was struck again that what Libby wanted most from me was my time . . . and to get down on the floor and play with her. She loves that! While kids like shoulder rides and the thrill of being tossed into the air from time to time, their main domain is the floor.

The perspective at floor level is so different from our normal point of view. You see small things you might normally miss. It's hard to try to impress someone while you're sitting down there. The clock is farther away. Life's a little less complicated a few feet lower than our normal headspace.

Ann Voscamp has written a poignant book called *"One Thousand Gifts: A Dare to Live Fully Right Where You Are."* In one chapter she tells about allowing her little girl to borrow her camera and take pictures around their farmhouse. As they reviewed her daughter's first efforts at photography together, Ann was amazed at what she saw. She writes:

> "Yet her photos surprise, every single one. Why? It takes me a moment to make sense of it. It's the vantage point. At thirty-six inches, her angle's unfamiliar to me and utterly captivating: the study ceiling arches like a dome, her bed a floating barge. The stairs plunge like a gorge.
>
> She's Alice in Wonderland all the world grown Everestlike around and above her.
>
> "Do you like them, Mama?" She pats my cheek with her laughter-drenched hand.
>
> I can only murmur, flicking through her gallery. "Marvelous . . . just marvelous."[12]

Perspective. Maybe it's not a view from the heights we need, but a view from the floor. *You could always go lower.*

9. Humility Helps You Find Greatness in Unexpected Places

I have a huge gratitude list that keeps growing every day. (Did I mention you should read *One Thousand Gifts?* Just checking.) Way up in the very top of that list are the three children God gave Don and me. They're each uniquely gifted, genuinely kind, loving people, and I live for the times when we're together, especially with the addition of their wonderful spouses and those adorable grandkids.

Kristi, our oldest, is an amazing wife and mommy (whose home is their neighborhood's *go-to* place for all the kids on the block) with a huge heart for the people of the world. Our son, Mark, is a gifted musician (I melt when I hear him play guitar) with a brilliant mind and a creative, compassionate spirit. And Jana, the youngest, has always been our songbird. Growing up she shared a bedroom with Kristi, six years her senior. From the time she was tiny, Jana sang. And even before she talked, she hummed. At night Kristi used to plead, "Mom! Jana's humming herself to sleep again . . . make her stop!"

Jana developed her vocal talents in high school with the help of a great voice coach, Vicki Judd (my best friend, who is now her mother-in-law!), and an excellent high school choir director, David Judd (who is now her father-in-law! How's *that* for providence!). It wasn't unusual for Jana to sing the National Anthem at games and sporting events in our community. She received the Outstanding Musician award when she graduated from high school. In college she sang in specialized choirs and ensembles, performed vocal solos, and led worship for chapel services. She also recorded music and traveled with a music ministry team to represent the university.

There's really a point to this, besides the fact that I'm proud of my kids, which I'll admit to in a chapter about humility, no less! Because Jana *so* loved music (and began to write and perform her own songs), as she neared the end of her college years, she wondered if she might be able to do even more with those gifts.

But the doors she hoped would open (for recording and traveling to do concerts) never did.

Jana had also sensed God's call to ministry on her life and had graduated from college with a major in pastoral studies and biblical studies (along with a minor in music) so she was excited to join the staff at a church in the Seattle area. Along with her other responsibilities, she sang and helped lead worship but the longing to use her musical gifts to a fuller degree pulled at her heart.

One day we had one of those mother-daughter heart-to-heart talks about Jana's dreams. In addition to her musical ardor, I also knew her intense passion to help the most hurting and broken people—those far from God who were unlikely to walk into a church on their own. She had read David Wilkerson's *The Cross and the Switchblade*[13] as a girl and had always been deeply moved whenever Teen Challenge choirs visited our church. (Teen Challenge, founded by David Wilkerson, is a world-wide faith-based recovery program for people with life controlling issues, especially drug and alcohol addictions. It was started to help teens but actually works mostly with adults these days.)

HUMILITY HELPS US ENCOUNTER GREATNESS IN UNEXPECTED PLACES.

As we talked, I asked Jana if she might consider new ways to combine her love for music with her desire to help broken people. I asked what she thought about becoming a volunteer at Teen Challenge. What if the audience she was supposed to sing for during this season of her life wasn't in a church or concert venue but in a treatment center?

I love to hear Jana sing, but I love her heart even more. She volunteered at the two local Teen Challenge Women's Centers where she hung out with the women, became a mentor and teacher, led chapel services, and yes, sang for those who had lost their own song. For the last few years she has also put on benefit concerts for Teen Challenge to raise money for this outstanding program.

Way leads on to way . . . and because she loved her ministry with Teen Challenge (and the women in the program) so much, she decided to check out her church's jail ministry. That's when she met Dorothy who (according to Jana) is an "amazing, classy woman, now a widow, who has a penchant for calling people 'Dear Heart.'" Dorothy and her husband spent many years investing in Young Life, a nondenominational ministry that reaches out to adolescents through relationships and offers camps, clubs, and the chance for students to get to know Jesus.

Even after her husband passed away, Dorothy stayed active in her church and began to sense a calling from the Lord to jail ministry, so she became a chaplain, and a beloved one at that. When I asked Jana to tell me a little more about Dorothy, she wrote: "One of my favorite quotes of hers is, 'We're just standing at the gates of Hell redirecting traffic.' Although she's forty to fifty years my senior, Dorothy is the brave one who introduced me to the world of jail ministry *and* public transportation as we rode the city bus to downtown Seattle one blustery January day to serve at the King County Jail. She will always be a hero to me."

Dorothy took Jana under her wing and behind bars, literally. Now Jana often sings to women who've lost their freedom. She still sings in church and helps her worship pastor husband, Chris, lead worship at their local church. But her "concert hall" these days is frequently a small prison chapel, and her audience is made up of inmates who weep when she sings about freedom in Jesus. *You can always go lower.*

Romans 12:16 says, "Do not be proud, but be willing to associate with people of low position. Do not be conceited." Jana would tell you that rather than being "the great person" in those settings, she has encountered greatness in others. She's met nobility in people like Dorothy and the women who valiantly fight their demons of addiction, overcoming years of abuse, poverty, crime, and family dysfunction to become whole again.

Humility helps us encounter greatness in unexpected places. That's definitely worth singing about.

10. Humility Protects Us from Crashing

Just about every verse that tells us humility leads to honor also tells us that pride leads to a fall. Here are a few verses we looked at earlier, but with a different emphasis. *"Before his downfall a man's heart is proud,* but humility comes before honor" (Prov. 18:12, emphasis mine). *"When pride comes, then comes disgrace,* but with humility comes wisdom" (Prov. 11:2, emphasis mine). "All of you, clothe yourselves with humility toward one another, because, *'God opposes the proud* but gives grace to the humble'" (1 Pet. 5:5, emphasis mine).

Downfall . . . disgrace . . . having God as an opponent. Those are things I would like to avoid, thank you very much! When you're doing the high-wire act of pride it's easy to get off balance, and it's a long way down when you fall. On the other hand, it's not so far to fall when you're already on the floor. Floor exercise falls hurt, for sure—but high-wire falls are deadly. Humility protects Jesus-hearted leaders from that kind of disastrous plunge so they can live to lead another day . . . from the floor.

• JODI'S COACHING QUESTIONS •

- When you look at the ministry/leadership traps Jesus warned against in Matthew 23, which one do you think is most easy to fall into these days? Why?

- How do you feel when you're around a prideful person? What can you do, especially as a leader, to put others at ease?

- Is it surprising to you that honor is part of the package that comes with humility? Have you ever seen a humble leader receive honor? How did that person respond? What could you learn from that person that would prepare you if God decides it's time for you to take the podium of honor?

- Think about the statement "you could always go lower." What might "lower" look like in your current setting or life circumstances?

• A LITTLE LESSON FOR NEW LEADERS •

When we're taking our first tentative steps into leadership, it's not always easy to distinguish between true humility and a basic lack of personal confidence (the gracious kind). Continually putting yourself down is *not* being humble. It might help to remember that it's less about what you do to yourself (including negative self-talk) and more about how you view and treat those around you. Don't forget, humility is a "to" thing.

• HEART-DEEP IN THE WORD •

Read Deuteronomy 8:2–3. What do these verses indicate about how God views and develops humility in His people?

_____

_____

_____

_____

_____

Second Chronicles 7:14 links humility to answered prayer. Read the following passages and describe the part humility played in each setting:

- Genesis 18:16–33
- 1 Kings 21:1–29
- Jonah 3:1–10
- Luke 18:9–14

_____

_____

_____

_____

_____

_____

_____

Generally speaking, do you believe most people still think it's important to be humble in prayer? Why or why not?

_____

_____

_____

_____

_____

Read Philippians 2:5–8, which describes the humility of Jesus. This section begins by telling us to have this same kind of humble mindset with one another. How would we treat each other if we consistently lived with a Jesus-like humility? What would need to change?

_____

_____

_____

_____

_____

_____

_____

chapter four

TAKE THE STAIRS

LEADERSHIP QUALITY: STAMINA

· · · · · · · · · · ·

There are three stages in the work of God:
impossible, difficult, done.
—JAMES HUDSON TAYLOR, ENGLISH MISSIONARY

W alk into any high-rise hotel lobby at its busy season and you'll see the same sight. Clusters of people with nothing in common except their desire to go up will be standing in front of a pair of doors, waiting for them to open. The most impatient in the group (you know who you are) will have pushed the UP button several times although it's already lit, just to be sure. While there may be some light-hearted chatter among the group, all eyes watch for the doors to open.

If you walk away from that huddle, around a corner or two, you'll find another door. There's no group gathered there, and the door doesn't open with the push of a button. You actually have to turn the knob and give it a shove. The sign above it says, Stairs.

Some people are what I call "elevator leaders"—they want a quick and easy ride to the top, skipping everything in between. But the strength to lead well when you get to the top, and the stamina to stay there, is built by taking the stairs . . . by putting one foot in front of the other, dealing with incremental levels of leadership.

Here are a few differences in elevators and stairs that apply to ministry leadership as well.

1. With an elevator, you have to push the right buttons and wait for just the right timing for the doors to open with a ding, offering a quick ride to the top.

I've known too many women who linger in front of that magic door of prospective leadership, hoping it'll open for them. They stand around waiting, pushing all the buttons they can see. They wait, and wait, and wait . . . for the perfect position (with the great salary), or for the ideal ministry opportunity—the one tailor-made for their gifts, and that just fits their schedule, of course. They're frustrated and disappointed when the doors don't open right away.

2. By taking the stairs, you can start the trek up at any time, from wherever you find yourself—even the lowest level.

With stair leadership, you don't have to wait for the doors to magically open; you open the door yourself and start to climb step by step. (I might add that by *climbing* I don't necessarily mean in rank or position, although that can happen. I'm referring to ascending toward stronger, wiser, more capable, and God-honoring leadership.)

Ecclesiastes 11:4 says, "Whoever watches the wind will not plant; whoever looks at the clouds will not reap." I really like the way the New Living Translation puts it: "If you wait for perfect conditions, you will never get anything done." Stair leaders don't wait for a lucky break or the right doors to open before they serve and grow. They start where they are, with what's in front of them.

3. If the elevator malfunctions, you're stuck.

While we all need people to help us (and even sponsors, as we discussed in the last chapter), pinning our hopes on someone else to do the heavy lifting for our leadership growth—expecting another person or organization to our carry all our weight, to become our "lift" (as they call elevators in the UK)—is a mistake.

Let's take a closer look at Joseph's cell mates in Genesis 40. During their time in prison with him, he interpreted both their dreams. His "night-vision" analysis, in fact, was spot on. The chief baker was executed for his crime, while the cupbearer was exonerated and restored to his original position as Pharaoh's butler. When they were still locked up together, Joseph had pleaded with the butler to remember him and his innocence to Pharaoh. But here is the sad statement of what actually happened (40:23, emphasis mine): "The chief cupbearer, however, did not remember Joseph; *he forgot him.*"

It wasn't until two years later that Pharaoh's strange dreams jogged the butler's memory (41:9, emphasis mine): "Then the chief cupbearer said to Pharaoh, 'Today I am reminded of *my shortcomings.'"* There you have the breakdown of a "lift" if there ever was one!

4. Since stairs are decidedly low tech, you're only stuck if you choose to be.

As long as you keep putting one foot in front of the other, it might not be easy but you'll eventually get to the place God wants you to be in your ministry and leadership. Even the good intentions of others toward us will malfunction at times, and we can wait in vain for them to take us where we want to go. In Joseph's case, (since it was an actual physical prison) his door remained locked. But most of us have access to an unlocked door; it says Stairs over the top.

As Christ-followers, we're familiar with the instruction to "bear one another's burdens and so fulfill the law of Christ" from Galatians 6:2. But just below that is the balancing truth we need to remember as stair leaders (6:4–5, emphasis mine): "Each one should test his own actions. Then he can take pride in himself, without comparing himself to somebody else, for *each one should carry his own load."*

Jesus-hearted women who are stair leaders appreciate the help they get from others but are also willing to do their own heavy lifting.

5. With an elevator, even when the doors open, it may be too crowded to get on.

Let's face it. Sometimes there are just more people than there are positions when it comes to certain key ministry and leadership opportunities. Not all of us can be CEOs, and that "dream ministry position" may seem pretty elusive. Sometimes the doors open, but we find the elevator is full. Or perhaps just as we're ready to step in, to take that last spot, someone squeezes ahead of us.

6. Stairs will accommodate an unending stream of people who can climb together—if they're willing to follow someone ahead and lead someone behind.

Rather than trying to squeeze in where there is no room, stair leaders are willing to try a different path—that "road less traveled" is often the stairs. That might mean asking to shadow a leader or to serve as a volunteer intern. It could involve pioneering a new ministry. It might mean using your gifts to serve in a secular (gasp!) organization where you can "do ministry" where it's often needed most: the world. Even within the local church, it usually means finding an unmet need and filling it.

I was talking to a friend and colleague in ministry a while back. She told me about a conversation with a woman (I'll call my friend *Linda* and the woman, *Susan*—not their real names) who had recently gotten her ministerial credentials but felt stuck (a common story!) when it came to finding her place in ministry. Linda asked Susan what she was hoping for and her response

AS LONG AS YOU KEEP PUTTING ONE FOOT IN FRONT OF THE OTHER, IT MIGHT NOT BE EASY BUT YOU'LL EVENTUALLY GET TO THE PLACE GOD WANTS YOU TO BE IN YOUR MINISTRY AND LEADERSHIP.

was that she would love a pastoral staff position at her large, multi-staffed home church. But, Susan continued, whenever she approached the lead pastor about it, she got nowhere.

Very wisely, Linda asked this woman a great question: "What significant need do you see in your church that no one else is filling?" Without hesitation, Susan replied, "The ushering! It's a mess, completely disorganized—and they can't get enough volunteers, which, traditionally, have all been men."

Linda encouraged Susan to go back to her church, volunteer to meet that need, and bring her A-game to the task. In just a few weeks, Linda got a call from Susan who had done just that. She had volunteered to take a job nobody really wanted, had enlisted a lot of sharp people to help her (including women, which was breaking new ground), and had pulled together an excellent ushering team that benefited the whole church.

The pastoral staff took notice. Susan bubbled with excitement when she told Linda her great news: they had asked her to join the pastoral staff, the first woman to ever do so in that church. Susan was a "stairs leader." She willingly followed the advice of a seasoned leader, and she inspired others to follow her own leadership, as well. By taking a different approach—the stairs instead of the elevator—Susan arrived at the place she had hoped to serve.

7. Elevators are usually fast and easy, but they do nothing for your health.

People who live or work in a multistory building have a daily choice. They can climb into a small, box-like room and be lifted up and down to their desired destination. Or they can follow the advice of numerous doctors and fitness experts and take the stairs. The first choice is by far the easiest, but it will do nothing to take off those extra pounds, promote cardiac health, or build strength in the legs.

Moses had the perfect leadership elevator awaiting his ride to the top. After all, being raised as the son of Pharaoh's daughter certainly had its perks and could open doors. After the basket and bulrushes episode, we often fast-forward and think of Moses as the stuttering, wilderness shepherd who bumped into leadership at a burning bush. But he had a life, and other opportunities, between the basket and the bush.

In Acts 7, Stephen, who was delivering his defense and preaching the last sermon of his soon-to-end life, talked about that "in-between season" for Moses. He said: "When he was placed outside, Pharaoh's daughter took him and brought him up as her own son. *Moses was educated in all the wisdom of the Egyptians and was powerful in speech and action"* (Acts 7:21–22, emphasis mine). Sounds to me like he was all set for a rapid ride to the top! But God had other plans, and they wouldn't be so quick and easy, that's for sure. Hebrews 11:24–25 says, "By faith Moses, when he had grown up, refused to be known as the son of Pharaoh's daughter. He chose to be mistreated along with the people of God rather than to enjoy the pleasures of sin for a short time."

8. Stairs build stamina. People who use them regularly develop muscles that serve them well on the level they arrive at after their climb.

Moses *would* become a great leader but not the elevator-kind. Due to his own dismal failures, an obstinate Pharaoh, and stubborn followers, he learned leadership on the stairs . . . step by painful step. But God, the One who called him and went with him on that course, knew Moses would develop deep humility and amazing stamina as a leader on his long march toward the Promised Land.

• WHICH WAY TO THE STAIRS? •

I've noticed that elevators are usually in a prominent place and easy to spot. But unless you're familiar with the footprint of a building, it may be difficult to locate the nearest stairway. When it comes to developing as a leader and as a minister, there are two major staircases to watch for.

Education

Sometimes the opportunity for formal higher education eludes us. That seemed to be my case in my earlier years (as I described in chapter one). However, along the way I took advantage of every kind of informal education possible. I read voraciously, attended workshops and seminars, listened to teaching tapes (that was before CDs or the Internet!), and took extensive notes on what I was learning. I also sought out wise leaders as examples and mentors.

When I got the chance to go back to school, I took it eagerly. I'll admit that at times it felt like a long, grueling staircase with no upper landing. Many nights when I worked my way through one of those convoluted and . . . shall we say . . . densely-worded books, I thought, *now . . . why am I doing this again?* And when I worked on a lengthy paper, writing bleary-eyed into the wee hours of the morning, I thought, *I'm way too old for this!*

But even in those moments of exhaustion and self-doubt, I knew I wouldn't trade the great friendships in my cohort, all I was learning from amazing professors, and my growth as a person, a leader, and a Christ-follower, for anything. And, oh, the stamina I've developed on this academic staircase!

So if you want to rise in your leadership and you have the opportunity to further your education (at any age, but especially when you're young), take that set of stairs! You'll be doing a favor to yourself and to those who follow you.

Recently I spoke with a bright and busy young woman who could finish her undergraduate degree if she chose. I told her about a concept called the equity of exchange, which goes something like this: when you meet someone casually for the first time, you're comfortable swapping surface-level pleasantries. ("Hello, my name is Lisa Smith. How are you?" "Hi Lisa. I'm fine, thanks—and you?") But generally speaking, you must be confident that the other person is at least equally matched or even superior to you in things like comprehension and intellect, perhaps life experience or education, and maybe even empathy and emotional intelligence, for your trust to be engaged in a manner that allows the conversation to go deeper, where real influence occurs.

Let's break this down. Normally, you wouldn't meet someone for the first time and, without knowing anything about her, begin telling her your marital troubles. That is—unless your introduction to her goes something like this: "I want you to meet Lisa Smith. She's a licensed marriage and family therapist in our town." Right away, even though you don't know her, the effort she's put into her education and credentials has given her an instant equity of exchange for a deeper, more influential level of conversation.

Here's the thing. Lisa Smith without the education and credentials might actually be just as good at helping troubled marriages as Lisa Smith with the education and credentials. But you would have no way of perceiving that unless you had time to develop a more intimate and lengthy acquaintance, something that doesn't always happen in our busy world.

As I explained to my young friend, furthering her education is one way to have a greater equity of exchange sooner, at a deeper level, and with more people. It's not the only way, but there's a credibility that comes from taking the long climb up the steps of academic studies.

And for anyone reading this who can't go back to school for various reasons (or perhaps you've already finished your schooling), keep learning and growing through whatever means available. There are more ways to learn these days than ever before, especially with the Internet and media technology. It all adds up! One of my favorite quotes is by Charles Kingsley: "Have thy tools ready. God will give thee work."[14] Being a lifelong learner is one way to have your tools ready. Please, take these stairs!

Experience

While educational opportunities may be limited for some of us, the staircase of experience is available to all of us! In her excellent book, *Life Equity*, US Congresswoman Marsha Blackburn says it like this:

> "Here is exciting news: there is a key truth that will unlock all of these extraordinary possibilities for you—one that forms the central message of my life and of this book.

That simple but powerful truth is this: your accumulated skills go with you. The ordinary, everyday tasks you have been performing are actually the foundation for getting you where you want to go. In even the most unglamorous roles, you have built real leadership ability that has prepared you for bigger things."[15]

I love that! "Your accumulated skills go with you."

Sometimes when we view a person at certain levels of leadership, we forget the years of struggle and toil, unseen and un-applauded, in her history. But God sees, and He doesn't waste even one of the things we go through in a life surrendered to Him.

Looking back, I can see how God was using the experiences of my life to prepare me for what I'm doing these days. Those years of studying for, writing, and teaching a weekly women's Bible study for eight years was amazing preparation for the opportunities I have now to speak to various groups throughout the country about God's life-changing truths. It was just a small group of precious women that met together for all those Tuesday morning Bible studies, but we knew God was doing big things in our hearts.

Serving informally alongside my husband as pastor's wife for more than three decades provided a wide range of experiences that have been invaluable in the development of my leadership abilities. I couldn't even guess how many services, special events, outreaches, retreats, training sessions, and holiday programs I helped plan and carry out through those years. And because I wasn't doing any of it by myself, I learned much about working with people and leading teams.

In those years, Don and I did a lot of counseling together as parishioners came to us with their personal difficulties, spiritual challenges, and relational struggles (especially in the area of marriage and family). He was the one with the degree in counseling, but we made a good team, and I was getting a priceless informal education in how to help people move beyond their past and over their obstacles. I know those experiences helped develop many of the skills I use today as a certified coach: focused presence, deeper level listening, asking powerful questions, offering insights, and designing action-steps for progress.

Even in the area of writing, experience has been my favorite teacher, though I might not have recognized it as such at the time. When I speak to groups about writing, I tell them that *all* their writing matters, if they put their hearts into it. So when I was writing little notes on the napkins that went into my kids' sack lunches for school, or writing cards and letters of encouragement to friends, or writing a variety of newsletters (for a dental office, for our church, for our ministry network, and even the annual family Christmas newsletter), or writing crazy skits for the annual women's retreat, or drama and narration for the church's Christmas program, or helping edit one of Don's sermons or articles—or one of the kids' homework essays or writing in my journals—thoughts, ideas, prose, prayers . . . *all* of it counted. Each laboriously scrawled word, each phrase I've typed, deleted, rephrased, and retyped (repeat that many times over, by the way) to get it *just* right, has honed me as a writer.

To be honest, some of my most valuable lessons—things that go much deeper than the skill level—have come through excruciatingly painful experiences I would just as soon have skipped. Family struggles with our offspring who were making choices that brought us much worry (and us not always handling those things in the wisest manner at the time), the tug-of-war between time pressures and true priorities, big decisions about ministry direction, financial strains, the battle to develop personal and spiritual disciplines, conflicts with colleagues in ministry, even emotional stress leading to a season of panic attacks—yes, these have been my teachers, too.

You can be sure I would have taken an elevator right past those learning levels if I had been given the choice! But had that been the case, I would have missed developing some of the character qualities (still very much an ongoing process, by the way) that have served me best in leadership and ministry. In fact, the chapter titles of this book would make a good list of those traits God was at work to increase in me through my most painful experiences. Not the least of these has been stamina—just continuing to continue, one step at a time.

• STAMINA ON THE STAIRCASE •

We've examined how stamina is built by becoming stair leaders instead of elevator leaders. But if you've ever climbed a really, *really* long flight of stairs, you know you also need stamina for the climb itself, not just for the sake of how it will serve you when you reach the top.

A few years ago, Don and I got to spend about ten fabulous days in England with two other couples. London is a history lover's dream. If there's one person on the planet who qualifies for that title, it's Don—and he's definitely drawn me into his fascination with antiquity. We and our friends had a blast tromping down quaint cobblestone streets, poking into old bookshops, touring castles, and visiting the homes of notables like Florence Nightingale, Winston Churchill, Charles Dickens, and the like.

Another highlight (and it was truly *high* in a literal sense) was our tour of St. Paul's Cathedral. Besides its stunning architectural features and air of holy beauty, it sits atop the city's highest hill offering visitors a breathtaking view of London from 365 feet in the air. The only caveat? To enjoy this magnificent vista you have to climb a narrow, winding staircase with 528 steps.

> **THERE'S SOMETHING ABOUT KNOWING WE'RE NOT ALONE AS WE FACE MINISTRY AND LEADERSHIP CHALLENGES THAT GIVES US STAMINA.**

Back then, Don and I were both a few (okay, several) pounds heavier than we are now, but we weren't about to let that stop us from this once-in-a-lifetime chance to see London from Mary Poppins' vantage point! So we huffed and puffed our way to the top . . . calves burning, hearts pumping, lungs on fire. The things that gave us staircase stamina for St. Paul's Cathedral can also help us on our long, sometimes grueling climb as leaders. Here are a few things that kept us going when we *so* wanted to turn back:

Camaraderie

My guess is that if any of us had been alone, we might have talked ourselves out of this challenge. My thoughts would have run along these lines: *Why would I want to spend all that time climbing, getting all tired and sweaty, just to see a bunch of rooftops? I think I'll just skip it and go get an ice-cream bar!*

But because we climbed together, we spurred each other on and had great fun along the way (even if it had something to do with laughing at each others' red faces and labored breathing!).

There's something about knowing we're not alone as we face ministry and leadership challenges that gives us stamina. In the verses below, Paul described a time and a situation where he really needed stamina—and notice how he found it in his friends!

> "I have great confidence in you; I take great pride in you. I am greatly encouraged; in all our troubles my joy knows no bounds. For when we came into Macedonia, this body of ours had no rest, but we were harassed at every turn—conflicts on the outside, fears within. But God, who comforts the downcast, comforted us by the coming of Titus, and not only by his coming but also by the comfort you had given him. He told us about your longing for me, your deep sorrow, your ardent concern for me, so that my joy was greater than ever." (2 Cor. 7:4–7)

It was another person, Titus, who brought great comfort (even joy) to a harassed, conflicted, downcast, and even fearful leader. We don't often think of Paul in those terms, but that's how he described himself. Time with Titus, and the message of support that he delivered from the Corinthian believers, helped give Paul the stamina to keep going. Stair leadership is not a solo endeavor. Be sure you climb with a friend!

Joy

I mentioned we were having fun on the climb to the top of St. Paul's dome. In fact we laughed ourselves up each of those 528 steps—it's probably the real fuel that kept us going.

I believe God doesn't intend all the pleasure to be waiting only at the end of our destinations; He sprinkles it all along the way. He knows how invigorating a little joy is in the middle of our labors and challenges. Nehemiah 8:10 is a verse that has been turned into a song. But it's not just a song. The joy of the Lord really is our strength.

Where do you find joy? When was the last time you were intentional about making room for fun in your day and in your heart? I'm thinking today might be a good time for laughter; it's the effervescence that propels us forward when we would like to give up.

Stops

When we were climbing the stairs at St. Paul's in London, we were grateful for some little ledges—places to stop and rest—that the long-ago architects had built into the winding stone steps. They knew something that we often forget. Stamina to reach the top is enhanced by periodic stops along the way up.

THERE ARE TIMES WHEN STOPPING IS YOUR BEST NEXT STEP.

As leaders, we're all about the next step—it's go, go, go for us! But there are times when stopping is your best next step. In a profoundly insightful little booklet called, *Ready, Set . . . Rest,* my friend Alicia Britt

Chole says that rest is more than a reward for faithfulness; it's a prerequisite for fruitfulness. She writes, "God did not design us to live to the end of our abilities every day. We are supposed to have a buffer. If we live each day to the end of our rope, there is nothing left to hold onto when an unanticipated problem calls for something more."[16]

Stopping gives stamina on the stairs.

Hope

In the chapter on humility, we talked about going lower. And now we're focusing on going higher . . . what's up with that? As believers in Jesus, we never climb for the sake of climbing—just for reaching some pinnacle of success or acclaim. In fact the only verse in the New Testament I could find about reaching for something high was Philippians 3:14 (KJV) "I press toward the mark for the prize of the high calling of God in Christ Jesus." The NKJV describes it as "an upward call."

But there are several places where we're told to grow, and to grow up! That's the reason we take the stairs—we have hope that there's something better above the level where we're living now. To rise above the sinfulness, the immaturity, the pettiness, the selfish focus that keeps us stunted in our growth and ineffective in our leadership—that's why we put our foot on the next tread and push upward. We take the stairs in hopes of gaining a new perspective that we just can't get from staying at street level.

When we and our friends finally emerged from that long climb up the stone staircase at St. Paul's Cathedral, we were breathless at the view of the city. London stretched out before us as far as the eye could see. We began to pick out landmarks.

"Look! It's the River Thames . . . and over there, Shakespeare's Globe Theatre!" There was a grandeur from this perspective that we would never have experienced if we had avoided the stairs. It was worth every step . . . all 528 of them!

• WHY JESUS-HEARTED WOMEN NEED STAMINA •

When my sweet little grandmother (we called her Ma Ma) was in her eighties she fell and broke her hip. She had been healthy most of her life so being in the hospital was new to her. At that point, early-stage dementia was starting to set in, which left her a bit confused about where she was and why.

As my parents visited in her in the hospital room after hip surgery, Ma Ma looked at them pathetically, sighed, and said, "If I had known it was going to be like this, I wouldn't have come."

Sometimes we can feel that way in ministry leadership: *If I had known it was going to be like this, I wouldn't have come.* It's easy for those who look on to think that life in the ministry (especially vocational ministry) is always exciting, a little glamorous, and full of spiritual highs. That's because they've never spent much time there. I hate to burst that bubble, but ministry life is often *hard—* and being the leader of anything is frequently an uphill struggle. Neither is for the faint of heart!

There are certain things we face that require special stamina if we're to be effective Jesus-hearted leaders in this broken-hearted world. Some of them are obvious: dealing with conflict and difficult people, the constant wear of decision-making, working on large tasks and long-range projects, guiding and motivating teams, and working through transitions, to name a few.

Sometimes it seems too much to keep going when the struggles of leadership become intense and multilayered. But I've discovered that so many situations find their resolve when we just keep showing up, letting time and God's faithful, relentless grace do their work of transformation.

However, having stamina doesn't mean that you never leave a position or stop serving in some capacity. It's just that when you do stop, it's for the right reasons, which might include one or more of the following:

- You're done; you've finished what you started.
- The setting is an unhealthy or unsafe place to serve.
- God is giving you a new focus, and it's the right timing for change.
- You have no choice in the matter; others in leadership have made a decision that brings your season of service to a close.

I once asked a friend of mine who is a wife, a mother, a minister, and a prosecuting attorney, no less, how in the world she managed to keep going with all the demands upon her life. Her reply made me chuckle, but it sure cast a new light on stamina. "I figure I can do anything for eighty years, or so," Tina said. "This life isn't forever so I'm going to keep going for it while I'm here."

Here's the thing. There will be a last time you turn the key in that door where you serve. No matter how hard it is or how long it lasts, you will drive away from that building, say good-bye to that group of people one day. We sometimes forget that this life is temporary and no setting is permanent. But it matters that we are Jesus-hearted leaders who don't leave the assignment God has given us before He lets us know it's time.

• STAMINA HELPS IN OTHER WAYS •

There are a couple of other things we need stamina for that might not be quite so obvious.

Slow Starts

When you're starting out in ministry and leadership, it can seem so hard to gain any real traction. You may have completed your education and gained the appropriate credentials. You may have worked hard at developing your skills, have lots of great ideas, and be filled with passion. Yet it seems like no one notices or is willing to take a chance on letting you lead.

There are certain books that just won't stay on my shelf. I buy a few copies and end up giving them all away (including the one that was supposed to be reserved for me), only to do it all over again. Alicia Britt Chole's outstanding book, *Anonymous: Jesus' Hidden Years . . . and Yours* is one of those books. I've given many copies of this little treasure away, especially to those just beginning their ministry journey.

Alicia starts chapter one with these words: "Have you ever felt hidden? Have you ever moved to a new place or entered a new environment where no one knew who you were, what you could do, or what dreams ignited your soul?"[17] If you would answer those questions with a disappointed yes, then I'm pretty sure that stamina for this season of slow starts is the fuel that will keep your light from sputtering out. It might not seem like it now, but God has His eye on you and you are not invisible to Him.

Michael Hyatt, former CEO of Thomas Nelson Publishers, has a great blog for leaders, and I was struck recently by something one of his guest bloggers, author Jon Acuff, posted: "This is just your beginning. Give yourself the gift of time. *Love your dream and your adventure enough to allow it to grow slowly.*"[18]

Jon also made another statement in that same blog that I've passed along to beginning leaders who are eager to come into their own but feel like all the action is happening to other, more seasoned leaders: "Never compare your beginning to someone else's middle." Stay on the stairs, my friend! The stamina you're developing today will serve you well tomorrow, and you'll get there. I'm sure of it!

When I think of start-up stamina, I wish you could see the beautiful, vibrant, red-head who comes to mind. My good friend Dr. Ava Oleson may be petite in stature but don't kid yourself, she's a classy powerhouse! To look at her now, as an accomplished minister of more than twenty-five years who has served on staff at one of the largest churches in the Pacific Northwest . . . was one of the first female presbyters in the Northwest . . . is a respected leader with a Doctor of Ministry degree who teaches seminary classes . . . whose service in ministry and as a marriage and family therapist has taken her to places like Southern California, Belgium, Argentina, and Toronto . . . you would never guess the stamina she needed to start her ministry journey.

> **IT MIGHT NOT SEEM LIKE IT NOW, BUT GOD HAS HIS EYE ON YOU AND YOU ARE NOT INVISIBLE TO HIM.**

Ava grew up in a family of ten in a small town in Manitoba, Canada. There was little Christian influence there at that time, and her parents went through a painful divorce that rocked the family. Eventually, the alcohol her dad had struggled with for many years took his life. This left her mother overwhelmed with the task of raising eight children on her own.

Ava says, "I got lost in the mix and had little direction or purpose. In middle school, a teacher began talking to me about Jesus. I couldn't believe that God wanted to have a personal relationship with me! Gratitude and a dramatic understanding of the power of God to change lives overcame me. I was like a lifeless doll that had magically sprung to life!"

SO MANY THINGS ABOUT US ARE INCOMPLETE: OUR DREAMS, OUR LONGINGS, OUR SENSE OF SELF, THE MATURITY OF A FULLY CHRIST-LIKE CHARACTER.

Ava and her entire family experienced a dramatic conversion to faith in Christ. Later, as a young adult who was captivated by the love of God and His power to radically transform lives, Ava decided to enter full-time ministry. She felt compelled to tell the world about the power of Christ.

However a huge obstacle stood in Ava's path. There was no way she, nor anyone in her large family, could afford the private Christian university that would provide the necessary training. Ava's problem-solving skills went into high gear, and she determined to find a way. The steel of stamina was forming in the fiber of her young soul.

About that time, Ava got wind of a high paying job so she packed up and moved to Northern Ontario, Canada. There, she worked through the bitter cold winter in an iron ore mine (the only female on that job), saving every single penny for her tuition. With a laser-like focus on her goal, she persevered. Each morning at 5 a.m. Ava climbed aboard a rickety old bus with the other miners for the one-hour trip into the darkness of the mine, where she worked ten hours a day. She remembers being so cold and alone that the tears would trickle down her cheeks. Still, convinced this was the gateway to her future, she persisted. That's stamina!

A year and a half later, Ava packed her little car, a ten-speed bike, two suitcases, and drove 3,000 miles across country. She made this trip from Toronto, Canada to Orange County, California all by herself at the ripe old age of twenty. "I was absolutely scared to death!" she admits. But she followed her humble little map (no GPS systems in those days!) to Southern California College (now Vanguard University). She was soon to discover that this was her door into a brand new world, and her life would never be the same.

Recently I had the privilege of sitting with Ava and several others as we shared a lunch break at the seminary where she serves. I couldn't help but overhear her encouraging words to a beginning seminary student who was overwhelmed by the writing projects required for her classes. "You know," Ava said kindly, "you just tell yourself, one more sentence. I'll just write one more sentence . . . and pretty soon you'll have that paper finished." Knowing a little of Ava's story, I smiled. *Stamina.*[19]

Living with an Unfinished Dream

Having stamina for beginnings is one thing, but there might be another season where it is needed even more. I read Philippians 1:6

during my "Jesus-time" in the Bible this morning. (I call it Jesus-time as a reminder to myself that it's not about just learning some new truth or mastering theology, or even gleaning insights to share with others. It's primarily about spending time with my friend, Jesus.) That verse says, "He who began a good work in you will carry it on to completion until the day of Christ Jesus."

The way the word *completion* is tied to the future implies an unfinished now. A lot of our angst in life has to do with what is undone. If you've ever had a deadline hanging over your head and still far to go to meet it, you know what I mean. But it's more than being unfinished in what we have to do that troubles us. The thing that often unravels our peace is that *we* are unfinished. So many things about us are incomplete: our dreams, our longings, our sense of self, the maturity of a fully Christ-like character. They lay in cluttering stacks, like half-painted canvases tossed about the room by some would-be artist—not quite good enough to spend more time on but with too much promise to throw out altogether.

Something specific may have come to mind when you read that last sentence. Perhaps the book you want to write. You know it's in you, and something will be missing until you give it your best shot. Maybe the spouse you hope to marry. You don't talk much about that inner ache for a life companion—you've even prayed for God to take away the longing—but it's still there. Possibly the travel or mission work you long to do. Something just tugs at your heart when you read about far-away places and hear about the great needs on the other side of the globe.

For others, that sense of the unfinished is about things that are much more vague and hard to describe . . . yet the uneasiness is the same. It might be that you want to be truly joyful . . .

you try valiantly to put on a smile as you go about your days but the downward pull of depression is never far away. Maybe it's the memories from a broken childhood that rise up and demand answers to your cry of why. Perhaps it's the disgust at your inability to do the things you know are good for you: eat properly, exercise, get enough sleep, be on time, get organized, make time for friendship, keep your house clean, volunteer, stop procrastinating . . . or a hundred other *shoulds* that point an accusing finger during the day and scold you as you drift off to sleep each night. *Unfinished.*

We're all unfinished in some part of our lives. Like Abraham waiting for the child of promise, like Joseph waiting for the dream, like Anna waiting for the glimpse of Messiah, like the whole creation waiting, groaning for redemption, we wait, unfinished.

Sometimes I think that faith, at its most basic level, has a lot to do with being patient with God. We know He's patient with us—unendingly so—and we're grateful. But we have to learn to be patient with Him, too. That might sound audacious, but I think He understands—and I think I'm onto something. Look at the following passages and notice the correlation between faith and patience:

> "We do not want you to become lazy, but to imitate those who through *faith and patience* inherit what has been promised. And so *after waiting patiently,* Abraham received what was promised." (Heb. 6:12, 15, emphasis mine)

> "Do not throw away this confident trust in the LORD, no matter what happens. Remember the great reward it

brings you! *Patient endurance* is what you need now, so you will continue to do God's will. Then you will receive all that he has promised." (Heb. 10:35–36 NLT, emphasis mine)

"For in this hope we were saved. But hope that is seen is no hope at all. Who hopes for what he already has? But if we hope for what we do not yet have, *we wait for it patiently."* (Rom. 8:24–25, emphasis mine)

"Dear brothers and sisters, you must *be patient* as you wait for the LORD's return. Consider the farmers who eagerly look for the rains in the fall and in the spring. They patiently wait for the precious harvest to ripen. *You, too, must be patient."* (James 5:7–8 NLT, emphasis mine)

"Wait patiently for the LORD. Be brave and courageous. Yes, *wait patiently for the LORD."* (Ps. 27:14 NLT, emphasis mine)

Did you catch who we are to be patient with in these verses? With *God.* As we deal with so much that's unfinished in our lives, being patient with God is an expression of our trust that "not done yet" is not the same as "will never be done."

Ephesians 2:10 says we are God's workmanship, His project. The New Living Translations says we are His "masterpiece." And unlike some of us, He always finishes what He starts. *Always.* Knowing that will give you stamina as you wait patiently for God to complete His good work in you.

• JODI'S COACHING QUESTIONS •

- Think about a ministry leader you know who has displayed stamina. What does that look like? How do you think she or he developed it?

- When it comes to ministry and leadership, have you ever been tempted to take the elevator when you needed to take the stairs? Which did you take and what was the result?

- At what points (or circumstances) in your life and ministry have you most needed stamina? Why?

- What are some of those unfinished areas where you need to be patient with God—to wait on Him to finish His work in you? How can you develop stamina while you wait?

• A LITTLE LESSON FOR NEW LEADERS •

A few years back in the middle of a long trip, I got extremely impatient when I had to stop for road construction. I just wanted to get to my destination as quickly as possible. Then I remembered the sign I had just read a few miles back: Road Work Ahead—Expect Delays. As I thought about it, I realized that a delay now meant safety later and a smoother ride down the road. It would've been silly to get out of my car and abandon the trip just because I had to wait a while.

If you're in a season of stops, it's likely that God is doing some road work ahead of you that will make the trip a better one in the long run. Expect a few delays now and then, but don't abandon your vehicle.

Stamina will keep you on the right road and move you forward when God says *go!*

• HEART-DEEP IN THE WORD •

In 2 Corinthians 11:23–30, Paul discusses the hardships he's been through as a believer and a spiritual leader. Read through those verses. What role do you think stamina played in Paul's life in these situations? What can you learn from Paul's example about the need for stamina as a leader?

_____

_____

_____

_____

_____

The Bible talks about steadfastness and endurance—other ways to describe stamina. What do the following verses teach about these qualities?
- Romans 5:3–4
- James 1:2–4
- James 1:12–18
- Hebrews 10:35–36
- Hebrews 12:1–3

_____

_____

_____

_____

_____

_____

_____

_____

Romans 2:6–7 says, "God will repay each person according to what they have done. To those *who by persistence in doing good* seek glory, honor and immortality, he will give eternal life" (emphasis mine). Knowing that God sees your persistence and will reward your stamina, how does that make a difference in your ability to endure? What are some other biblical examples of stamina that was rewarded?

_____

_____

_____

_____

_____

_____

_____

chapter five

THE CRINGE FACTOR

LEADERSHIP QUALITY: RESILIENCE

· · · · · · · · · · ·

I don't believe in the resurrection of Christ when
I live like all the painful things are all the final things.
—ANN VOSKAMP

I lay flat on my back looking up at the circle of children's faces staring down at me. Some seemed worried and others just curious or amused. The ground felt hard and cold, and my head pounded. Most of all I wondered why I couldn't catch my breath.

It was the first time the wind had been knocked out of me. I was in the third grade and thought I had finally mastered the agile feat of skipping two rungs as I swung my way, hand by hand, across the monkey bars. Now I was in the league with those bigger kids I admired on the playground at Morris Elementary. But somehow, as I gave a mighty swing forward and grasped at that distant third rung, I couldn't quite get a grip. The momentum caused my feet to fly upward, and I came down with a loud *thwump*. The next thing

. . . .

**GREAT LEADERS
OVERCOME REGRET
WITH RESILIENCE.**

. . . .

I knew, I was lying there gasping for breath, scared and embarrassed at the same time.

Once I regained my breath and picked myself up (while trying not to cry), I had a choice to make: head to a safer part of the playground and join a group of my more docile friends playing four-square with one of those big maroon-colored rubber balls or climb back up the ladder and take another grab (literally) at those treacherous monkey bars. I was little but feisty, and four-square seemed boring that day. Pretty soon I was swinging with the best of my monkey-bar buddies again. I'm not bragging, but before I left Morris Elementary I could skip three rungs. That may be my biggest athletic accomplishment to date!

I did say that was the *first* time the wind had been knocked out of me, didn't I? Though it hasn't happened again physically, on a spiritual and emotional level there've been many times since when I've found myself flat on my back, embarrassed, scared, and gasping for breath. And the things that put me there often make me cringe when I think of them later.

If you've been in ministry leadership for any time at all, you'll look back at things you or others have done, and cringe. Leaders are learners, and learners make mistakes—sometimes those really knock-the-wind-out-of-you kinds of mistakes. But here's the thing: *great leaders overcome regret with resilience.* It's possible to cringe and then continue. And that's true whether the blunder was done *by* us or *to* us (or some combination of both, which is often the case).

In the previous chapter we considered the leadership quality, *stamina*. Some might wonder about the difference between stamina and resilience. It's like the difference between telling a person to *continue,* and telling her to *resume.* The latter implies that there has been some kind of break in the action—something has stopped that person and she needs to start again.

I promise you this: you'll need resilience if you're going to be a Jesus-hearted woman who lasts in leadership, especially when you deal with three of the "cringe factors" most common to leadership life. These are the things that cause us to wince in revisited pain, or shrink back in embarrassment, when we think about them. They may even tempt us to give up, to find a safer game to play. I call them *my bad* (missteps of our own making), *their bad* (the things others do that negatively affect us), and *too bad* (when life's circumstances go awry).

• MY BAD •

I have a good friend in ministry who has served Jesus all her life. (I have her permission to write about a few parts of her painful story. But to respect her privacy, I'll call her by a different name . . . let's go with Cindy.) For years Cindy was a missionary with a stellar record of making a difference in many lives, both in the United States and in the distant countries where she served. Sadly, she got embroiled in some legal problems as she tried to help a family member handle an estate issue.

Even with the advice of an attorney, things spiraled out of control and (to keep a long and complicated story a little shorter) Cindy ended up being charged with a felony. Though her intentions had been right, she regretted allowing herself to be pulled into this awful ordeal. She had taken unwise actions, albeit out of good-hearted naiveté. Still, the result was confusion and pain on all sides. She hoped someone would realize the misunderstanding and mistake—that the truth would come out and she would discover it was all just a bad dream. It wasn't, and they didn't.

CINDY SAW HER FELLOW INMATES AS A NEW MISSION FIELD AND PURPOSED TO MAKE HER TIME BEHIND BARS COUNT FOR JESUS.

Cindy lost her ministerial credentials, her good name among a number of her peers (except those of us who knew more about the "rest of the story" and believed in her character), and the profession she had poured her life into as a single woman in ministry. Not only that, she eventually lost her freedom and was sentenced to a year in prison. I'm not writing this to convince you of her innocence (though it's something I believe in), but to hold up to you a real-world picture of resilience through what followed.

You can't think of a more unlikely inmate than my friend. Seriously, you can't. Kind, funny, intelligent, people-loving, and passionate about Jesus—those words don't exactly describe a "hard-core criminal." At the time of her incarceration, Cindy could have just pulled a blanket over her head and said, "Done! I've served Jesus all my life, and now one stupid saga has ruined everything. I'll become a recluse and wait for heaven." The wind had been knocked out of her—*slammed* out of her, is more like it—and she could easily have run to a safer part of the playground, allowing regret to extinguish the lamp of ministry leadership that had burned brightly for so long.

Instead, my friend took an altogether different perspective. Cindy saw her fellow inmates as a new mission field and purposed to make her time behind bars count for Jesus. Here, in her own words, are some thoughts about her experience:

Those first twenty-four hours are a blur. There were never-ending strip searches, supervised showers, mug shots and fingerprinting, transport in shackles, and humiliating taunts. The first month was spent in the medium security prison side with lifers and much more dangerous women. Eventually, I was moved to minimum security where things settled into a routine.

Yes, there were a few dangerous times and, yes, there was the total lack of anyone in the system believing I was innocent. You do lose all rights to what you do, what you wear, what you eat, personal hygiene, or any private time or space. The conditions were not comfortable, but I've seen far worse. The food was not always my favorite, but I was thankful for all that I had. My biggest determination when I walked into that place was never to let bitterness begin and not to waste any time trying to find out why this was happening to me. God granted those requests.

I knew it would be easy to fall into several traps if I didn't have a plan, with God's help, to avoid them. I could become discouraged, depressed, angry, vindictive, hopeless, or worldly in that environment. To have lights and noise 24/7 is wearisome, and to be constantly subjected to filthy language could affect my thoughts and speech. So I prayed daily that God would protect my mind and keep my thoughts, words, and actions pleasing to Him.

I set up my own routine so I wouldn't just lie on that steel bunk and let my thoughts wander. I started early every morning on the exercise bike for several miles. Then after a shower, I had my oatmeal and settled at the same table with my Bible and note paper where I worked hard on reading and developing a teaching outline for every book in the New Testament. Then I walked several miles around the yard outside and worked as much as possible. I learned to run an industrial sewing machine/serger and then was accepted as a tutor in the Basic Education and GED program.

I spent as much time as possible reading my Bible during restricted periods on my bunk, in the evenings, or when there was nothing else to do. A new believer there was determined to read the Bible all the way through. She had many questions but kept at it. I knew I could do no less, so the challenge was on to finish, as well.

What wonderful times I had in tutoring sessions when I was asked about my faith. I walked over 3,000 miles and many of those were spent with someone alongside asking me about my beliefs in God. Prison officials made comments about my faith. Some women actually defended me, protected me, vouched for me, and respected me because of my trust in Jesus.

How did they know about my faith? I was being watched 24/7. They saw my devotional routine, my work ethic, and my smile. They saw me humming or grinning as I walked outside on that never ending oval, thanking God for the sunshine, the grass, the birds, the clouds, the flowers, the occasional animal that passed by our fence. They saw me thank God for every meal, and they heard my speech that never included vulgarity. They watched me walk away and turn my back to inappropriate television programming, and they noticed that I refused to laugh or join in the angry or bitter talk around the tables. My missionary experience was paying off. This was just another culture that needed Jesus.

This chapter behind bars showed me that learning to stay spiritually strong is vital in every culture. All people want to be respected, and when we listen to God, He will give us the words to reach anyone with His love in any situation. There are many spiritually hungry women in our society who are never reached with the gospel message.

Sometimes that's because they've been hurt by the church or its people. Sometimes it's because they've lived in a very different culture from the one most church-goers know. They've grown up in families that are generations away from knowing anything about Jesus. In spite of lifestyle, language, tattoos, and piercings, these women wonder if there's something more to life and a God somewhere who cares.

The greatest common fear I encountered in these amazing women from such a different world than mine was related to death. During my time in prison, my father passed away. It was difficult not to be with my siblings and to miss the funeral of my dad, but God gave me an amazing sense of peace and His presence during those days.

This turned out to be the biggest door-opener for sharing my relationship with Jesus Christ. I had many come to me and ask how I could handle this so calmly and peacefully. I told them of my hope and God's peace. Their lives are filled with fear about death. Most of these women have been surrounded with death through abuse, violence, gangs, drugs, and much more. They're scared to death of dying. Without hesitation, as I explained my hope, they wanted to know more. Yes, it was hard not to be at home through those days, but I would never trade the opportunities God gave me there.

Resilience. My friend has shown me what this leadership quality looks like—and in vivid colors. When Cindy got out of prison, she was determined to go through the necessary processes to restore her ministry credentials, and reclaim her good name—something she's still following through on today.

As far as doing ministry? Although it looks a little different than before, she serves vibrantly on a ministry team in her church and is impacting her community. They love her there, and she's making every day of her regained freedom count for eternity. Resilience won over regret, and our world is better for it.

Recently I asked Cindy, "What would you say to anyone who is struggling to get past the paralyzing pain of regret?" Her response was, "Let it go and move on. You really can't waste time going back over things you can't change. Any of us could go there in our thoughts but that would just continue to make a person sad or angry, so don't go there. Focus on others and quit searching within. It's amazing how God can heal and change our hearts when we let our problems go and focus on sharing His love with others."[20]

No Rewind, Only Redemption

My bad. Those two words have become modern vernacular for "it was my fault," or "my mistake." Everyone reading this has regrets, and for some they've become heavy, damp, flame-smothering blankets of depression that bury the glow of future ministry potential—maybe even the possibility of joyful living. This is for you, my friend: *there is no rewind. There is only redemption.* But a redeemed life is even *better* than a rewind because through it, Jesus showcases hope to others who feel their mistakes have left them unqualified for significance and service.

News flash: Jesus didn't come because we have it all together and never get ourselves into messy circumstances of our own making (usually with contributions and complications from others). In fact, that's precisely *why* He came—because we *do* blow it, both intentionally and unintentionally. Why, as believers, can we emphatically believe and express this to those who don't know Jesus yet can't see it for ourselves?

The Bible is filled with people who loved God but at some point in their lives did stupid and sinful things. Moses and David

> JESUS DIDN'T COME BECAUSE WE HAVE IT ALL TOGETHER AND NEVER GET OURSELVES INTO MESSY CIRCUMSTANCES OF OUR OWN MAKING.

were each murderers (add lust, lying, and adultery to David's wickedness). Naomi was bitter, Samuel was a negligent parent, and don't even get me started on Solomon and all those extra wives! We've already discussed Peter's hypocrisy toward the Gentiles (not to mention that little incident of denying his Lord), and Paul had such strong conflicts with co-ministers that they had to go their separate ways. Yet they, and we, would have missed so much if they had just given up when they missed the mark.

I like what Paul wrote in 1 Timothy 1:12–14: "I thank Christ Jesus our LORD, who has given me strength, that he considered me trustworthy, appointing me to his service. *Even though* I was once a blasphemer and a persecutor and a violent man, I was shown mercy because I acted in ignorance and unbelief. The grace of our LORD was poured out on me abundantly, along with the faith and love that are in Christ Jesus" (emphasis mine).

Even though. We all have an "even though." Can we move past our past, those regrets of sin and failure, to an "even though" resilience, and a willingness to resume service for our God?

In the verses following (15 and 16) Paul goes onto say, "Here is a trustworthy saying that deserves full acceptance: Christ Jesus came into the world to save sinners—of whom I am the worst. But for that very reason I was shown mercy so that in me, the worst of sinners, Christ Jesus might display his immense patience as an example for those who would believe in him and receive eternal life."

I'll say it again: a redeemed life is better than a rewind because others get to see the "immense patience" of Jesus on display! When you, as the recipient of His mercy, are resilient and determined to get back up and move forward, others will believe there is hope for them to do the same.

You might be thinking, *but Paul's "even though" was before he was a believer. Mine was after.* Listen, Peter had already spent three years with Jesus, in the flesh no less, before his "even though." Are you kidding me? There are whole books in the New Testament written almost entirely for the purpose of correcting the mistakes of believers whose sinful or stupid behavior had knocked the wind out of them! If God had no purpose in mind for them beyond their mistakes, why would He inspire those books to be written?

As a reminder, here are a few New Testament "even though" moments:

- My brothers and sisters, some from Chloe's household have informed me that there are quarrels among you. (1 Cor. 1:11)
- You are still worldly. For since there is jealousy and quarreling among you, are you not worldly? Are you not acting like mere humans? (1 Cor. 3:2)
- It is actually reported that there is sexual immorality among you, and of a kind that even pagans do not tolerate: A man is sleeping with his father's wife. (1 Cor. 5:1)
- The very fact that you have lawsuits among you means you have been completely defeated already. Why not rather be wronged? Why not rather be cheated? Instead, you yourselves cheat and do wrong, and you do this to your brothers and sisters. (1 Cor. 6:7–8)

- Come back to your senses as you ought, and stop
  sinning; for there are some who are ignorant of
  God—I say this to your shame. (1 Cor. 15:34)

Those are just a few verses from only one New Testament book! Do you think the Corinthians may have had a few "my bad" issues? Yet Paul includes these words as he wraps up this book: "Be on your guard; stand firm in the faith; be courageous; be strong. Do everything in love" (1 Cor. 16:13–14). That doesn't sound like he was addressing a group whom he, or God, had written off because of their failures.

I love these verses in Hebrews right in the middle of a chapter that describes how God disciplines us to produce holiness: "Therefore, strengthen your feeble arms and weak knees. 'Make level paths for your feet,' so that the lame may not be disabled, but rather healed" (Heb. 12:12–13). It's like the Lord is telling us, "Yes, I know all about your weakness and spiritual disabilities, but it's time to regain your strength and get healthy again. I have places for you to go!"

You Are Not Defined by Your Mistakes

My son-in-law, Jesse, is one of the nicest guys you'll ever meet. He's also strong and smart—which makes him so good at his job. Jesse is a registered nurse and has received many commendations and expressions of appreciation for his service at the hospital where he works. If you're ever hospitalized, you'll want a nurse like Jesse.

But Jesse's big heart and desire for excellence almost took him out of his profession a while back. One of his patients, a man who'd had surgery and seemed to be doing just fine afterward, died on his watch. As a nurse, Jesse has experienced the death of many people through the years—it comes with the territory. But he had really connected with this particular man and his wonderful family. And all had seemed to be progressing normally in his recovery . . . then suddenly, he was gone.

Jesse agonized over the details and wondered if he might've missed something or could've done something else to prevent this man's death. His medical colleagues, who did a thorough review, all assured him he had done everything correctly—that this was just one of those sad, unpredictable things that sometimes happen in the world of medicine. But in the days after this incident Jesse was inconsolable and thought about giving up his career. He might have followed through, too, if it weren't for a pep talk from one of the doctors he knows and respects.

This doctor heard of Jesse's discouragement and took him aside for a frank and surprisingly vulnerable talk. He told Jesse that when he was a young doctor he actually *had* made an error that cost a patient his life. He described his deep angst and how he had wanted so badly to give up medicine as he dealt with the repercussions that followed. Somehow he had found the courage and resilience to continue, though, and this is what he wanted Jesse to know from his years-later-down-the-road perspective: many more people

YOU ARE NOT DEFINED BY YOUR LAST BIG MISTAKE.

are alive today, who otherwise wouldn't be, because he didn't quit when he felt like it. He had made a costly mistake, one that would always make him cringe with regret, yes. But he learned from it, never repeated it, and brought those valuable lessons forward with him in a way that benefited countless other patients.

You are not defined by your last big mistake. If it was sinful, repent and stop it. (Did you catch that? *Stop. It.*) If it was stupid, learn from it and figure out how to keep from repeating it. Here's the thing . . . you *will* get a chance to choose between smart and stupid, between wise and unwise, between grabbing the bar or landing flat on your back again, as time goes on. To some degree, those situations that call us to do better arise almost daily, in one way or another. And many more people will experience life because you are resilient despite your regrets.

My sweet friend Jen Annan (now in her eighties and still a mentor to many) quoted Ralph Waldo Emerson in her "Jennuflections" devotional e-mail a while back and then added an important charge of her own:

> "Finish every day and be done with it. You have done what you could. Some blunders and absurdities no doubt have crept in; forget them as soon as you can. Tomorrow is a new day; begin it well and serenely and with too high a spirit to be cumbered with your old nonsense. This day is all that is good and fair. It is too dear, with its hopes and invitations, to waste a moment on yesterdays."
>
> —Ralph Waldo Emerson

All of you are loved and forgiven—and all of you love and forgive—so keep walking on in love. That is how we carry on a legacy.

That is how, indeed. And that is resilience.

Dumb Mistakes

Most of us, thank God, won't end up serving time for our gaffes. But, believe me, some of my less dramatic mistakes have made me want to crawl into a cave and hide for a decade or two. And sadly, I've had friends in ministry who have pretty much done just that.

I once did a training event called the "The Top Ten Dumbest Things I've Done in Ministry Leadership." The count could've gone much higher, but ten is a good round number, and I figured that was just about all the humility I could handle in one setting. We laughed a lot that day. The participants loved it and appreciated learning at my expense. By the way, when you have an opportunity to learn from the mistakes of others, go for it. It's much easier than learning from your own!

Unfortunately, my years of ministry and leadership experience *still* have not rendered me incapable of an occasional faux pas (or worse) now and then. Recently, I was offering spiritual counsel and mentoring to a lovely young woman in ministry who, due to some extremely difficult circumstances, had begun to experience panic attacks. We prayed together, and I ended the conversation by telling her, "You are *not* going down!"

A couple of days later, I was praying for this friend and decided to text her and reinforce that message of hope, "You are not going down." Sounds like a good plan with great intentions, right? Unfortunately, after telling her I was praying for her, I texted these words, "Remember, you are going down!" (Not exactly a good thing to say to someone who is battling fear. Cringe!)

Thankfully, when my friend wrote back a sweet response, I re-read my previous text message and had a chance to make amends. I apologized profusely and explained what I had meant to text: "You are *not* going down, you are *not* going down!" She replied that she knew what I had meant to say and thought the whole thing was hilarious, maybe even something God used to bring laughter into her day. My bad . . . *sheesh!*

I'm not the only one who's gotten into trouble by omitting a word in a text or an e-mail. Another friend told me about a group e-mail that was sent out to inform several ministers about a colleague who "went to be with the Lord." The sender, however, left out the word *with,* rendering it: "We wanted to let you know about our dear brother who went to be the Lord." (I think I know some of those dear brothers!) In another e-mail missive meant to reference "our deaf churches" one letter was changed. It read instead, "our dead churches."

Those blunders make me laugh and feel a little better, but remind me that I've plenty of my own material when it comes to silly mistakes. Some of those things, often from years ago, still make me cringe when I think of them. Like the day I completely bungled a radio interview and couldn't seem to string two complete sentences together. Or the time (as a young pastor's wife in our first church) when I didn't write down a telephone message about a particular deacon being sick and asking the pastor for prayer—which means I forgot to pass the message along to said pastor, which the aforementioned deacon happened to mention publicly (bless his heart) at a subsequent church service. (Note to self: make notes to self!) There've been times when I've said the wrong thing, done the wrong thing, and hurt others by my words, attitudes, or actions. *Cringe!*

Post-Partum Ministry Blues

For more years than I care to admit, I've been responsible for organizing all kinds of events, retreats, and conferences—large and small. And it's been my privilege to speak at all kinds of events, retreats, and conferences—large and small—across the nation. Here's the unvarnished truth: my first thoughts afterwards are almost always on what didn't go as well as I had hoped, what transition seemed awkward, what I omitted, what I should have omitted, who I forgot to acknowledge, etc., etc., etc. My mind, unchecked, spins off into all directions. *And the strange look on the face of that woman sitting in the fourth row on the left-hand side . . . what did that mean, for heaven's sake? Did I offend her in some way?*

When I'm finished speaking publicly, I sometimes think of what Winnie-the-Pooh said:

> When you are a Bear of Very Little Brain, and you think of things, you find sometimes that a thing which seemed very Thingish inside you is quite different when it gets out into the open and has other people looking at it.[21]

Yes, Winnie . . . *I know just what you mean.*

I remember driving home from one conference, in particular, feeling totally defeated. Never mind that numerous women had come up to me saying how God had used this event to inspire, instruct, and even change their lives. Never mind all the months of passion, effort, prayer, and preparation our whole team had put into this conference—and all the things that went really well. I had my focus on the few glitches, those small details that weren't quite right. And since I was the leader, the responsibility landed in my lap.

I have an acronym for this pathetic condition common to leaders and speakers: PPMB. It stands for Post-Partum Ministry Blues. (It sounds female, but men can have it, too. Also, small group leaders, worship leaders, teachers, professors, and those doing one-on-one ministry are not immune from this malady.)

PPMB occurs when you pour your heart and soul into giving birth to some form of ministry. Afterwards, when you're emotionally, physically, and spiritually spent, you look at the "baby" you've just birthed . . . and cringe. With no disrespect intended you say to yourself, "Yikes! What an ugly baby!" Then you think, *I shouldn't be doing this . . . I'm really not capable of handling these kinds of responsibilities . . . Someone else could do a much better job . . . Why am I putting myself through this? . . . Why am I putting others through this?*

There's nothing wrong with a good, honest post-ministry evaluation, especially when it's done with a group of trusted, spiritually-healthy colleagues. In fact it's crucial to look at what went right, what went wrong, and how it can be improved next time, or even if there should be a "next time" for the event. But that isn't PPMB.

PPMB is a fixation on the negative aspects of a ministry effort, especially as it relates to our performance in that event or situation. It's coupled with the complete disregard of anything we did well or any successful outcome. And though we may not realize it, it makes *our* efforts (and what we, or others, think of them), more important than what God may have been up to in the secret places of the heart.

I've learned, through my own dealings with PPMB, that it's best to give myself a few days to rest and replenish emotionally and spiritually before I delve into reviewing a ministry event I've just led or a speaking engagement I've just completed. Only then do I have the emotional equilibrium to handle what needs to be fixed without being debilitated by it. At the same time, I can celebrate the wins, and have the spiritual discernment to perceive the less obvious things God may have been up to in that setting.

My bad. As much as we wish we would never have to say that again, never have to own up to any weakness or error, until we stand in the presence of the Faultless One, it's a line that will (in some form or another) be part of our vocabulary. Still, we can own our flaws without being forever incapacitated by them.

> **IT'S BEST TO GIVE MYSELF A FEW DAYS TO REST AND REPLENISH EMOTIONALLY AND SPIRITUALLY BEFORE I DELVE INTO REVIEWING A MINISTRY EVENT I'VE JUST LED OR A SPEAKING ENGAGEMENT I'VE JUST COMPLETED.**

In his book *Abide in Christ,* Andrew Murray put it like this:

> The Christian often tries to forget his weakness: God wants us to remember it, to feel it deeply. The Christian wants to conquer his weakness and to be freed from it: God wants us to rest and even rejoice in it. The Christian mourns over his weakness: Christ teaches His servant to say, "I take pleasure in infirmities; most gladly will I glory in my infirmities." The Christian

thinks his weakness is his greatest hindrance in the life and service of God: God tells us that it is the secret of strength and success. It is our weakness, heartily accepted and continually realized, that gives us our claim and access to the strength of Him who has said, "My strength is made perfect in weakness."[22]

By all means, my friend, cringe if you must. But then continue.

• THEIR BAD •

True or false: Most people are decent. Most people have good intentions and don't start their day with the goal of making your life miserable. Did you answer true to those statements? So did I.

However once in a while we all run into folks who are not "most people." They *do* seem to have it in for us, for whatever reason, and can find all kinds of ways to create misery in our lives. Not all bullies are found on the grade school playground. These folks seem to thrive on intimidating others, maybe just because they can.

I wonder if Paul was referring to a bully when he wrote these words in 2 Timothy 4:14–15: "Alexander the metalworker did me a great deal of harm. The LORD will repay him for what he has done. You too should be on your guard against him, because he strongly opposed our message."

It was on my first real summer job (other than picking Oregon strawberries in the hot sun to earn money for school clothes) that I ran into my first grown-up bully. I worked at our local elementary school as a janitor's assistant, of sorts, where I earned a whopping $1.25 an hour doing building maintenance projects like painting and helping to clean up after summer students. It was hard but enjoyable labor, for the most part, made better because my good friend from church, Sharon, was working with me.

One warm afternoon, Sharon and I finished all our regular duties early and had nothing left on our to-do list for the day. We got along well with the head maintenance guy—a quiet, easygoing fellow—who was our boss, and we decided to surprise him. Here was our plan: the maintenance storage room had become quite a mess so we would clean it up without being asked. Sharon and I scurried around, organizing the strewn supplies and tools, cleaning the littered floors, and putting everything in spick-and-span order. We were tired but pretty proud of ourselves when it was all done. And we couldn't wait to see the look on our boss's face when he saw the results of our efforts.

A little while later, as I walked down the hall I heard voices and laughter coming from inside the maintenance room. I thought I recognized the only adult voice as belonging to the stocky woman who cooked lunch for the summer school kids. We had never actually met beyond a hello since my duties didn't take me into her kitchen. The few times I had seen her, she always seemed to be wearing a scowl along with her ever-present hairnet and dingy-white apron, so it surprised me to hear her talking so jovially with her crew of teen girl helpers.

As I got closer, though, I had a hard time believing what I was hearing. "Yeah," she said, "we'll show them—the little goody-goodies." (This remark brought loud chortles from her young subordinates.) "They're from that church on the edge of town . . . bunch of crazy Christians, that's what they are! Let's see how they like . . . "

About that time I walked through the doorway into a bizarre sight that, in its ridiculous meanness, seems surreal to this day.

There was the school cook dumping garbage from the big trash can all over the floors. In one sweeping glance I took in the room's disarray that, less than an hour earlier, Sharon and I had worked so hard to clean. The cook's crew must have gotten wind of our little surprise and for some crazy reason, decided to put us in our places by undoing all our efforts.

I was stunned with hurt and anger—the cook looked up in guilty surprise. The big broom, which I had been returning to the room, dropped out of my trembling hand, its wooden handle clattering loudly on the floor.

"Don't you have . . . have *anything* better to do with your time?" I stammered before turning on my heel and running to find the maintenance man. With hot tears streaming down my flushed cheeks, I told the older man what had happened. My gentle boss just shook his head, his eyes sad, and told me not to worry about it.

I'm not sure what, if anything, was ever done to the cook in the form of a reprimand. Perhaps my boss thought it too small an incident to pursue with his superiors—or perhaps he'd had his own run-ins with her and wanted to steer clear. In retrospect, it really wasn't such a big deal, but it was one of the first stand-out times when an adult directed malice towards me, personally. And I had no idea why.

MOST PEOPLE, EVEN WHEN THEY INADVERTENTLY HURT YOU, HAVE GOOD INTENTIONS.

My best guess, considering the comments I overheard, is that her motives involved some long-held grudge against our church (though she had never attended during the years my parents had been pastors there), or someone in it. Or maybe she was striking out against Christianity in general, and I just happened to be a handy target that day. Since it was a small town, she likely knew I was a local preacher's kid. Perhaps it had nothing to do with faith at all—maybe she just didn't like me.

On that summer afternoon, I was dazed by just how mean people can be. Decades later, I still am. And frankly, the more active you are in ministry and leadership, the more of a spite-target you become for some. I should repeat here, *most people do not fit in this category.* Most people, even when they inadvertently hurt you, have good intentions. Still, there are those who seem to relish nothing more than slinking in to undo your best efforts, to pour garbage over your acts of service and kindness.

Hatefulness comes in many forms, even in ministry life:

- The unsigned letter telling you all the ways you're failing
- Sarcastic, cutting comments that keep you awake half the night wondering how in the world to respond
- The subtle withdrawal of friendship or support when you make a leadership decision that doesn't meet with approval
- Crossed arms and stone-faced stares from the audience when you're up front trying to minister or lead
- The use of phrases like "A lot of people are really unhappy . . . " or "Everyone is saying . . . "
- Spreading of half-truths or untruths
- Forming of disgruntled coalitions

I really, really hope none of these are familiar to you. But if you've been in ministry leadership for a while, it's likely that at least a couple are. And any of these (or other similar types of human nastiness) can knock the wind right out of us. Sometimes our detractors feel like a demanding, extra-critical audience at an ice-skating show. The skaters, who are doing all kinds of intricate steps, graceful spins, and flying leaps (often backwards, on one foot, while wearing a razor-thin blade, on the world's most slippery surface—mind you) are being judged by people in the stands who couldn't even stay upright on the ice while wearing rubber-bottomed street shoes with cleats! But they have their opinions, nonetheless, and are not afraid to let them be heard. I think you catch the parallel.

Right now, I'm thinking of one amazing friend who did a fantastic job of leading her first big event. Afterwards, while there were many positive comments and affirmations, she received some pretty stringent criticisms about one thing—just one small thing—that happened over the course of those two days. That did it. She vowed never to take on something like that again . . . and she never has. Regrettably, the true leadership potential in my friend has been minimized, to everyone's loss.

Encounters with Mean People

Mean people are nothing new. In his first letter to the Thessalonians (2:2), Paul wrote, "We had previously suffered and been treated outrageously in Philippi, as you know, but with the help of our God we dared to tell you his gospel in the face of strong opposition." "Suffered" . . . "treated outrageously" . . . "strong opposition." Sounds like Paul knew something about painful encounters with mean people.

Sometimes other leaders can create the most angst and be your biggest obstacles, even those "God-fearing women" who believe they're doing His bidding when they give you grief. That was the case in Acts 13:49–52 (emphasis mine):

> The word of the LORD spread through the whole region. But the Jewish leaders incited the *God-fearing women of high standing* and the *leading men* of the city. They stirred up persecution against Paul and Barnabas, and expelled them from their region. So they shook the dust off their feet as a warning to them and went to Iconium. And the disciples were filled with joy and with the Holy Spirit.

Shouldn't we strive to resolve conflicts and work to live at peace with everyone as far it depends on us, like Romans 12:18 says? Absolutely! There are many wonderful training resources and great books that deal with conflict and how to resolve it in a biblical manner. Peaceful resolution has to be our default, and we must be willing to work hard and show patience with the process.

But sometimes it's beyond us—sometimes those we are in conflict with are unmovable in their animosity. In his insightful book on this subject, *Necessary Endings,* psychologist Dr. Henry Cloud says, "Some people are out to do you harm. If you do not accept this reality, then you are going to spend a lot of time wasting time, money, energy, love, resources, your heart, and everything else that matters to you on people who will either squander it or destroy it."[23]

We can't fix everyone's negative opinion of us, but we can use up every last drop of energy trying. We may need to learn, or re-learn the Acts 13:52 lesson about how to shake the dust off our souls and bruised egos, and be on our way, filled with the Holy Spirit and with joy.

As a woman in my mid-fifties, I'm finally learning to be at peace with the fact that not everyone I meet will like me. (Such a pity, though.) They may not like my mannerisms. They may distrust my motives. They may not appreciate my quirky sense of humor—to their great loss, of course. (Or . . . maybe not.) I can be okay with this when I know that, in good conscience, I've acted with kindness toward them, done nothing intentionally to hurt or offend them—or if I've offended, I've also done my best to make amends and repair any relational breach.

Since becoming a religion columnist for *The Seattle Times* back in 2007, my skin has had to get a little thicker. When you write about issues of faith for a secular newspaper in one of the most unchurched regions of the country, you expect that not everyone is going to love what you write. Thankfully, through the years I've had mostly positive feedback and reader responses (via e-mail). Actually, I'm often brought to tears by the details and personal stories of how my column spoke to someone and helped that person at a crucial time. These have been such an encouragement to me that I've saved most of them in a file.

But I also get e-mails that could singe your eyelashes off. Here are a couple examples mild enough to include:

You may be small town but you have maintained your simple mindedness.

Jodi, it sounds like your parents were wise and prepared. It was a nice story and you have a nice descriptive writing style. You then start blathering, "Proverbs this, Psalms that." Here is the rewrite. My folks saved my bacon because of their foresight. Have good friends nearby. Sometimes one has to pull up their big-girl panties and do uncomfortable things. Prepare, and believe in yourself, even when it's scary and don't panic. See? No God.

I've been called a variety of colorful names, been accused of hearing voices from invisible "pretend friends" akin to the Tooth Fairy and the Easter Bunny, and told that I'm trying to brainwash the public.

I'm learning many lessons along this journalistic journey but here's a big one that applies to other parts of life too, especially if you're a leader: *while I may need to have tough skin, I never want to develop a hard heart.*

I could pretend that the vitriolic comments don't sting. I could have a "What do they know, anyway? They're just a bunch of unbelieving imbeciles!" attitude, which would, in effect, contradict my message of compassion and grace. So what *is* the right response?

I think Lettie Cowman captures this well in her *Streams in the Desert* devotional entry for February 10:

> The apostle Paul said, "None of these things *move* me." (Act 20:24 KJV). He did not say, "None of these things *hurt* me." It is one thing to be hurt, and quite another to be moved.[24]

If we acknowledge the hurt and stay tenderhearted, without being moved from what God has called us to do, then we can be Jesus-hearted women who also happen to be endearing and effective leaders.

So when I get a reader's e-mail that hurts, I let it. But I've determined to pray for that person, to try to understand where he or she might be coming from, and to learn from the objections. Actually (here's a little secret), it makes me glad to know that my column is being read by someone other than the already convinced, even when they post withering comments on *The Seattle Times* Web site for all to see!

By the way, did you know you can actually pay for an online service that promises to "manage your reputation" by searching the Internet for damaging posts or articles about you, and then removing them? Oh boy! If that www technology had existed in Jesus' day, just think of the fortune this company could've made by dealing with all the negative press He got; that is, if He had wanted them to. But I'm pretty sure He wouldn't have, since He seemed perfectly content to let the Father be His reputation defender. We would be wise to do the same.

• TOO BAD •

On Saturday, February 27, 2010 at 8:30 in the morning, an empty Boeing 757 jetliner was being towed along the taxiway at Sea-Tac airport in Seattle, Washington, not far from where I live. Unfortunately the tow went awry and the huge plane went off the taxiway into the strip of soft ground beside it.

As you may have heard, we get a good deal of rain in the Pacific Northwest (okay, we get drenched, but that accounts for all the beautiful green landscape you'll see when you visit), and that February had been no exception.

A 757 jetliner contains roughly the same square footage as an average three bedroom house in America (1,950 square feet) and weighs about as much as a diesel train locomotive. Still it can easily break the bonds of gravity while holding more than two hundred people to soar 37,000 feet up in the air at speeds in excess of 500 mph.

Yet on this day, this mighty bird was stuck . . . in six inches of mud! It took crews all day, about nine hours, to finally free the earthbound jetliner from the mire. In actual flying hours, the 757 could have flown most of the way to New York and back in that same period of time. But those mere six inches of mud kept it from moving six feet. "Too bad," people might have said when they heard this story. "Must have been a real bummer."

I've felt like that grounded jetliner from time to time, stuck in the mud when I should be soaring. And it's not due to *my bad* or *their bad;* it's just that life is in one of those *too bad* seasons. These are the times when circumstances beyond our control make us feel stuck.

Your six inches of mud may look different than mine. It may come in the form of financial struggles that keep the dreams in your heart under lock and key. It may show up as health issues—those frequent and debilitating headaches, that growing lump in your breast, or your six-year-old's cough that won't go away despite repeated rounds of antibiotics.

It may have its source in a natural disaster, like the flood that ruined your home and destroyed your wedding pictures. It could be related to your deepest unmet desires to find your spouse or to have a child. Sometimes it stems from something as mundane as too much clutter and too little energy—or too many extra pounds and too little willpower. It may show up in the form of a rejection letter from your publisher or a pink slip from your boss. It just might be a simmering frustration that the wonderful goals for your ministry, the ones you were pretty sure God gave you, are not even close to being met.

Without resilience, your six inches of mud—whatever it looks like—can keep you stuck for a long time, much longer than the jetliner's nine hours.

To be honest, I feel I'm emerging from one of those *too bad* seasons as I write this. Life took quite an unexpected turn for my family and me a few months ago. Don and I were in the Dallas, Texas airport on our way home from a national leaders' conference when we got word that our thirty-four-year-old daughter was being taken into emergency surgery to deal with a ruptured (and heavily bleeding) ovarian cyst. We were assured that the procedure would be pretty straightforward and would involve only a short recovery period.

Upon landing in Seattle, I immediately unpacked and repacked to head down to Oregon to help my daughter's family during her recovery. Kristi and her husband, Jesse (whom I wrote about earlier), have three precious little girls, including a four-month-old (at the time) baby so I knew they could use the extra help.

But things didn't go well. During surgery, the doctor decided to remove Kristi's right ovary and fallopian tube and, in the process, accidentally perforated her bowel, which lead to a massive septic infection. Several times in the following days, she was extremely close to death, her body fighting off raging fevers that left her with hallucinations and horrible pain. As her mother, it tore at my heart to watch my firstborn's agony. There were many prayers where I pleaded, with a mixture of faith and fear—I must admit—for God to spare her life. She underwent a second surgery to remove part of her small intestine, and then a third to insert a drain to deal with the increasing infection.

Kristi was in the hospital (much of the time in ICU) during most of December. She missed baby Mira's first Christmas and middle daughter Libby's seventh birthday. When she could finally go home (probably a little earlier than would have happened otherwise, had she not been married to a great nurse), she was under doctor's orders to do almost nothing for several weeks and was told to expect that full recovery would take many months.

So, upon this writing, I've spent a big part of the last few months either with Kristi in the hospital, or helping to care for her girls, part of the time in my home and part in theirs, trying to be a calming presence in the midst of difficult circumstances. During that same time period, all three girls had respiratory infections that required antibiotics, Libby almost broke her arm (I spent three hours in the emergency room with her—on Christmas Eve), I got a severe steam burn on my right hand (not so good for changing diapers), and we lost power for a few days due to a severe snow and wind storm. None of these things were *my bad* or *their bad*—there was no person to blame. It was just a season of *too bad*—when life, which is already tricky, got even harder.

Treasures from the Dark Places

Although I'll admit to being drained, even exhausted, throughout those days (there are good reasons why women usually don't have babies in their fifties!), there are also amazing treasures from the dark places we walked through that will always be with me . . . like the sweet hours and days of just being with my girl and her lovely family during a recovery period that could not be rushed. Isaiah

45:3 (ESV) says, "I will give you the treasures of darkness and the hoards in secret places, that you may know that it is I, the LORD, the God of Israel, who call you by your name."

This was the longest I'd ever taken care of my grandgirls, and we linked hearts on a completely different level. We played games, baked Christmas cupcakes, and worked on crafts to take as gifts to their mommy in the hospital. Feeding baby Mira in the late night or early morning hours became sacred prayer encounters as I held that precious little life, so fresh from God, to my heart. As I rocked her, I lifted up another near-to-my-heart life, Mira's mommy, who was so precariously close to leaving us. Bright treasures in dark places, indeed.

GOD HAS CALLED US TO A LIFE OF RESILIENCE EVEN WHEN THINGS ARE *TOO BAD.*

Today, Don and I are beyond grateful that our daughter is alive and slowly getting better. I tell Kristi the long reddish slash on her abdomen is her MOTB (mother-of-the-bride) scar—it means she gets to be the MOTB at her daughters' weddings someday. I'm not sure she's buying it, but she chuckles and we both sigh with a mixture of regret and gratitude. Regret that all this happened, yet gratitude that God brought her through.

Helping Kristi and her family was a great privilege and one of the things I was put on this earth to do. I truly don't begrudge a minute of it. So please don't think that what I'm about to say next is a *poor me,* or that I'm comparing my stress during this season with what our daughter and her family went through, because it doesn't even come close. And I know that many reading this have experienced a devastatingly different outcome for a beloved family member or friend who didn't make it, despite all the prayers.

Here's the truth, though. When it comes to the things I was focused on before Kristi's health crisis, I feel like someone knocked the wind out of me. My plans and to-do list (including my doctoral work and writing this book) went topsy-turvy even though I was right where I was supposed to be and *wanted* to be. I'm really tired and wish I could just pull the covers over my head for a year or so. It would have been easy to cancel speaking engagements and leave this book manuscript untouched, based on my stuck-in-six-inches-of-mud feelings.

But God has called us to a life of resilience even when things are *too bad*. With His strength, and with help from friends and family (which I had in abundance), He wants us to pull ourselves out of the mire, whatever its source, and find a way to soar again. I did take some time to rest, and I think I'm finally back on the runway . . . at least waiting in line for my turn to lift-off again.

One of my favorite greeting cards says this: "Everything will be okay in the end. If it's not okay, it's not the end." Lots of things in life are "not okay," but as Jesus-hearted women, we know we haven't reached the end when everything really will be okay. And until we do, we move forward steadily. Resilience makes that possible.

Even better than a greeting card are my favorite resilience verses for *too bad* times:

What, then, shall we say in response to these things? If God is for us, who can be against us? He who did not spare his own Son, but gave him up for us all—how will he not also, along with him, graciously give us all things? Who shall separate us from the love of Christ? Shall trouble or hardship or persecution or famine or nakedness or danger or sword? *No, in all these things we are more than conquerors through him who loved us.* For I am convinced that neither death nor life, neither angels nor demons, neither the present nor the future, nor any powers, neither height nor depth, nor anything else in all creation, will be able to separate us from the love of God that is in Christ Jesus our LORD. (Rom. 8:32, 35, 37–39, emphasis mine)

We are hard pressed on every side, but not crushed; perplexed, but not in despair; persecuted, but not abandoned; *struck down, but not destroyed.* (2 Cor. 4:8–9, emphasis mine)

Though the righteous fall seven times, *they rise again.* (Prov. 24:16, emphasis mine)

How's that for resilience!

I know it's easy to get stuck in the muddy waysides of life. When that happens, we can lose heart and wonder if we've still got what it takes to soar. Circumstances may leave us with a sense of defeat. F. Scott Fitzgerald said, "Never confuse a single defeat with a final defeat." Please don't. That really would be *too bad.*

• JODI'S COACHING QUESTIONS •

- Is there a particular *my bad* (a mistake that was your fault) memory that still makes you cringe? What did you (or can you) learn from it that will serve you in the future?

- Have you ever had a case of PPMB (Post-Partum Ministry Blues)? If so, how did it affect you? How can you move from PPMB to a more healthy evaluation of your ministry efforts?

- How can you recognize a spiritual or emotional bully? What are the main things you want to remember when someone is trying to bully you?

- Have you ever felt stuck in "six inches of mud" when you wanted to be soaring? What did that look like? How did you become "unstuck"? When it comes to resilience, what's the greatest lesson you've learned so far?

• A LITTLE LESSON FOR NEW LEADERS •

When you start out in ministry and experience a cringe factor, it's easy to feel like that episode will stain your whole life as a leader. It doesn't have to if you learn to be resilient and keep moving forward. People really can come back, even from big mistakes. It's called grace: God's priceless gift to fallible people. Don't color all the pages of your ministry picture book with the darkest crayon of one bad experience.

Most messy situations mellow with time (and God's active mercy); you can probably outlive the smirkers and outlast the skeptics—even the ones in your head. And about those people who might fall into the "their bad" category? While it's okay to be cautious, don't be quick to write people off, even if they've hurt you. You may be able to out-love a bully or two until they become a friend. Stranger things have happened. There was this guy named Saul, later called Paul . . .

Finally, if you're stuck in the mire when you should be soaring, by all means, tell someone who can help you get moving again. That 757 jetliner would still be sitting by the runway if someone hadn't radioed for help. Everyone gets stuck from time to time. Seriously, *everyone.* The only shame is in staying stuck for good. Find someone who's trustworthy and enlist her prayer support—then ask what she would do if she were in your six inches of mud. The wheels will slowly gain traction (be patient, but keep trying), and you'll be soaring again before you know it.

• HEART-DEEP IN THE WORD •

Revisit the story of Joseph in Genesis chapters 37 and 39–45. What were the circumstances in which Joseph displayed resilience? What situations do people face today that might parallel some of Joseph's troubles? How have you seen resilience make a difference in these circumstances?

_____

_____

_____

_____

_____

_____

Read Genesis 40:2; 5; 20–23. Also read Genesis 41:25, 38–52. What is the common thread in these verses? How does believing the promise given in Hebrews 13:5 help us to have the resilience of Joseph?

_____

_____

_____

_____

What do the words of Paul in Philippians 4:11–13 have to do with resilience?

_____

_____

_____

_____

Read 2 Corinthians 4:7–10, 16–18. What lessons about resilience can you learn from these verses? What stands out to you most from these scriptures?

_____

_____

_____

_____

_____

chapter six

POCKETBOOK PUNCHES

LEADERSHIP QUALITY: COURAGE

· · · · · · · · · · ·

Courage is not simply one of the virtues
but the form of every virtue at the testing point.

—C. S. LEWIS

I t was a shocking news story with video footage that had the
entire country holding its collective breath. On December 14,
2010, an ordinary school board meeting in Panama City, Florida,
quickly turned into a scene of terror when a gunman, Clay Duke,
walked to the front of the room and spray-painted a red circle and
a "V" (for *vendetta)* on the wall. He then ordered everyone but
the male board members out. For the next several minutes, Duke
waved his gun around and ranted about the district firing his wife,
a special-education teacher.

One of those ordered out of the room was board member
Ginger Littleton. As she considered the danger her colleagues
were in, Littleton made a courageous (though some would call

it foolish) choice. Cameras set to capture a routine school board meeting showed instead a brave woman sneaking up behind the gunman with the only "weapon" she had at hand—her purse.

In a matter of seconds, Littleton drew back her arm and swung the brown pocketbook with all her might, hoping to knock the gun out of Duke's hand. Instead, the glancing blow only alerted the gunman to the valiant woman's presence. As Ginger Littleton fell to the floor, Duke aimed the gun at her but for some reason, refrained from shooting.

> **COURAGE. IT'S ONE OF THOSE LEADERSHIP QUALITIES THAT'S NOT ONLY ADMIRABLE BUT NECESSARY—NO ONE LASTS LONG WITHOUT IT.**

The whole frightening scene could have ended more tragically than it did. As the gunman fired point-blank at the seated board members, miraculously just missing each of them, another hero entered the room. Security guard Mike Jones exchanged fire with Duke, hitting him in the side. Moments later, the gunman ended his own life, and the ordeal was over.

Later, in a *Today* show television interview, Ginger Littleton had this to say: "My guys were lined up like ducks in a pond, so I could either walk away and try to live with myself because I knew something bad was going to happen, or I could try to defend, delay—somehow or other divert—hoping that the cavalry would come soon. My guys had three-ring binders and pencils to protect themselves, so I whacked him with the purse, hoping I could get him to drop the gun. Obviously that didn't work. I did not have a Plan B."[25]

Courage. It's one of those leadership qualities that's not only admirable but necessary—no one lasts long without it. Hopefully you've never had to face a gunman (thank God!) but, as a leader, you may have felt a bit like Ginger Littleton at times. The odds are against you, someone else holds all the power, and the things in your hand seem pathetically weak.

Even your motivation may be a lot like hers. Ministry is not your hobby—lives and eternities are at stake. So, even when there seems little chance at success, you gather your courage and your pocketbook and come out swinging. Great leaders make gallant efforts and take risks, even when the odds are overwhelming and the outcome uncertain.

Where does courage come from? Are some people just a little gutsier by nature? Is courage a gift from God, or perhaps a virtue that can be developed? We'll explore these questions and see what a brave, Jesus-hearted woman might look like as she leads others through a dark world into the light of grace.

• I'M SCARED •

We humans are an interesting conglomeration of timidity and valiance, fear and fierceness, cowardice and courage. We're rarely all of one without traces of the other. Have you ever been on the back end of the fight or flight syndrome but discovered that it's hard to run when your knees are knocking together and your heart is playing its own drum-solo version of *Wipeout?* Yeah . . . me too.

I am, however, consoled by all the scaredy-cats (that's what my kids would have called them) in the Bible:

- The first excuse a human ever gave to God for missing an appointment with Him? *I was scared.* (Gen. 3:10)
- The first time a human lied directly to God, it was due to fear. Mrs. Beautiful herself, Sarah, fibbed to God. Genesis 18:15 says, "Sarah was afraid, so she lied and said, 'I did not laugh.' But he said, 'Yes, you did laugh.'" Ummm . . . trying to pull the wool over God's eyes? Now that's laughable!
- Fear was the motivation behind one of the first biblical accounts of intentional deception. Abraham was so sure his beautiful wife, Sarah, would get him killed by the Egyptian men who wanted her for themselves that he concocted a plan to pass her off as his sister. (Gen. 12:11–13) He even repeated this ruse years later with Abimelech, King of Gerar. (Gen. 20) And, following in his father's fainthearted footsteps, Isaac applied the same subterfuge with *his* wife, Rebekah! (Gen. 26:7–9) How would you like to have been married to those *great-faith* guys?
- After fleeing Sodom, a frightened Lot lived in a mountain cave and completely isolated his two daughters from any other human contact. *That* did not turn out well. (Gen. 19:30)
- In Exodus 2:14, a fearful Moses ran for the desert after learning his crime (murdering an Egyptian who had mistreated a fellow Israelite) had been discovered.
- The sixth chapter of Judges recounts the story of Gideon, a man so afraid of the marauding

Midianites that when we first meet him he's hiding out in a winepress to thresh his wheat. He seems anything *but* the "mighty man of valor," referred to in the angelic greeting. And when God tells him to tear down his father's pagan altar, he does it at night because he's so scared of his own family and neighbors. (Judg. 6:27)

- Saul, the tall warrior-king, was afraid of David. (1 Sam. 18:12)
- David, the mighty giant-slayer, was afraid of Achish, the king of Gath. (1 Sam. 21:12)
- Elijah, God's bold spokesman who had just faced down four-hundred prophets of Baal and won, was so terrified by the death threats from one woman, Queen Jezebel, that he went into hiding. (1 Kings 19:3)
- Peter was panicked by the wind and the waves. (Matt. 14:30) Later he was so intimidated by the comments of a little servant girl that he denied knowing Jesus. (Matt. 26:69–75)

Are you starting to see a pattern here? Even the boldest among us can be frightened at times. And yet, even the most cowardly can become courageous. That gives me hope when I face my own fears.

• BRAVER THAN YOU BELIEVE •

When I consider courage, I like what English author and humorist A. A. Milne's character, Christopher Robin says to Winnie-the-Pooh: "Promise me you'll always remember . . . you're braver than you believe, and stronger than you seem, and smarter than you think."

It's difficult to nail down the source of courage. Some people seem to have a pluckier disposition from birth. They're the four-year-olds who grab the microphone from the adult leader in the Christmas program while their timid siblings hide behind the stage curtain and refuse to be coaxed out. They're the rambunctious six-year-olds who insist on going down the big slide at the park on their backs and head-first. Or better yet, they'd prefer to jump from the top! They think garden snakes make great mommy-presents and can't understand why she won't hold the cute little creature.

IT SEEMS COURAGE CAN BE NURTURED AND DEVELOPED WITHOUT FANFARE, USUALLY CHOICE BY SMALL CHOICE.

However, disposition alone cannot account for the bravery displayed by ordinary people down through history. It seems courage can be nurtured and developed without fanfare, usually choice by small choice, act by unobtrusive act, until the occasion arises when a hero is needed. Then suddenly, the Ginger Littleton's of the world stand up, grab their pocketbooks, and deliver their best punches. Afterwards, they shake their heads in disbelief at their own actions—they've surprised even themselves. Yet they wonder why people consider them heroic. "I just did what needed to be done," they say quietly.

So what needs to be done when it comes to courageous leadership? Some women in the Bible were *braver than they believed, stronger than they seemed, and smarter than they thought.* By looking at their lives we glimpse why Jesus-hearted women must be brave if they're going to lead and last. They will need courage:

- **To deliver a dream**—Jochebed's story (Exod. 2:1–10)

It couldn't have been a worse time to bear a child, especially a baby boy. But in a slave-hovel somewhere near the Nile, Moses was born. And as her breasts began to leak drops of nourishment into his tiny mouth, defiant delight rose in Jochebed's heart. This child was beautiful, and she was glad he had been born, despite Pharaoh's edict that all male Hebrew babies should be killed.

For more years than she could count, her people had been pleading to God, dreaming day and night about finding liberty from their tortuous oppression. Maybe the risk-laden delivery of *this* child would somehow deliver *that* dream of freedom. Her eyes darted about the room and landed on the reed basket in the corner. *Yes,* she mused, *now if I can only find some tar.*

Hebrews 11:23 says, "By faith Moses' parents hid him for three months after he was born, because they saw he was no ordinary child, and they were not afraid of the king's edict." That's courage.

What is your dream? My friend, Dr. JoAnn Butrin's dream is to deliver compassionate health care to under-resourced people around the world. To her, social justice and a holistic approach to the mission of God are not just the latest fads. They're components of the dream that compels her to fly to sites of tsunamis and massive earthquakes; they bid her to work in the poorest of countries with HIV/AIDS patients and the orphans left behind. Like Jochebed, she looks into faces given a virtual death sentence and dares to dream life for them instead. That's courage!

- **To protect the powerless**—Esther's story. (Esther, chapters 1–10)

Everyone in the kingdom knew what happened to defiant queens. They disappeared. Queen Esther had just learned something else—though she wished she hadn't. Her cousin Mordecai managed to get word to her that their own people were the target of a murderous plot by one of the king's right-hand men, Haman. The Jews were slated for mass genocide, and it was perfectly legal. It was all so maddening! Her people were defenseless, but what did they expect *her* to do about it? Everyone knew what happened to defiant queens.

"Have everyone fast," she told her cousin, "and I mean *everyone.*" As she paced through her part of the palace, she eventually found herself in the cooking quarters, perhaps because her own stomach was rumbling from lack of food. It was there a plan began to take shape. *Yes, it would definitely be risky,* she considered, as her fingers traced soft lines through the fragrant spices in a small pottery bowl, *but maybe a meal might help—or even two . . .*

What will you and I do when we're called to protect the powerless? One of my lifetime heroes is Corrie ten Boom, who helped hide Jews from the Nazi holocaust during World War II.

Her book, *The Hiding Place,* is a classic must-read for anyone who wants to know what courage looks like in the direst of circumstances. But her bravery cost her dearly.

Their family, who'd been betrayed by an informant, was arrested and imprisoned; her father died ten days later. Corrie and her beloved sister, Betsie, ended up in the notorious concentration camp, Ravensbruck. And although she experienced a miraculous release just before she was to be gassed, Betsie died there. After traveling the world for decades with her message that God's love can overcome humanity's cruelest evil, Corrie died on her ninety-first birthday. But her legacy lives on in the lives of the powerless she protected, and in the example of courage she left behind.[26]

A little closer to home, I have other protectors-of-the-powerless heroes, though they wouldn't identify themselves as such. Some of them (like my daughter, Jana) mentor at-risk youth. Others deliver meals to elderly shut-ins or take in foster children. My good friend Dr. Beth Grant helped found and now co-leads a remarkable ministry called Project Rescue (PR). Beth has made it her mission to protect the powerless victims of sex slavery in India, Nepal, and Moldova—and anywhere around the globe where women and girls are forced into prostitution. This beautiful, bold woman has walked into some of the world's darkest hellholes and emerged with precious souls who will find restoration in one of PR's Homes of Hope. As I told her recently, her courageous example inspires and convicts me—and I need both.

- **To win the war**—Deborah's story. (Judg. 4 and 5)

His reaction surprised her. Surely after twenty years of cruel oppression by Jabin, the king of Canaan,

Barak should be glad to hear that God had finally said, "Enough; it's time to fight back. I will give Sisera, commander of Jabin's army, into your hands."

Barak couldn't doubt that this message was truly from God, could he? After all, Deborah had faithfully led Israel as prophet and judge for many years; God's hand upon her leadership and His voice speaking through her were undeniable. All Israel came to her for wisdom under the tree they called The Palm of Deborah, and she gave it freely.

"Go, and you will win this war," she told Barak. But instead of heading off to rally his army, he held his gaze on her and said, "If you go with me, I will go; but if you don't go with me, I won't go."

Such a thought! Deborah, a mother in Israel, off to war with ten-thousand men? Deborah, the wife, the mother, the judge, the prophet . . . yes, she was all of these. But Deborah the *warrior?* Warriors often died in even lesser battles, and Israel's military track record in recent years had been lamentable.

Still, God had said there was a war to win, and this battle was the place to begin. Deborah cast her eyes about and saw her heavy cloak lying at the base of the tree, where she'd tossed it that morning. *Not much protection from a flying arrow or the sword's sharpness,* she thought, *but it will do.* Her eyes met Barak's. "Very well," she said, "I will go with you."

When I think about Deborah's courage, the face of a modern-day counterpart quickly comes to mind. This sweet face belongs to my mother, Louise Lankford Dunlap. That she was born on the fourth of July should tell you something about her nature and character—strong, brave, a little bit independent when she needs to be, and with a sparkling personality that lights up any room.

Mother served right alongside my dad, fully immersed in every element of pastoral ministry for decades (Barak and Deborah, off to battle!) until Daddy's health failed. Then, for more than a decade, she was his loving caregiver, bearing up under a load that would break stronger backs.

After Dad's passing, Mother continued to minister to the people around her—teaching classes in her church and small group, volunteering in children's ministries, and being a good friend and neighbor to all she met. With a lifelong interest in writing, she was always composing a piece of poetry, music, or prose as I was growing up (guess where I got my writing bug!), yet never had much of a chance to develop her works for publication. But at the age of almost eighty, Mother went to her first writer's conference, all by herself. She carried her little suitcase up three flights of stairs to her room and jumped into the learning experience with both feet. And guess who has had articles published right and left ever since? Yep, my eighty-something mother! I'm so proud of her for all these things, but it's another incident from years ago that most reminds me of her Deborah-like courage.

My parents had been camping by a beautiful lake when Mother took their dog, Brownie, for a walk down the trail toward the campsite's restroom facilities. When Brownie suddenly planted all four paws in the dirt and began emitting a low, throaty growl, Mother knew something was wrong. There, coiled just off the path, lay a large diamondback rattlesnake within striking distance. Instead of putting herself in reverse and hightailing it back to camp (as any sane woman would have done, we all told her later), Mother looked around for a weapon. Spotting a couple of large rocks, she grabbed them and aimed for the rattler's raised head. A few minutes later she walked back into camp—with a big, dead rattlesnake draped over the end of a long stick.

When we asked why she didn't just turn and run, my mother's answer revealed both her character and courage: "So many people use that path. I couldn't run away knowing that someone else might come along after me and be bitten."

Sometimes the wars we're called to win (perhaps over things like gossip, dishonesty, anger, overspending, or pride) are as much about someone else as they are about us. If we don't deal with these "snakes" in our paths, those behind us will feel the fangs and experience the pangs of their soul-corrupting poison.

I've also seen my mother, not content to let sleeping snakes lie, wage a decades-long battle of intercessory prayer for the souls of her children and grandchildren, and now the "greats." She's a fierce prayer-warrior, and I pity the forces that oppose her on that battlefield.

Yes, the Deborah-spirit lives on in those who are willing to go into battle so those they lead now, and those walking a few steps behind, can go forward, free from harm. That, too, is courage.

- **To hold the holy**—Mary's story. (Luke 1:26–38)

Mary knew she shouldn't be tired, not at her young age. But it seemed like she was always waiting, along with her whole nation, for something she couldn't quite put her finger on. It had been so long—centuries, even—since any word from a prophet, any message of hope or call to repentance, had come to shatter the soul-deadening stillness. Life was the same predictable routine, over and over, day after endless day. It was wearying.

And then, that electrifying moment—an angel, a mystifying greeting, a baffling pronouncement. *Breathe, Mary,* she told herself. *Give birth to God's Son? Hold the Holy One in my womb and in my arms? But I'm a virgin—I have never been with a man . . . how can this be?* Suddenly she realized her thoughts had formed themselves into spoken words. She was questioning an angel of the Lord!

As she tried to focus on Gabriel's response, it was the last part that kept ringing in her ears. "For nothing is impossible with God . . . nothing is . . . impossible with God." Without realizing it, Mary's right hand had lifted slightly and found a place on her flat abdomen. Glancing down, she hoped her courage to hold the Holy would grow along with her womb. "I am the Lord's servant," she answered, her weariness gone. "May it be to me as you have said."

Some people make you thirsty for Jesus just by their presence, their demeanor, their capacity to express holiness in laughter as easily as through carefully chosen words. A number of my friends have that effect on me, such as Alicia Britt Chole, whose passion to make room for the holy has influenced thousands of others like me to want to do the same.

Alicia is a bountifully gifted woman—to read her books or listen to her speak is like savoring a delicious, five-course gourmet meal in which equal care has been given to flavor, artistic presentation, and healthful nutrition! I've observed many times that this level of giftedness often brings with it an overloaded existence. I'm pretty sure Alicia could look at the abundant places of her life—her writing and speaking schedule, her ministry to leaders, the prayer retreat and mentoring center she directs (called Rest Inn Rivendell—I'm going there some day, God willing! www.restinnrivendell.com), not to mention the three special-needs children she mothers with great care—and conclude that her life is quite occupied, thank you very much. Make room for unhurried encounters with the Holy One? Create time for quietness and rest? *How can these things be, seeing I have a schedule . . . and a family . . . and a ministry?*

But Alicia, probably more than anyone I know, models what it means to intentionally make room for the holy—to know that her yes to God means spiritual stretch marks galore, but to say yes anyway. Her life has become a show-and-tell (with, perhaps, more emphasis on *show* than *tell)* of increasing intimacy with God in the ordinary moments of life.

This comes at the courageous price of saying a relentless no to the encroachment of a thousand other things (even good things) that stand in line to plead for a piece of the space and time Alicia has reserved for Sabbath rest, and for truly knowing Jesus. Capacity costs.

But for those who've learned to hold the holy—who've experienced the quiet exhilaration of an expanding soul—the cost of a well-placed yes and no (no matter how many times they must be spent and re-spent) is quite a bargain. In a world that values speed, activity, and productivity over almost everything else, *that's* a courageous exchange.

- **To transport the truth**—Phoebe's story.
  (Rom. 16:1–2)

Phoebe took a deep breath and shifted her weight from one foot to the other, as if doing so would somehow help balance the load and lighten the task before her. Not that she was unaccustomed to heavy responsibilities. As a deacon in the church at the seaport city of Cenchrea, she knew what it meant to bear the burden of ministry and leadership—to care for the souls as well as the practical needs of those who had left their worship of many gods for the one true God, through His Son, Jesus.

She looked from the wizened, leathery face of her beloved friend Paul to the papyrus scrolls he held out to her. Phoebe knew how long he had labored over this letter to those in Rome who now followed The Way. She was well aware that each word had come at the cost of deep, aching concern and countless prayer-filled nights during his ministry in nearby Corinth. She also knew that by placing this letter in her hands Paul was bestowing upon her a sacred trust—to transport God's life-giving truth to those who would be changed forever by its message of hope, correction, and instruction.

Phoebe's eyes stung. She blinked back tears as she considered this affirmation of her calling and the old apostle's confidence in her reliability. Honor or not, however, it was no small undertaking. The 616 mile trip from Corinth to Rome would require courage, stamina, and, in all likelihood, more than one good pair of sandals.

Phoebe carefully took the scrolls from Paul's weathered hands and placed them gently in a large leather pouch for safekeeping. Soon it would be time to gather a few belongings and provisions for her trip. A growing realization that she would play a part in the transformation of those who would receive this hallowed delivery—who would know and love Jesus better, simply because she was willing to . . . to walk—made her eager to be on her way. She looked down at her feet and thought of the miles ahead. *Hmmm,* she wondered, *where can I find another pair of sturdy sandals?*

While many females in our day enjoy the luxury of an occasional pedicure (count me in), there are no feet so lovely as bona fide *Phoebe-feet* on a Jesus-hearted woman. Isaiah 52:7 says, "How beautiful on the mountains are the feet of those who bring good news, who proclaim peace, who bring good tidings, who proclaim salvation, who say to Zion, 'Your God reigns!'"

Make no mistake, though. Transporting the truth takes just as much courage today as it did in Phoebe's day. We may not have to carry papyrus scrolls more than six hundred miles, but we may be called to convey God's Word to hearts that are even greater distances from Him.

I know a woman with the most beautiful "Phoebe-feet" you can imagine! My friend Carol Kent probably has more frequent-flier miles than she and Gene (her husband, traveling buddy, and ministry companion) know what to do with. When I consider Carol's ministry, I don't think about air miles or highway miles, but heart miles. Carol is willing to go the distance to bring truth and hope to those who need it most. And for her, that distance means walking into maximum security prisons as willingly as she walks into the auditoriums and churches filled with women who've read her books and are eager to hear her speak.

If you don't know the road Carol and Gene have traveled with their son, JP, who is incarcerated with a life sentence in Florida, then you need to read her powerful books *When I Lay My Isaac Down, Between a Rock and a Grace Place,* and *A New Kind of Normal.* The kind of adversity Carol and Gene have walked through—one of the most anguishing parents can know—would have stopped many in their tracks. But, by God's grace (as she would tell you), it has only fueled Carol's passion to transport the truth of that grace to wherever her "Phoebe-feet" will carry her. And like her scroll-carrying, first-century counterpart from Cenchrea, Carol knows life transformation is waiting at her next destination.

• THE BASIS FOR BRAVERY •

These faithful and faith-filled women, past and present, remind us that we need courage to deliver the dream, to protect the powerless, to win the war, to hold the holy, and to transport the truth. But the call to gather our nerve and step up doesn't stop there. To be a Jesus-hearted woman may also require other forms of bravery:

- Getting comfortable with the sound of your "speaking up" voice, the one that respectfully offers a perspective different from those around you.
- Being the only woman in the room at times, or perhaps one of very few.

- Listening to valid criticism with a willingness to own your mistakes when you're rightfully called out.
- Keeping a confidence that's so tempting to tell to a few "trusted friends."
- Walking into a roomful of women who seem to have it all together but embracing the truth that none of you do.
- Sitting at a new table of leadership where the learning curve looks like Mt. Everest.
- Intentionally putting yourself in the company of people whose core beliefs are different from your own.
- Trying a new approach to an old ministry.
- Seeking out a mentor, or a new friend—or looking up an old friend with whom you've lost touch.
- Lifting the lid off your simmering dreams and letting someone else peek inside.
- Cleaning out your inbox, your closet, your preoccupations, and even your relationships—being willing to lay aside what is unhealthy, excessive, or no longer a fit for who God is calling you to be.

I want to be this kind of woman; honestly, I do. My guess is, if you're reading this, you do, too. But what do we do with the pinpricks (or gaping holes) of fear that deflate our soul's capacity to live courageously? While it's possible—even likely—to feel afraid while acting bravely, if you give fear the upper hand it will displace courage every time. And if those who serve in ministry don't deal with their personal specters of fear, they will be stunted as leaders—or possibly taken out of the game altogether—no matter how gifted they are otherwise.

Perhaps because fear is such a part of the warp and woof of our human condition, as well as the default response to so many situations in life, God has gone to great lengths in the Bible to counter our faintheartedness. He has a message for frightened people from a wide variety of backgrounds, in all kinds of circumstances— Abraham, Hagar, Moses, Joshua, Hezekiah, David, Mary, Peter, Paul, Mary Magdalene, Salome—the list goes on and on. It extends to my name, and yours. He wouldn't have to say it so many times if it weren't so true of us—we *are* often scaredy-cats with every hair standing on end. But we're *beloved* scaredy cats with a mysterious, Spirit-infused capacity to become lion-hearted. He knows this about us, and so He says it again and again. "Do not be afraid. Fear not."

WE'RE *BELOVED* SCAREDY CATS WITH A MYSTERIOUS, SPIRIT-INFUSED CAPACITY TO BECOME LION-HEARTED.

I think my favorite courage verse is Isaiah 41:10. I've penned it in countless cards and letters to friends who were facing frightful, stomach-churning situations. I've scrawled it on a three-by-five note card and set it where I could see it daily when my own courage was slipping away: "So do not fear, for I am with you; do not be dismayed, for I am your God. I will strengthen you and help you; I will uphold you with my righteous right hand."

The word *dismayed* in that verse means something like, "to look around in a panic."[27] Oh, I'm quite good at that! I look at my measly resources next to what's required of me . . . and I panic.

I look at knotted tangles of conflict I can't hope to untie . . . and I panic. I look at child abuse statistics and headlines about war . . . I look at families I love who are falling apart . . . I look at trends showing the decline of orthodox faith in God among young adults . . . and my heart drops. I look around in panic.

That's when God uses this verse to "snap" His fingers and draw my attention upwards. *Hey, Jodi . . . up here! Focus, and listen carefully to what I'm about to tell you . . . again. Do not fear; I'm right here with you.*

This is the bottom-line basis for any bravery I have. God, *my* God, is with me. Since He is not only *with* me, but *for* me (as Rom. 8:31 promises), I believe Him when He says "I will strengthen you and help you; I will uphold you with my righteous right hand." When I panic, those are the three things I need most: strength, help, and to be upheld by Someone who is wholly good.

I'm not the hero in my story. Jesus is. I'm more like the sidekick character in Tolkien's *Lord of the Rings* trilogy, Samwise Gamgee, who accompanies Mr. Frodo (the real champion) on his daring mission. Samwise becomes brave and does heroic things only because of the presence and influence of his hero-friend. It's his devotion to Frodo that grows gallantry in the heart of Samwise.[28]

If ever an ounce of courage springs up in me, it's only because I love my hero, Jesus. As I follow on His mission, His presence and influence slowly infuses steel into my otherwise cowardly heart and helps me dare things I wouldn't dream of on my own. And, as our adventure together unfolds, He also chooses the most unexpected times, places, and ways to teach me lessons about overcoming my destructive foe, fear.

• STALL WARNINGS •

I closed my eyes tightly and squeezed my seatmate's hand, glad she was a sister in Christ. Our quiet prayers together belied the desperation rising in my heart. As our little single-engine Cessna bounced around over the fog-smothered ocean below, that harsh alarm, sounding like the cross between a grating buzzer and a stuck car horn, seemed to grow louder and louder. I recognized it as the plane's stall warning and knew what it meant.

I'm sure aviation technology has changed a lot but back then (in the mid-1970s), the stall warning alerted pilots that their airspeed was too slow and altitude too low to continue flying much longer. When it sounded the plane was in danger of stalling and falling. In other words, it was time to land—*now!* I'd heard that severe sound many times before, always just seconds before we touched down on the runway.

But there was no runway below us that day. We were circling over the choppy waters of the Pacific, waiting for the fog to clear so our pilot, who was only visually rated to fly, could find the landing strip of that little North Bend, Oregon airport. *Buzzzz!* I wondered why in the world I had ever thought this would be a fun adventure. We were going down; I just knew it.

Almost a year earlier, Don and I had moved to Eugene, Oregon, so he could pursue his ministerial studies. I soon landed a job for a local periodontist and was excited to learn he was also a pilot who flew to the coast monthly to perform oral surgeries— and he took his two assistants along to help out! Going up in the small plane was exhilarating, even though it got a bit bouncy at times, and I looked forward to our trips. I would crane my neck to watch the landscape and earth-bound objects below grow smaller and smaller. It filled me with a sense of wonder to fly into canyons of swirling white clouds that dwarfed the sturdy little Cessna.

But on this particular day, the only wonder I had was wondering if I would make it back home to my new husband, alive and in one piece. We circled and bounced above the waters for about forty-five minutes while the loud stall warning blared with an intensity that could be felt in our bodies. Nancy and I sat, white-faced, hands clenched together, praying harder than we had ever prayed before. Eventually the fog cleared enough for our pilot to spot land and that longed-for airport. When we finally touched down and climbed out, I was weak-kneed. If it hadn't been necessary to keep my uniform clean, I would've plopped face down on that runway, arms outstretched, and given the ground a big hug.

THE TYPE OF STORM VARIES, BUT WE ALL FLY THROUGH THEM AT ONE TIME OR ANOTHER.

Upon inspection of his plane, our dentist-pilot figured out what was behind our noisy arrival. Apparently, when we flew through a small ice storm on our way over that wintry morning a chunk of ice bent the mechanism designed to activate the stall warning. So what was meant to be a safety device no longer gave an accurate read of real danger. It blared as loudly when the plane was doing just fine as when a stall was imminent.

It was such a relief to know we had just experienced the ultimate false alarm—big emphasis on *false!* But, since there were no means to fix the device where we were, we had to wear earplugs during our return trip with the stall warning blasting the whole way. It was a long, loud flight, and I wasn't the only one who went home with a headache.

I've thought about that scary episode many times since. In fact, I think it may have been the genesis of a fear of flying I battled for years. Through it, however, I gained a few valuable insights into the common physiological and psychological fear-responses we experience in a scary world.

Sometimes, when we're "flying" through life on our way to some God-ordained assignment, we go through storms of one kind or another. Perhaps colleagues we thought were our friends oppose us. Or the budget falls apart, leaving us embarrassed and scraping for ways to keep from going under. Maybe a teen decides to rebel or a spouse says he's not sure he wants to stay in the marriage. The storm might come in the form of strange, hormonally-induced physical symptoms that seem to defy a rational diagnosis. We may be thunderstruck by roiling clouds of church conflict or icy shards of criticism. The type of storm varies, but we all fly through them at one time or another.

Here's the thing: whether we realize it or not as it happens, our "stall warnings" can get bent by the trauma of the storms we go through. In practical terms, that means even when we're out of the storm and beyond immediate danger, we might still hear an internal alarm that says, *you're going down*. Especially when we encounter any kind of turbulence, our emotions go on high alert and panic sets in. We feel it in our tightened neck and shoulders; it sits like a scorching coal in our guts. *This time, I'm not going to make it. I'm really going down.*

Fear can serve God's purposes when it warns us of real danger; it's an excellent motivator to take action and find safety. But here's what I have discovered: if I find myself frequently living on "high alert" with my internal stall warning constantly blaring, even when there's no cause for alarm, I probably need a spiritual, mental, and emotional recalibration. That correction happens when I engage truth, *God's* truth, to rework the mechanisms of my soul, especially those meant to alert me to danger or trouble.

Proverbs 3:25 has often intrigued me, especially as it is rendered in the King James Version. "Be not afraid of sudden fear." During a period in my life when I battled panic attacks, I learned it's quite possible to get caught in a cycle of being more afraid of fear itself—that sense of losing emotional control—than whatever triggered it in the first place.

I began to gain victory over this struggle when I learned my panic attacks were fundamentally a physiological response (which, for me, included heart palpitations and rapid breathing) to an intense feeling of fear. In other words, I was afraid of being afraid. But I found great hope in learning that my feelings could be significantly influenced by the way I thought. And how I think is ultimately the result of what I put into my mind as truth. Enter, God's Word.

As I poured over Scripture and found statements countering the natural propensity to fear ("fear not" . . . "do not be afraid". . . "why are you so fearful?"), as well as multiple promises of peace for those who trust in the Lord, feelings of panic gradually lost their grip on my heart. I didn't have to be afraid of a sensation that would soon pass. And I could hold onto a peace that would not.

Maybe you've never experienced a full-fledged panic attack, but you know what it's like to go through a storm that leaves you with a defective stall warning. You recognize the all-too-familiar moods that accompany worry-filled days and sleepless nights. Certain people or situations trigger a dread-heaviness in your chest or that ball-of-barbed-wire feeling in your stomach. It could be time for a recalibration of truth and a new infusion of God's peace.

In re-reading an old journal, I came across a prayer I had written during one of my own seasons of recalibration:

> Lord, sometimes I do battle with an unnamed uneasiness . . . a free-floating anxiety not tethered to any concrete source. I have nothing I can point my finger at and say, "there—that's what's wrong." Consequently, I have nothing I can tackle or fix to change my disquietude. Today is such a day. Help me to remember that, even when I can't name my anxiety, my restlessness, I can trust it to You. Your omniscience takes it all in, and your omnipotence covers every potential struggle with grace to help in time of need. When unnamed uneasiness arises, I call on *Your* name, Jesus.

On my refrigerator, I have a magnet with a quote by William Shakespeare that reminds me not to live in an ongoing state of emergency: *Every cloud engenders not a storm.* The old Bard of Avon was right; it doesn't. Every time I feel like I'm going down—in my job, my ministry, my marriage, my finances—I'm not. And neither are you.

• EBAY AND UNEXPECTED ENDINGS •

Remember Ginger Littleton and her hard-hitting handbag? When the terrifying incident with the gunman was finally over, what good did her courage do, anyway? After all, she didn't succeed in knocking the gun out of Duke's hand and she could've gotten herself killed in the process. She probably bought some time for those on their way to help. But were there any other tangible benefits to her bravery?

I had the chance to speak with Ginger by phone in the process of writing this chapter and asked her that question, along with a few others.

When you have a conversation with Ginger, it doesn't take long to develop a comfortable ease, like you're talking to a trusted friend you've known for years. The warmth and quick wit of this dedicated civic leader (education is her passion), who's also a wife and mom, draws you right in. As I've come to expect from brave people, Ginger never thought of herself as a particularly courageous person and doesn't see herself that way now. But as she explained to me more of the details from her harrowing experience, I would have to politely disagree.

"You know, Jodi," she told me, "Everyone got up on that morning, put on their shoes, and combed their hair. This was just an ordinary day. The other guys on the board and I were laughing together before the meeting started—making bad jokes about head lice (one of the issues on the agenda) like, 'I hope no one gets nit-picky today' . . . *bad* jokes! But everything turned from light-hearted and fun to this really dangerous situation in a matter of seconds."

That's when Clay Duke, the gunman, ordered everyone out of the room except the men on the board. Ginger explained she and one other woman were the last ones to exit. Except she *didn't* exit; not completely, that is. The door through which she was to leave was at the front of the conference room in direct line with the dais where the other board members were sitting. It was part of a small corridor area that provided the board members their own entrance and exit to the room, and had a restroom attached for their use.

When Duke ordered her to leave, Ginger paused in that little passageway, which was out of sight from most viewpoints in the larger conference room, though there was no door between the two. She hates the question, "What was going through your mind at that time?" but I asked it anyway.

"It's hard to actually remember my thought processes," Ginger explained. "But there were some." She knew, if she walked out the door to personal safety, she would not be able to come back in without the gunman hearing her—this was a once-and-for-all decision about whether or not to act. She claims her choice to stay was selfish in nature—that she couldn't have lived with herself if anything had happened to "her guys," as she affectionately labels them, knowing she might've made a difference and hadn't tried. (What Ginger calls *selfish*, I call incredibly caring.)

So, there Ginger stood in her own "courageous choices corridor": on one side was a door to personal safety—and on the other, an opening back into the atmosphere of danger and risk, where injury or even death were real possibilities. Security or courage—those were her options.

To complicate matters, when Ginger looked around for a possible weapon, the only thing she spotted was the fire extinguisher. But that wasn't a good choice because taking it off the wall would've been noisy. All she had was there in her hand: a faux-crocodile leather purse given to her by her eighty-nine-year-old mother-in-law who had decided it was too heavy to carry.

In the meantime, Duke moved forward to stand at the end of the dais, close to the board members who were still sitting in their chairs. His back was to Ginger as she stood in the corridor area.

"Jodi," Ginger told me. "You have to understand . . . my frame of vision contained Duke's back, his gun, and my guys looking back at him. And there was nothing between them. I couldn't exit that room without trying *something* . . . the purse was it! I do need to work on my backhand, however." The rest, as I explained earlier, is history. Courageous history.[29]

But there's more—kind of a P.S. (that would be *purse script,* of course) to this story. The brave security officer who wounded Duke and saved the board members lives? Turns out the retired police detective, Mike Jones, prefers being more of a gentle citizen than an action hero. More than twenty-seven years prior to the school board shooting incident, he became known as Salvage Santa when he started repairing and restoring old or broken bicycles to give to underprivileged children in the community at Christmas. Since that time, the charity formed around his actions has given away literally thousands of like-new bikes and other toys to needy kids, with many from the Panama City community pitching in to help.

So someone came up with the idea to auction Ginger's now-famous purse on behalf of the Salvage Santa charity, and she was more than eager to go for it. One eBay auction later, a little over $13,000 had been raised by that faux-crocodile purse! But it gets even better. Brahmin, the New England handbag company that made the purse, heard about the auction and agreed to match the winning bid. So Ginger's pocketbook brought in more than $26,000 to Salvage Santa, and a lot more children have reasons to smile as a result.

But that's still not the end of this handbag's history. Last year, Ginger told me, the Panama City Beach Library Foundation held a "Power of the Purse" event in which her bag, under lock-and-key in a glass case, was the guest of honor. The event organizers also honored Ginger as The Courageous Woman of the Year and made her honorary co-chair, which she informed me *really* meant she had no opportunity to mess anything up. The occasion raised more than $15,000 for the library—and they're planning a repeat event this year.

"I would define courage as doing something even though you're unsure the outcome will be positive," Ginger said, when I asked what the word means to her. "Those in the military, first responders, parents, and teachers are courageous on a daily basis. That also makes many of us going through our daily lives, and meeting daily challenges, courageous people. I just caught the interest of the public. Of course, having the whole thing filmed in high-definition and living color helped a bit!"

"I WOULD DEFINE COURAGE AS DOING SOMETHING EVEN THOUGH YOU'RE UNSURE THE OUTCOME WILL BE POSITIVE," GINGER SAID.

Ginger and her celebrated purse remind me that more is accomplished by our courage than we think, even though it may take the passing of time to reveal it. When you step up to take a group of junior-high girls on their first missions trip . . . when you swallow hard, clear your throat, and speak to a roomful of strangers . . . when you trade a day at the mall for a trip to the homeless shelter . . . when you know acting like Jesus means doing things others won't understand—your valor has an often underestimated value that will pay big dividends down the road.

I don't want to live a safe life—not at the cost of courage and the opportunity to make a difference for someone else. Psalm 138:3 says, "When I called, you answered me; you greatly emboldened me." Another version puts it, "you made me bold and stouthearted." That has become my prayer lately: *Lord, make me bold and stouthearted.* Like my new friend, Ginger, I want to grab my purse and come out swinging.

• JODI'S COACHING QUESTIONS •

- When you hear the word *courage,* who most personifies that virtue for you? Why?

- Have you ever experienced a "bent stall warning" scenario? If so, what triggers that sense of alarm in you? Can you trace it to a particular "storm"? What will you do to recalibrate your alarm system?

- In this chapter, I write about some of the reasons Jesus-hearted women need courage: to deliver the dream, to protect the powerless, to win the war, to hold the holy, and to transport the truth. Which of those most speak to your need for courage? Why?

- David had his sling and Ginger Littleton had her purse. What are some of the unassuming weapons we might overlook when fighting our big and little battles in life and leadership?

- What verse (or section of Scripture) has given you comfort and courage when you were afraid?

• A LITTLE LESSON FOR NEW LEADERS •

You don't have to *feel* brave to *act* bravely. But you do have to "think bravely" and "trust bravely" to develop godly courage. Find verses from the Bible that correlate to the areas where you need courage and write them on three-by-five note cards. Let these truths soak into your spirit.

The next occasion you have to be either cowardly or daring, act on what is true rather than how you feel.

And one more thing—spend time with courageous people whenever you have the opportunity. Courage from a bold heart often unwittingly sends a tiny spark of bravery into a timid heart. That small spark may smolder in secret, unrecognized for a time, but when the need arises, it can flash up into a bright flame of bravery that will bring about remarkable acts of courage.

• HEART-DEEP IN THE WORD •

Read 1 Samuel 25:2–42. How do you see courage displayed in Abigail's words, attitudes, and actions? What resulted from her bravery?

_____

_____

_____

_____

Read 1 Chronicles 28:20. How significant was David's example of bravery to his son Solomon? How can we impart courage to our children?

_____

_____

_____

_____

Read Romans 8:14–16 and 2 Timothy 1:7. What factors in these passages produce courage in your heart?

_____

_____

_____

_____

_____

_____

_____

Psalm 31:24 (NLT) says, "So be strong and courageous, all you who put your hope in the LORD!" What role does hope play in helping us to be courageous? What helps you to be hopeful?

_____

_____

_____

_____

_____

_____

chapter seven

TERRA-COTTA WARRIORS

LEADERSHIP QUALITY: SELF-AWARENESS

· · · · · · · · · · · ·

*If someone isn't going to give you a self-awareness
shot in the arm every so often, you can't grow and get better.*
—ANDREA JUNG, CEO, AVON

t's going to take some doing, but I want to go there—to China's
Lintong District, just east of Xi'an. For some reason, of all the
amazing bucket-list things to view in this big world of astonishing
sights, I really want to see these guys. I've studied their pictures
in books and on the Internet. At first glance they look like a force
to be feared, all decked out in their battle regalia, standing at
attention in military-straight lines that stretch on and on. Their
fiercely grave expressions, each just slightly different from the
other, seem to indicate they are prepared for anything.

But these soldiers neither take new territory nor defend
against an old enemy. Never have, never will. This militia is
magnificent to behold but utterly helpless in battle. They are the

more than 8,000 life-sized terra-cotta warriors created for Qin Shi Huang (259 BC–210 BC), the first Emperor of China. Apparently Emperor Qin wanted subjects to rule over and an army to protect him, even in the afterlife. So, at great cost in suffering and human life, approximately 700,000 people worked for more than eleven years (some estimates are much longer) to give him what he wanted. When he died in 210 BC, they buried the army of clay men with him. His mausoleum, which was larger than most cities of the world at that time, held many other treasures and works of art including 130 chariots, more than 600 life-sized clay horses, and approximately 40,000 real bronze weapons. And the workmen who built the mausoleum? They were killed in order to maintain its secrets.[30]

On the other hand, while he was still living Emperor Qin outlawed and burned numerous books and even had some scholars buried alive. It seems he feared what could have been most beneficial to him and invested heavily in what would prove to be useless. Emperor Qin may have been exceedingly wealthy and extraordinarily powerful, but he was not very insightful.

• WHO'S GOT YOUR BACK? •

I wish I could say Emperor Qin was the last one to lead without self-awareness, the final "in charge" person whose main concern was that underlings had his back. He wasn't. Self-protective leaders still abound, and it's never a pretty sight. Even as followers of Jesus who are leading the way for others, we can spend an inordinate amount of time and energy trying to amass a little force to safeguard our power or position. More than we'd like to admit, we may fret over who has our back.

That's not always a bad question. Healthy loyalty towards healthy leadership is a good thing. Who doesn't want a team of people to work with who are trustworthy and true-blue? But to some, loyalty is defined as unquestioning compliance and absolute protection from those who might question their motives, methods, or outcomes. They will not stand for anyone to challenge how they treat a colleague or to question the faulty rationale behind a decision. Essentially, they expect their team to act as human shields to ward off any arrows of criticism or perceived opposition. This stance virtually assures the stunting of self-awareness, which is one of the main components of emotional intelligence[31] and so crucial to healthy leadership. Those without this quality will not really know themselves or how their leadership affects others.

A wise, Jesus-hearted woman in leadership will guard against defensiveness and self-protectionism. Surrounding yourself with people who tell you only what you want to hear—those who have your *back* to the detriment of your *heart*—is like building an army of terra-cotta warriors. When the real battles come, they will crumble, and you will not only be defenseless against outside forces but also against the one who is often your own worst enemy . . . the "you" that lacks self-awareness and insight.

Some Emperor Qin-type leaders appraise successful leadership primarily by the quantity of people they lead. What matters most is having the biggest platform, the largest audience, the most Facebook friends, and the highest number of followers on Twitter. Their sense of self hinges on how many pairs of eyes are staring back at them, or how many heads in the boardroom are nodding a yes in their direction. Like Emperor Qin, they go to great lengths to build more followers.

But there's no strength in numbers if those numbered aren't strong. It doesn't really matter how many people follow me, virtually or any other way, unless I have at least a few people nearby who are stout enough to tell me the truth, even when it stings a little—or a lot. These bold souls are my "insight increasers."

When the Bible says, "The heart is deceitful above all things and beyond cure. Who can understand it?" (Jer. 17:9), it's talking about my heart, and yours. My heart often tells me what my ego wants to hear. *You weren't the one in the wrong. It wasn't your fault. You're just misunderstood. You're the leader—you don't have to stand in line; those rules don't apply to you.*

Thankfully, if we let Him, God constantly changes and renews us, replacing unbridled self-deception with a keen self-awareness. We don't have to live with a deceitful heart till the day we die. And interestingly, even though solitude and introspection are part of the process, you don't acquire self-awareness by being shut away in a room by yourself. A big component of self-awareness is to understand how we affect others by our words, attitudes, and actions. So one of the primary ways God develops this much needed quality is through our interactions with those around us. Proverbs 27:17 says, "As iron sharpens iron, so one person sharpens another." I need to pay close attention to those around me because the "outsight" of others brings insight to me.

> THANKFULLY, IF WE LET HIM, GOD CONSTANTLY CHANGES AND RENEWS US, REPLACING UNBRIDLED SELF-DECEPTION WITH A KEEN SELF-AWARENESS.

• HONEST INPUT FROM OTHERS •

As a little girl, I loved it when the Avon lady came around to visit my mother, especially because she left behind an assortment of sample-sized beauty products and fragrances for us to try. I even tried selling Avon myself in the late 1970s. That lasted a whole three weeks before I realized I was not cut out to be a door-to-door merchant of any kind.

Fortunately for Avon, Andrea Jung, who became the CEO in 1999, brought a lot more to the company and has lasted much longer than I did. Perhaps her ability to lead Avon through a difficult period of declining sales into a season of transformation and renewed success comes, in part, from the priority she sets upon developing her own self-awareness. Jung is quoted in *How Remarkable Women Lead: The Breakthrough Model for Work and Life:*

> I still have things to work on. It's a constant process of reinvention, a constant process of self-improvement. It's human nature to want people to point out the things you do well. Having people who honestly tell you the truth is critical. When I look at CEOs who have failed, I really always see a lack of self-awareness. If someone isn't going to give you a self-awareness shot in the arm every so often, you can't grow and get better. So that's what I try to look for in my network.[32]

Leaders love to hear "you are the man" or "you are the woman"! But when Nathan, the prophet, told King David, "You are the man," it was *not* a compliment. (2 Sam. 12:7) I'm certain those words pierced David's heart, but that wise wounding allowed light to penetrate a part of his soul that had grown extremely dark. There are times when we need a rebuke even more than we need a compliment. And there are moments when a challenge to our ideas and desires (which can feel like a rebuke) benefits everyone if we respond with insightful leadership.

A while back, I presided over a meeting of leaders gathered from around the country. For some of us, it was the first time we had met in person and most of those present were new to my leadership. In my preliminary remarks, I let everyone know I'm not easily-offended and I value dialogue and respectful push-back.

As the day progressed, we eventually came to a couple of somewhat controversial agenda items. I could read "is this really a safe place to say what I'm thinking when it differs from what the leader is proposing" in some of the eyes around the table. With the opportunity and a little encouragement, one woman spoke up. She was respectful, but strong, in her opposing perspective of what I had just presented. And she had some very valid points.

THERE ARE TIMES WHEN WE NEED A REBUKE EVEN MORE THAN WE NEED A COMPLIMENT.

Somehow I could sense this was a watershed moment for the formation of trust and the cohesiveness of this team under my leadership. Perhaps more than any organizational prowess or the ability to hatch and articulate great ideas or the skills required to run a meeting smoothly, my response to this healthy challenge would set the tone for my leadership in that environment and would determine what kind of team we would be.

It seemed like the whole room breathed a sigh of relief and the tension broke when I sincerely thanked this team member for her comments and gave her perspective credence by inviting others to weigh in with their thoughts on the subject. We had a vigorous discussion with lively input on all sides of the issue. And we were on our way to being a team instead of a group of people withholding their best thoughts because to speak up would be equated with disloyalty and not having the leader's back.

• OPEN INTERACTION •

It amazes me that even Jesus, the Lord, Creator, and Master of the Universe provided a safe environment for open interaction with His followers. On more than one occasion Jesus rebuked Peter. But it's striking to me that Peter also felt free enough to rebuke Jesus. In Mark 8, Jesus told His disciples about His upcoming suffering and death, and Peter just couldn't contain himself—he had to straighten Jesus out. Verse 31 says, "He spoke plainly about this, and Peter took him aside and began to rebuke him."

Okay, this is about the time I would expect lightning to strike or the earth to open up and swallow Peter. But while Jesus minced no words in responding back to his mouthy follower (how would you like to be called Satan by the Lord?), the reprimand was for Peter's wrong-headed ideas not for his rebuke . . . for his content not his confrontation. Jesus didn't say, "How dare you correct me or give me advice! I'm the leader here so just keep your mouth shut from now on!"

Apparently that same safe environment, which allowed for open expression, carried through to the night of the Last Supper when Peter strongly opposed something Jesus was doing.

"No," said Peter, "you shall never wash my feet" (John 13:8). Once again, Jesus' response was to correct Peter's thinking not his outburst.

Jesus modeled for us a non-fragile leadership that cultivated authentic loyalty while allowing for honest expression of thought. The only One who fully deserved it didn't require that His followers always have His back. In fact He hand-picked men whom He knew would *not* have His back on the night He most needed defending, at least by human standards.

As we read farther into the New Testament, Peter is on the other end of being rebuked by someone younger in faith and newer to the early church scene. (I mentioned this story in chapter two but it's worth looking at again from a different perspective.) Galatians 2:11–21 shows Paul, far from the demure, got-your-back underling to Peter, publicly confronting the venerable apostle's hypocritical stance towards Gentile Christians. And my guess is that Peter was all the better for it. On the other hand, in Acts 5, Sapphira had Ananias' back. Brush up on that account; it didn't turn out well.

Please don't read into this something I'm *not* saying: that it's okay to be discourteous towards those in authority, that any form of rebuke or verbal opposition towards a leader is acceptable, or that good leadership means allowing people to treat you rudely. None of those are true, and the Bible is rich with wisdom about how to respectfully address those with whom we disagree. First Timothy 5:1 is a good example when it tells us, "Do not rebuke an older man harshly, but exhort him as if he were your father." The subsequent verses tell us to treat each other as family members. Families sometimes have their squabbles, but the healthy ones know how to keep the words and tone honoring.

My real concern here is for leaders, especially ministry leaders, who stunt their growth in self-awareness when they hide behind the out-of-context quotation of "touch not God's anointed" (1 Chron. 16:22; Ps. 105:15) or when they claim that those who see things differently than they do have a "Jezebel spirit." Sadly, I've watched too many people with great leadership potential sabotage themselves and wound others with this kind of self-protectionism.

• WHO SERVES ALONGSIDE YOU? •

In her brilliant best-seller, *Team of Rivals: The Political Genius of Abraham Lincoln,* author Doris Kearns Goodwin highlights one of the qualities that made our sixteenth U.S. president one of the greatest leaders of all time. After he was elected to the presidency, instead of surrounding himself with "yes men," Lincoln chose three of his former political rivals for the White House to serve on his cabinet, even though they had opposed him intensely and disliked him personally. But he knew they were well-suited for the job and had strengths in areas where he was weak. He also knew they would tell him the unvarnished truth.[33]

Emperor Qin, on the other hand, tolerated no back-talk, and when he ran out of living "yes men," he created 8,000 more out of terra-cotta. Who was the strongest leader, Qin or Abe? Whose leadership brought oppression and whose brought freedom? Are you willing to include people on your team who are stronger than you in some areas—and do you encourage them to use those gifts freely, even when it may seem they are showing you up? Who you invite to serve alongside you says much about your security as a person and your degree of self-awareness as a leader.

Again, Jesus is a profound example of strength-based vulnerability. John 18 recounts the story of Jesus' betrayal by Judas in the garden. Verse two says, "Now Judas, who betrayed him, knew the place, because Jesus had often met there with his disciples." Wow, did you catch that? Jesus had allowed a betrayer into a place of spiritual intimacy. . . multiple times. He had taken an unsafe person into His safe place.

I realize there's a fine line to walk, and one that requires much discernment, when handling issues like this. I don't think Jesus' inclusion of Judas means that we should expose ourselves, without thought or prayer, to dangerous or toxic people. On the contrary, the Bible also gives many cautions about linking up with people of bad character.

But when we go to the other extreme and filter out everyone who seems "risky," we build a wall of protectionism that blocks out valuable input from those who have much to offer. Camillo Benso, the Italian Count of Cavour, wisely said, "The man who trusts men will make fewer mistakes than he who distrusts them." Add those of the female gender to that quote, and I think he had it right.

• SAFE BUT NOT SUCCESSFUL •

When you boil it down to the basics, Emperor Qin wanted two things: to be safe and to be served, even after he was dead. Those are not good elements for healthy leadership. But, if the truth were known, sometimes we're more Qin-like than Abe-like. We have our own terra-cotta warrior tendencies we count on to serve us and keep us safe. Here are a few:

1. Conflict Avoidance

No one (who is healthy, that is) likes a fight, but some people are so "skirmish squeamish" they run from *any* situation where disagreements might arise. Yet conflict is not only unavoidable, it's often healthy since it allows people to air opposing viewpoints and broadens the perspectives of everyone involved—which results in superior solutions and greater accomplishments.

If you're skirmish squeamish and count on conflict avoidance to keep safe, I highly recommend you take a course on conflict resolution or mediation training. These are offered widely; my husband and I took one in our local community not long ago. Even though it wasn't faith-based, it was excellent and gave us some great tools and insights into something we all have to deal with sooner or later—conflict. And, no, running away isn't "dealing."

2. "Yes" People

While it may seem safer to be surrounded by people who tell you only what you want to hear or to *be* that person who never speaks up or says only what you think *others* want to hear, remember the terra-cotta warriors' fate. They ended up buried in a pit, crumbling away for centuries not far from their dead, despotic emperor.

Hey, leader! You're not made of clay—you won't break if someone else is right or has a better idea than you. In fact, you become stronger and more self-aware when you receive input from others. And as for being a "yes woman" to those in authority over you? Trust me; they can get old, fast—and who wants that? It turns out weak spines are quite expendable—terra-cotta warriors who look good but have no original thoughts in their hollow heads can easily be tossed aside for someone who thinks and has the courage to speak up now and then.

3. Buddy Up

The old adage "it's not what you know, but who you know" can become something of an unspoken, perhaps subconscious, personal mission statement if we're not careful. We can develop an over-reliance on familiarity to help us get what we want, or to be a safety net—even in ministry leadership. *If I can just know more people, or if I can just be buddies with the right people, then things will work out for me.*

While having lots of friends can be a good thing, and while God may even lead us into strategic relationships that open new doors and leverage our strengths, becoming someone's buddy for what we can get out of that person is being a *user,* plain and simple. Aim to be a true friend not just an opportunistic buddy.

• GROWING IN SELF-AWARENESS •

Once we stop relying on our lovely, but lifeless, terra-cotta warriors to defend and serve us, it's much easier to become people who grow in self-awareness. Let's look more closely at what that means and how it can help us to be Jesus-hearted leaders who endure.

While there are many perspectives on what self-awareness is (and how it's developed), I would describe it as the *keen perception into the complexities of my own life.* That would include understanding my:

- Strengths and weaknesses
- Personality type
- Family history and the influence of others on my life
- Effect on others (as we looked at earlier in this chapter)
- Emotional temperament
- Belief system and motivation
- Level of spiritual maturity
- Intellectual development
- Character

That's a long list but not exhaustive when it comes to being fully self-aware. When Psalm 139:14 describes us as being "fearfully and wonderfully made," I don't think the reference is solely to our physical bodies. We are, after all, created in the image of Almighty God! Is it any wonder that we are incredibly complex beings, layered with mystery? Proverbs 20:5 says, "The purposes of a person's heart are deep waters, but one who has insight draws them out." You're a deep well, my friend.

So how do we get this kind of understanding? Socrates said "the unexamined life is not worth living," but is the whole concept of self-awareness even biblical? While the term isn't used explicitly, many passages point us in that direction. The purpose of many of Jesus' parables was to show His listeners what was in their hearts. The story He told of the Good Samaritan in Luke 10:25–37 is a perfect case in point. (For other examples, see Mark 10:17–23; Luke 12:13–21; and Luke 7:36–50.)

Notice how many times the following verses tell us to think about, or examine, ourselves. (The italics are mine, and I've added some thoughts after a few of the verses.)

- Romans 12:3 says, "For by the grace given me I say to every one of you: Do not think of yourself more highly than you ought, but rather *think of yourself with sober judgment,* in accordance with the faith God has distributed to each of you." This passage calls us to honestly and realistically evaluate what God has put inside us. The J. B. Phillips version puts it like this: "try to have a sane estimate of your capabilities by the light of the faith that God has given to you." You can't have a "sane estimate" without knowing what's there, and that requires self-awareness.

- Proverbs 20:27 declares, "The human spirit is the lamp of the LORD that sheds light on one's inmost being." What an interesting verse. God uses your own spirit as a lamp to show you what's inside your heart, or your inmost being. Apparently He wants you to know!

- In 1 Timothy 4:16 we read, *"Watch your life* and doctrine closely." Because we're motivated to maintain biblical beliefs, we're accustomed to scrutinizing our doctrines. But this verse reminds us to watch our lives as well—and closely! It tells us to get out a spiritual magnifying glass and give ourselves a careful inspection.

- Deuteronomy 4:9, "Only be careful, and *watch yourselves closely* so that you do not forget the things your eyes have seen or let them fade from your heart as long as you live."

- Second Corinthians 13:5, *"Examine yourselves* to see whether you are in the faith; test yourselves."

It'll take years, no doubt, to develop self-awareness fully. Parts of who we are will unfold at different times and through various means. Blessing and success reveal some things about us; crisis and loss uncover other things. We may go on quests of self-discovery through coaching (I'm partial to this approach), by taking personality profile tests, or by doing a spiritual gifts inventory. Counseling can be valuable in unearthing who we really are and finding out what makes us tick.

In the end, though, our own best efforts at self-awareness will still fall short. That doesn't mean we should stop trying to know ourselves fully. But we must take an even bigger step of vulnerability and ask God to "know us," to examine our hearts and show us what is there. Using His Word as a mirror for the soul is one way to make that happen. James 1:22–25 talks about that. Verse 25 says, "But whoever looks intently into the perfect law that gives freedom, and continues in it—not forgetting what they have heard, but doing it—they will be blessed in what they do."

In one of my favorite Psalms, 139, David begins by acknowledging that God has searched him and knows him well. A few verses later, he ends this chapter with one of the most daring prayers ever prayed. The psalmist unflinchingly offers God an ongoing search warrant into his soul. Nothing is off limits. "Search me, God, and know my heart; test me and know my

> **BLESSING AND SUCCESS REVEAL SOME THINGS ABOUT US; CRISIS AND LOSS UNCOVER OTHER THINGS.**

anxious thoughts. See if there is any offensive way in me, and lead me in the way everlasting" (v. 23–24). That's a bold offer, one that has challenged me deeply.

• THE EXAMINED LIFE •

When I go away for solitude, reflection, and prayer during times of spiritual retreat, one practice I've adopted helps with the process of earnest self-examination. It sounds rather simple, but it's been powerful for me. At some point during my retreat, I take an opened spiral notebook and across the top of the two pages I write, "How am I doing . . . really?". Then on one of the pages I write out every great thing, every blessing, every way I'm getting life right, and all the good things I think God is accomplishing in and through my life. Since no one else will ever see this, there's no need for false modesty or to hold back. Fun, right?

Then, there's the other page—the one I often skip in daily life. On this page I pull back the heavy drapes of secrecy concealing the darkest rooms of my heart. With brutal honesty (and many tears of repentance, I assure you), I write down every wretched thing about my life—the ways I fail and the sins I commit. I include how I've disappointed others and myself, and how they've disappointed me. And since I'm being totally honest, I also write down the ways I feel disappointed by God and the things I don't understand about Him.

People talk about having a "come to Jesus meeting." This is mine. I don't rush this process, and I don't hold anything back. It may take hours, but in the end my soul feels as if it's had a vigorous salt-scrub that's removed layers of dead sin and thick callouses of doubt. I finish by joyfully refocusing on God's goodness, thanking

Him for the specifics of His faithfulness that I've observed in His world and in His Word. And then gleefully, we tear those pages up, He and I, celebrating a love that knows me that well, yet loves me that much. I walk away knowing myself better, for sure, but knowing Him better, too.

Here's the thing: Socrates may have been right about the unexamined life not being worth living. But I'm not sure I could handle such a comprehensive, painstaking examination of "the real me" all alone. I want to know myself, yes, but only in the presence of a living, forgiving, transforming, grace-offering God. Only He can make the converse of Socrates' statement true—the examined life *is* worth living. With Him it is, my friend. It is. No terra-cotta warriors need apply.

• JODI'S COACHING QUESTIONS •

- Why is it so easy for leaders to slip into the mode of self-protectionism and stay there?

- How are people affected by serving with an Emperor Qin-type leader versus an Abe-like leader?

- How do you want people to remember you? What do you need to do to make sure that happens?

- What are some other terra-cotta warriors that people create these days to serve them and keep them safe?

- What are some of the self-unaware things leaders do that drive others nuts? (Let me get you started: talking over people, needing to have the last word, taking credit for other people's ideas, "punishing" those who point out their mistakes . . . what else?)

- Look at this list related to self-awareness:

   Strengths and weaknesses
   Personality type
   Family history and the influence of others on my life
   The effect I have on others
   Emotional temperament
   Belief system and motivation
   Level of spiritual maturity
   Intellectual development
   Character

Which one, would you say, is the most challenging to grasp?
Which one would you like to work on next?

- My definition of self-awareness is the *keen perception
  into the complexities of my own life.* What things have
  helped you develop that keen perception into your life?

• A LITTLE LESSON FOR NEW LEADERS •

Have you ever tried to get ready for a special occasion in front of a
bathroom mirror covered with steam? It doesn't work very well, does
it? There's no problem with the mirror, and your eyesight is fine. But all
those crazy, miniscule water droplets obscure everything until you can't
see your own image.

Sometimes it's not one big thing that prevents self-awareness—it's
a thousand little things: staying too busy for self-examination; nursing
an un-forgiven hurt that creates a tiny layer of defensiveness; neglecting
to personalize scriptural truth to our specific situations; avoiding anyone
who doesn't have our back; forgetting to pay attention to the effect we
have on others. They may not seem like a big deal, but they add up to
"fog on the mirror" when it comes to knowing who we really are as
people and as leaders.

The great thing is, it doesn't take as much effort as we think to
clear things up. Grab a towel of truth and take a swipe at that fog. Tell
yourself the truth. Then invite God and others to do the same.

• HEART-DEEP IN THE WORD •

Read James 1:22–25. According to these verses, how is taking action on what we see in the "mirror" of God's Word linked with true self-awareness? Read the next two verses, 26 and 27. How do "religious people" sometimes deceive themselves? What can prevent that self-deception?

_____

_____

_____

_____

_____

_____

Read Proverbs 27:6; 28:23, and Psalm 141:5. According to these verses, what role do our friends play in helping us become who we're meant to be? Describe what the healthy "wounds" of a friend might look like.

_____

_____

_____

_____

_____

_____

Read Romans 12:1–8. Self-awareness is not only about recognizing our weaknesses but also about being familiar with our strengths and the gifts God has given us. What gift do you see, in this list, that He has given you, even if it's not fully developed? How can you begin to develop and use that gift?

_____

_____

_____

_____

_____

_____

chapter eight

FIRST-CLAPPERS

LEADERSHIP QUALITY: KINDNESS

· · · · · · · · · · ·

*Three things in human life are important: the first is to be kind;
the second is to be kind; and the third is to be kind.*

—HENRY JAMES

t can be bit awkward. Have you ever sat in an audience when no one knows if it's appropriate to clap or not? Is this the right time? Is the speaker or performer really finished? Is applause even proper for this setting? Except for a stray cough or the uneasy rustling of programs, all is quiet. Uncomfortably quiet.

Then, from a few rows back and to the left, some brave soul breaks the silence. She follows her heart and brings her palms together with a series of staccato claps while everyone else still waits. Soon the first clapper is joined by a smattering of others, though somewhat timidly, as if they might regret it. More and more join in—and before you know it, thunderous applause echoes off the walls.

We've looked at several essential qualities for enduring and endearing leadership, but none is more important than the one we turn to now. The heart of a great leader and her true effectiveness is based on, and sustained by, kindness.

Kind leaders are the kind of people others want to be near and emulate. That kindness can take many forms, some of which we'll explore in the pages ahead. But being a "first-clapper"—especially applauding those in the rookie stage of life and ministry—is a great place to begin. Start your kindness with those who are just starting.

SOMETIMES IT'S NOT WHAT WE DO THAT'S A KINDNESS BUT WHAT WE *DON'T* DO.

Jesus-hearted leaders affirm those who are just learning to minister or lead because they never forget what it's like to begin. They are first-clappers who cheer on those who've just given their underdeveloped best to a still-silent audience. While others are doing a mental critique to see if the newbie's performance is worthy of endorsement, Jesus-hearted leaders applaud enthusiastically.

Lewis F. Korns said, "Our regrets are the least for those past errors that were made on the side of kindness."[34] While I can think of many things I wish I could do over in my years of living and leadership, being too kind isn't one of them. And I'm absolutely sure I wouldn't be where I am, or have the courage to walk the path I'm on, without a series of first-clappers in my life. They endured my early efforts at writing, speaking, and leading, and *somehow* kept smiles on their faces. Maybe it was really a grimace, but they never let me see it that way.

Do veterans of ministry leadership, those who are polished and accomplished in what they do, need and deserve affirmation and a show of appreciation? Unquestionably. (And sometimes more than you would think.) But it's hard to imagine the heft of encouragement bestowed by a hand-written note from a seasoned leader to a young woman who spoke in a quivering voice before an audience for the first time. Or the wind-in-the-sails effect that comes when someone with more experience and authority publicly points out the good job done by a neophyte who led worship, or wrote a piece of prose, or taught a class, or organized an event. Novice leaders go a long way on the empowering commendation of a first-clapper.

As a leader, I have an adjuvant mission that runs like a golden cord through everything I do. And that's to cheer others on—frequently, specifically, sincerely, openly—as they become and do all God has designed for them. I'm determined to be a first-clapper, generously offering an *atta girl!* or *atta boy!* whenever I observe people trying to follow Jesus and make a difference with their lives.

I want to do kindness well, and being a first-clapper is just one piece of this complex but sweet fruit. There are days when I realize how far I have to go on this quest to fully implement Paul's instruction to "be kind and compassionate to one another" (Eph. 4:32). But I'm discovering some new, and even surprising, perspectives about what kindness in leadership looks like along the way.

• KINDNESS BY OMISSION •

Sometimes it's not what we do that's a kindness but what we *don't* do. In answer to Peter's question about how many times he should forgive, Jesus told the parable of the unmerciful servant in Matthew 18:21–35. In this story, a king decided it was time for those who owed him to settle their accounts. When one of his servants couldn't pay back an enormous debt, the king prepared to have him thrown into debtor's prison. He had the right to do so; it was both legal and customary in those days. But as an act of merciful kindness in response to the servant's plea, the king didn't follow through with the imprisonment. Instead, he forgave the man his debt.

The story doesn't end there, unfortunately. The servant who had just been released from his massive obligation turned right around and required back-payment from someone who owed *him,* even though it was a much smaller amount. When that person couldn't pay up, the ungracious servant immediately threw his insolvent friend into debtor's prison.

Both the king and the servant were within their rights to incarcerate those who couldn't pay what they owed. The king showed kindness by what he *didn't* do—that is until the unmerciful servant was exposed by his peers as a complete cad. It seems forgiveness, at least in part, is *not* doing what we have the right to do. And so is kindness.

We see another example of kindness by omission in the unique love story between Ruth, the widowed foreigner, and Boaz, the elderly "kinsman redeemer" from her dead husband's family. After Ruth followed the instructions of Naomi, her mother-in-law, and presented herself to Boaz on the threshing floor (an indirect marriage proposal, of sorts), the eighty-year-old man made an interesting statement to Ruth: "The LORD bless you, my daughter," he replied. "This kindness is greater than that which you showed earlier: You have not run after the younger men, whether rich or poor" (Ruth 3:10).

Boaz saw kindness in Ruth by what she did *not* do. She did not pursue younger men who, no doubt, would have been more attractive to her as potential husbands. Instead she chose to seek marriage (and provision for her mother-in-law) in a way that would honor and perpetuate her deceased husband's name.

What did you *not* do lately out of sheer kindness? If you're a Jesus-hearted leader, it's likely that you practiced kindness by omission when you overlooked someone's fault. This is probably the most common way to be kind by what you *don't* do—and the most needed.

Some of us remember The Pointer Sisters, a very popular female R and B group from the 1970s and 80s. (True, many of you weren't even born then . . . *sigh.*) I'm not sure if they're around anymore, but I'm afraid there are still "pointer sisters" of another kind among us. We can be so quick to pick out each other's mistakes and weaknesses; it's almost like we have a "pointing anointing."

But, have you noticed? In the same way applause can be contagious, so can pointing. Even kids can catch our "pointing syndrome." I found that out while being a mom-chaperone on my child's elementary school field trip years ago.

It was fun listening to the youngsters' chatter as we drove towards our destination that warm fall afternoon. One of the little boys was the son of an associate pastor from a church in our community so I was glad, for my son's sake, to know there was more than one PK (preacher's kid) in the bunch. Sure enough, the topic of conversation eventually turned to church—but sadly, church conflict—with my little PK passenger friend leading the discussion.

"Yeah," he said in his most blustery, I've-got-life-figured-out-now-that-I'm-eight voice. "I could line all those people in our church up against the wall, point down the row, and say, 'Sheep, sheep, goat, sheep, goat, goat, sheep, goat . . . '" It was all I could do to hold back an explosion of laughter. But in retrospect, it's only funny in a tragic sense. That little guy had caught a bad case of *point-itis* from someone, and I shudder to think of the ramifications.

First Peter 4:8 says, "Above all, love each other deeply, because *love covers over a multitude of sins"* (italics mine). Self-righteousness catches the mistakes and misdeeds of others. A sense of justice wants to chastise those wrongs. But kindness steps in and covers; it causes us to omit acts of retaliation.

• WWJND—WHAT WOULD JESUS NOT DO? •

Jesus did much to show us the kindness of God. But the things He did *not* do also revealed divine kindness. He did not:

- Cling to His rights as God (Phil. 2:6–11)
- Call down fire from heaven on a Samaritan village (Luke 9:52–56)
- Throw the first stone (John 8:1–11)
- Seek human popularity (John 5:41; 8:50)
- Allow His disciples to defend Him (John 18:10–11)
- Answer His accusers (Isa. 53:7; Matt. 27:12–14)
- Call for twelve legions (72,000) of fighting angels (Matt. 26:53)
- Come down from the cross (Mark 15:30)

We'll never match the magnitude of "omission-al kindness" Jesus showed. But as leaders who follow Him, here are some ways we can show kindness:

We don't correct every small error that others make.

I've watched prominent veteran leaders answer kindly to the wrong name, repeatedly, because they didn't want to embarrass the person making the blunder. Not every typo or wrong pronunciation, not every poor choice of words or less-than-stellar teaching illustration, not every mislocated scripture reference or slight flaw in biblical application requires our deft hand of correction.

That's not to say there's never a time or place for instructive words to rectify an error or to help others improve. But being endlessly nit-picky is not kind, and usually not productive because it creates resistance in those whose faults we're pointing out.

Proverbs 19:11 says, "A person's wisdom yields patience; it is to one's glory to overlook an offense." In other words, don't be a pointer sister. That will be a kindness, indeed.

We don't show others up.

On April 11, 2011 an Air France A380 Airbus jumbo jet, the biggest plane in the world at the time, was getting ready to take off. As it taxied toward the runway, its huge wing clipped the wing of a smaller commuter plane that had just landed, spinning it like a toy. Apparently one of the design flaws of the A380 is that its vast wingspan creates a blind spot for the pilot.[35]

This is something to watch for: the "bigger" (as in more visible and prominent, not more important) your ministry leadership and the larger your freight of authority, the easier it is to forget your wingspan and clip others, without even realizing it. Bumping others with your gifts and strong presence may not seem like a big deal to you—the Air France passengers reported only feeling a small rumble—but it can spin others into a sense of belittlement, making it hard for them ever to take off again.

It's not that we shouldn't be who we are and take to the skies, no matter the size of our gifting, influence, or opportunities. But we've all seen folks with a "move over, dear, and let a pro show you how it's really done" attitude that smacks of competition and pride. Sometimes it's a kindness to shine less for a while so that others can shine more. Watch your wingspan, my friend.

We don't insist that others lead like we do.

My husband and I have made a few trips to Pennsylvania Amish country, and we've loved every mile of each visit. While driving past acre after acre of beautifully groomed farms, we notice certain road signs we never see around the Seattle area. They're bright yellow with the black silhouette of a horse-drawn Amish buggy painted in the center and say simply, Share the Road.

THERE ARE MULTIPLE WAYS TO DO JUST ABOUT ANYTHING, AND MOST PEOPLE FEEL THEIR WAY IS BEST.

Now there's a useful concept for ministry leaders! Even though we're on the same journey, going in the same direction, with the same destination in mind, there will be differences in how we get there. Count on it. (I'm referring to the variety of ways to lead and do ministry, not how we get to heaven. That's completely settled and unchangeable; Jesus is the *only* way.)

More than five decades of living has taught me this: there are multiple ways to do just about anything, and most people feel their way is best. Worship music styles, biblical translations, attractional versus incarnational models of being the church—most of us have seen the hurtful conflict caused when being "right" on these issues, and a hundred others like them, becomes more important than spiritual unity and having a Kingdom-first outlook. It's pretty sad when we want to shut others down because their ministry or leadership methods are different from ours.

If it's any comfort, this is not a new problem. Jesus faced it with His original disciples:

> "Teacher," said John, "we saw someone driving out demons in your name and we told him to stop, because he was not one of us." "Do not stop him," Jesus said. "For no one who does a miracle in my name can in the next moment say anything bad about me, for whoever is not against us is for us. Truly I tell you, anyone who gives you a cup of water in my name because you belong to the Messiah will certainly not lose their reward. (Mark 9:38–41)

Many of us love having well-defined borders and knowing who's in and who's out. It's fairly easy to show kindness to people who think like us and act like us. Then someone comes along with a harebrained, outside-the-border idea and we find our capacity for kindness diminished. That happened with the Israelites on their way to the Promised Land. The story is recounted in Numbers 32 (the whole chapter), and it's an interesting one.

The Reubenites and Gadites (two of the twelve tribes of Israel) were "outside the borders" (OTB) thinkers; they wanted a different inheritance from their kinsfolk. They wanted to settle on the east side of the Jordan River rather than the west side, which God had vowed to give to Israel as the Promised Land. As a result, their kinsfolk, and even a wise spiritual leader like Moses, misjudged them.

Because they wanted something unique, he assumed they were shirkers and perhaps cowards (he said as much when accusing them of being like their fathers in verses 8–13). He was ready to call God's judgment down on them until they clarified a few things. They assured Moses that their choice of a different inheritance wouldn't stop them from being "team players" who would fight and work for the good of everyone. They committed to delay the fulfillment of their request until the whole nation found rest.

It's easy to misjudge OTB thinkers, even when we're spiritually mature. We can't understand why they don't want the same "promised land" we do. We might think they're lazy or they're cowards who've given up on battles worth winning. I cringe when I hear seasoned (and often more traditional) leaders criticize today's young church planters and leaders for approaching ministry in a way that's unique and definitely OTB.

Why would anyone want to start a church in a local coffee shop . . . or focus on reaching workers in the sex industry . . . or spend so much time writing a blog . . . or become a motorcycle chaplain—and as a *woman*, for heaven's sake? That's probably the best answer why OTB leaders want to try something different . . . *for heaven's sake.* And for the sake of those who've spent their lives outside the borders of God's love and grace.

On the other hand, OTB thinkers must resist the urge to be independent of the other "tribe" members. It would be easy to settle into a new comfort zone over there (wherever "over there" is) and let everyone else fend and fight for themselves. But in the body of Christ, we're all part of the greater tribe. No sub-group can act independently without, in some way, affecting the rest. There may be many skirmishes, but we're called to only one great battle—against evil. If I settle into my inheritance without thought for your struggle, I weaken both of us and invite God's displeasure.

It's kindness not to insist that everyone be just like us—to give others the freedom to lead differently, and minister from the perspective of their unique calling, and cheer them on when they do. After all, would you want a world occupied only by a few billion copies of you? I can barely handle *one* of me most days, so I sure wouldn't. Diversity with unity, within the framework of truth, is God's design.

You'll find a wide variety of vehicles on the highways and back roads of our world. There are racy sports cars, mom-style minivans, boxy SUVs, and luxury sedans. And yes, there are still horse-drawn buggies in Amish country. All of them, properly maintained and fueled (whether by gasoline or hay), will get you where you want to go, though the style and pace may differ. Remember that God has an astonishing amount of variety in His leadership fleet, too, so . . . *share the road.*

• KINDNESS BY COMMISSION •

For the leader who is serious about following Jesus, kindness is not an elective, not a nicety we choose for days when we feel like all is right with the world. It's a commission. "Be kind and compassionate to one another," Paul says in Ephesians 4:32. "Therefore, as God's chosen people, holy and dearly loved, clothe yourselves with compassion, *kindness*, humility, gentleness and patience," he adds in Colossians 3:12 (italics mine).

We're under orders to "wear" kindness. As Christ-followers, it's the daily uniform we wear when we go out to meet a broken world. At home, it's the comfy, well-worn jeans and T-shirt we put on as we interact with our family and close friends. It may look slightly different in various settings, but kindness is never optional attire that we can take off and throw aside altogether.

A Countenance of Kindness

When it comes to wearing kindness, your face is a good place to start. Your demeanor says more than you realize about the kind of leader you are—and whether or not you're a kind leader. There are many who are able to handle the tasks and responsibilities of leadership, but their countenances are so off-putting people have a hard time following them. What others see in your face affects them; it really does. Likeability makes a difference in leadership, whether we want to admit it or not.

Have you ever known people who put the mean in demeanor? Or perhaps, demean others by their demeanor? Their facial expressions are closed, at best, or openly hostile, at worst. They send out withering looks that seem to say *your presence annoys me.* Proverbs 6:17 warns us that God hates a proud look, or "haughty eyes." This indicates that we bear some responsibility for our visage, especially because it usually reveals what's in our hearts. It's interesting that one of the first indicators we have of Cain's downhill slide is that "his countenance fell" (Gen. 4:5–6).

- - - - - - - - -

YOUR DEMEANOR SAYS MORE THAN YOU REALIZE ABOUT THE KIND OF LEADER YOU ARE—AND WHETHER OR NOT YOU'RE A KIND LEADER.

- - - - - - - - -

Most of us only see our faces when we get ready in the mornings or occasionally at a bathroom mirror throughout the day. We have no idea what our expressions are conveying at other times. If you're feeling brave, ask a trusted friend what she sees in your demeanor during specific circumstances, like: when you're in a new situation or are just meeting someone for the first time; when you're challenged by others; when you're under pressure to make a decision; or (if you feel really brave) when you're angry. It could be pretty eye-opening!

Think of someone you know who could be described as winsome. What is it about that person's face that shows kindness? Is it the warmth of a ready smile, the sparkle of humor, an expression that says *I care* and *you matter?* Is it tenderness in eyes that don't look away when they view pain in yours? Maybe a softness in the mouth that doesn't condemn or offer easy answers?

Not everyone is a natural extrovert whose favorite pastime is smiling as widely as possible. And truthfully, not everyone who looks grumpy and mean really is. Some people appear somber (and maybe even mad), especially when they're deep in thought, even though they are absolutely kind. The thing is, others can't see the sweetheart behind that sullen expression. And certainly, if we hope to be Jesus-hearted leaders whom others want to follow, we should take responsibility for our own faces!

It won't work to put on a phony mask or to plaster on a fake "everything is fine" perma-smile. There are times when it's appropriate to wear expressions of sadness, displeasure (especially at evil), and even anger. But we don't have to forsake kindness altogether in the process. Proverbs 15:13 says, "A merry heart makes a cheerful countenance." Some of us need to ask God to merry up our hearts and cheer up our expressions. *Kindness* . . . it's what the best-dressed faces are wearing.

Healing Honey

I was tired, desperately so. And quietly sad. Few people knew about the private burdens I was carrying. But life doesn't stop when we're tired and sad. Then it happened. Someone said a few kind words. They were like a reenergizing time-out from my stresses, the "peace break" my spirit urgently needed:

> "Hey, Jodi! Nice job on your last column. I think you wrote it just for me! And thanks for all the work you put into the retreat. My sister—the one who just went through a divorce—she came with me and gave her life to Jesus. She'd been so depressed but she's making real progress now. Our family can hardly believe she's the same person!"

That dear person spoke less than a hundred words to me before hurrying on her way. I'm sure she didn't know the effect she had, but after hearing her, I knew I could keep going. I re-believed that what I was doing mattered.

Just a few, kind words make all the difference. Leaders need to hear them, and they need to say them. They need to read them, and they need to write them. Isaiah 50:4 says, "The Sovereign LORD has given me a well-instructed tongue, to know the word that sustains the weary." I want to increase my "kindness vocabulary" with words like these:

"I really appreciate you."

"You've been working really hard. Go take a break!"

"Nice haircut . . . you look great!"

"What you said made me think."

"I couldn't have done it without you."

"I'm so sorry I hurt you. Please forgive me."

"Your example has inspired me to dream big."

"I just want you to know, God used your leadership to change my life."

"I was really moved by your honesty and vulnerability. It gives me hope."

"Thanks for loving and accepting me as I am."

Kindness may show up on your face, but it becomes defined, specific, and life-giving to others through your words. If we could see beneath the surface, we would discover that most of the people we meet carry some degree of weariness and sadness in their souls. While it's true that words can injure, Proverbs 16:24 says, "Gracious words are a honeycomb, sweet to the soul and healing to the bones." I've been healed by sweet words, and it's likely you have been, too.

What would it look like to take that "healing honey," those words of kindness, and generously pour them on those we encounter each day? It might look like this:

- Writing a note on the napkin when you make your child's school lunch. (I used to do this with my kids, and they never got tired of a mid-day word of love from Mom.) Your husband will appreciate a Post-It love note left on the mirror when you're off to speak at a weekend retreat—and leaving a kiss on paper, via your lipsticked-lips, works just as well as words to remind him that you'll miss him! *Just sayin'* . . .
- Thinking carefully about the tone your words carry, even by e-mail. Brevity doesn't have to be cold; professionalism doesn't have to be divorced from graciousness. And while we're on the subject, are you sure you *really* want to post that sarcastic comment on Facebook or tweet in frustration about something you'll later regret?
- Taking the time to send a hand-written, thank-you note to someone who has blessed your life. I think it might matter even more to write one to someone who is *not* expecting it—like that administrative assistant who handled the details of an appointment you had with her boss. My daughter, Kristi, wrote a thank-you note awhile back to the man at her dry cleaners who was always so friendly and helpful. This older gentleman, an immigrant from India who

was working extremely hard so his kids could go to college, was moved to tears by her kindness.

- Making it a weekly habit to send a note of encouragement or a funny card that will bring joy to someone's life. My tip for this is to buy one of those nice, accordion-type file folders that look almost like a fancy briefcase or purse—they aren't expensive and they're a pretty addition to your home or office. Label the sections with all the different categories of greeting cards you'd like to have on hand. Then have fun over the weeks and months as you keep an eye out for great, affordable cards to fill it up. Because it has handles, you can take it from room to room and fill out a card or two while you're watching a favorite movie on TV in the evening. Keep stamps and return address labels in one of the sections, and you're all set to send tangible kindness anywhere, courtesy of the US Postal Service!

- Using your phone, Skype, or Google-Hangout or some other form of communication technology to connect with a young woman for a mentoring conversation that will pass along some of your hard-earned wisdom—and will mean the world to her.

- Finding specific things to praise about those who serve with you, over you, or under you. Whenever possible, commend them publicly and creatively. Words are wonderful, but words and a Starbucks card, or a salted dark-chocolate with almonds bar? Now that's sweet!

The options are endless because every day you have at your disposal over a million words in the English language (according to a 2010 Harvard and Google study[36]) with thousands more added yearly. (If you're reading this book in a language other than English, I'm sure your language is extremely word-rich, too.) With the possible combinations being virtually infinite, how will you blend a few words today to bring health, joy, and renewed strength to someone's life? Someone you meet in the hours ahead, or someone who crosses your mind, could use an expression of kindness, I assure you. So, honey . . . grab your sweetest words and start pouring!

• COMMITTING KINDNESS •

Earlier, we considered how we show kindness by what we omit. But we also commit kindness by what we do. Acts of kindness, big and small, help us fulfill the demands of love on any given day. And while our words, both written and spoken, are significant, it is our actions that make the message of God's love legible to others.

First Corinthians 13:4 tells us that "love is kind." I like how the New Living Translation puts 1 John 3:18: "Dear children, let's not merely say that we love each other; let us show the truth by our actions." Wear kindness, and speak kindness, yes; but don't stop there. *Do* kindness.

It's telling that when Paul wanted to explain the Creator God to a completely pagan crowd who worshipped Zeus in the city of Lystra, he talked about God's kindness. "Yet he has not left himself without testimony: *He has shown kindness* by giving you rain from heaven and crops in their seasons; he provides you with plenty of food and fills your hearts with joy" (Acts 14:17, italics mine). Notice that Paul connected God's kindness to His acts. He gives us rain for our crops and food to eat. He puts joy in our hearts. God *is* kind; therefore God *does* kindness.

I love speaking for women's retreats. Something special happens when we put aside our normal routines and workaday roles to get away together and meet with Jesus. God always has something up His big sleeve that's unique for each group, and I'm never disappointed.

Of the many retreats I've spoken for over the past several years, one in particular stands out. When my good friend Jeanette Webber, the pastor's wife from Parkway Christian Center in Grants Pass, Oregon, told me she wanted to try something a little different at their upcoming women's retreat, I was curious but up for it.

Instead of using the free time on Saturday for the usual shopping, napping, or other leisure activities, Jeanette divided the women up into groups of five or six and gave each of them five, one dollar bills. She instructed them to take a few minutes to pray with each other and decide how they could invest that money back into the community where they were retreating (which was not their own town). She also gave them the option to keep the money for themselves if they needed it—no one would ask any questions. They could also add funds from their own wallets if they desired, but there was no pressure to do so.

ACTS OF KINDNESS, BIG AND SMALL, HELP US FULFILL THE DEMANDS OF LOVE ON ANY GIVEN DAY.

As Jeanette explained this new "experiment in kindness," she urged the ladies not to identify themselves as Christians (unless it came up naturally) to the recipients of their gifts or to reveal that they were with a group in town for a retreat. There was no agenda but to display love and kindness in a quiet way, as led by God's Spirit. That evening, the whole group would meet and share their experiences.

Soon the room buzzed with groups of women praying or talking animatedly about what they wanted to do with their pooled resources. After spending even a few hours with this group of Jesus-hearted women, it did not surprise me to see the stashes of cash grow significantly as they generously chipped in. Then they went out into the community to commit kindness, wondering where this adventure would take them.

That night, as the group reassembled, there was an almost electric charge in the air. I still get tears in my eyes when I think about it. This was not the same group of women who had walked out the doors earlier that day. They could hardly contain their excitement. Jeanette had set aside a certain amount of time for the women to tell about their experiences, and then I was to speak. But it wasn't long before we both knew that I would not be speaking that night. God was speaking through these women whose hearts were set ablaze by intentional acts of spontaneous kindness. For hours they told their stories amidst much laughter and many tears.

One group decided to put together gifts for all the cleaning staff at the hotel where we stayed. Another group found themselves browsing through a little shop downtown. As they chatted with the owner, they discovered that she not only worked long hours trying to keep her small business afloat, she also worked a second job *and* took care of an ailing family member.

"Wow, what do you do to unwind?" they asked her casually. "Oh," she replied, "I love to take a relaxing bubble bath now and then, when I get the chance." They smiled at her as they made their purchases and went on their way. But soon they were back—with a large, lovely gift basket . . . overflowing with (you guessed it) every conceivable luxury bath product for the bubble bath of your dreams!

The shop lady was stunned. "Why did you do this?" she wanted to know. "Because you work hard, and we wanted you to have a relaxing time on us" they replied simply. As they walked out of her store, I'm pretty sure it was the smell of kindness, not soap, that lingered in the air.

Another group didn't have to go far before they found a recipient for their generosity. They saw the hotel's maintenance man fishing around in his pocket to buy a soft drink at the pop machine so they asked if they could buy it for him. As they got deeper into conversation, he explained that he had come to Jesus only a few months back, after years of drug addiction. He was going to be baptized in a couple of weeks along with his young daughter, and he was excited about it.

Although Jeanette had cautioned everyone about giving cash to individuals, this group collectively sensed that they were supposed to invest their money into this new believer. He was overjoyed by the faith-building generosity of God through these sisters in Christ.

When one of the other groups prayed together, they felt God direct them to go into one of the local grocery stores and pay for someone's groceries. They felt sure it was supposed to be a mother with young children. It took a while (and they felt like stalkers as they walked around looking for someone who fit that description), but finally, they saw a mom with a couple of young children and approached her, explaining that they'd like to buy her groceries.

She couldn't believe it but happily agreed! As they talked with her and got to know her better, the young girl piped up. "Guess what?" she said. "My daddy and I are going to be baptized in two weeks!"

I can only imagine the double-joy when that dad got home from his job at the hotel and talked with that mom who had taken her kids to the grocery store that day. I didn't have to imagine the double-tears and the double-wonder when those two groups of women came together and learned that God had used them separately, and without any knowledge of what the other group was doing, to bless one small family who was starting a new journey of faith.

As story after story (and there were many more amazing accounts of God's fingerprints upon this "experiment") spilled out, I heard one question repeated over and over in various forms. "Why don't we live like this all the time? Why don't I make this a normal part of my life?" Why, indeed?

I think God calls all of us to lives of "intentional spontaneous kindness." That may sound paradoxical, but here's what I mean. When we plan ahead and make provision for kindness and generosity, we're prepared to act in spontaneous obedience to the promptings of God's Spirit. For me, that's been as simple as keeping some "giving cash" tucked away in a special part of my wallet. It's ready when the Spirit nudges me to be generous to someone I encounter along the way.

It's also motivated me to emulate my coaching instructor and friend, Linda Miller. I'll never forget what she did when she hardly knew me some years ago during coaches' training in North

Carolina. At a break between one of our sessions, Linda and I were talking and I complimented her on the stunning necklace she wore. The break ended, and I didn't give it a second thought.

A few weeks later I received a small package in the mail with a return address I didn't recognize. When I opened the padded envelope, there was a small box. And inside the box was Linda's necklace. Her note explained how she just knew she was supposed to give me the necklace when I commented on it that day. It meant even more to me to know this was a necklace she really loved; parting with it had not been easy. But Linda loved being generous, like her Father, more than she loved the necklace. To me, it was divine kindness in a box, and I never wear that necklace without thinking about my kind friend Linda.

Since that time, I've determined to keep Linda's example of spontaneous generosity alive. To be honest, I've wrestled internally a bit when nudged to give away a favorite possession, sometimes on the spot. I was searching my closet high and low recently for this cute little jacket that I just loved to wear. Suddenly I remembered . . . it now belongs to a sweet friend in another state who admired it one day. It made me smile to think of her wearing it—and believe me, I'm not running out of things to wear!

> **I THINK GOD CALLS ALL OF US TO LIVES OF "INTENTIONAL SPONTANEOUS KINDNESS."**

I struggled with whether to include this glimpse into a private area of my life because I don't want to give the false impression that I've got this kindness thing all figured out. But I want you to see that kindness is a chain reaction—one that God set off and one that we can perpetuate. When my heart was brightened by being the beneficiary of Linda's unexpected, generous gift, it made me want another person to experience that same surprised joy. And as fun as it was to be the receiver, Jesus was right . . . it's even more fun to be the giver.

I've only scratched the surface, but I hope you'll do your own experiment with intentional spontaneous kindness. You never know what chain reaction you might set off.

• JODI'S COACHING QUESTIONS •

- To clap or not to clap—that is the question. Why is affirming others, like clapping, often influenced by those around us? Why is it sometimes harder for leaders to commend others?

- What do you think your demeanor says to others about you? What do you think it means to "wear kindness?"

- What would it mean to increase your "kindness vocabulary"? Describe a time when someone's words were like "healing honey" (sweet and health-restoring) to you.

- If you were to make provision for more intentional, spontaneous kindness in your life, what would you need to do?

- Has someone ever done an act of kindness that set off a chain reaction in your life? Describe what happened.

- How do you plan to "commit kindness" in the week ahead?

• A LITTLE LESSON FOR NEW LEADERS •

Throughout the history of our faith, Jesus-hearted leaders have chosen to curtail their preferences and limit personal freedoms to show kindness to those they wanted to reach with the Good News. There are times when the assertion of what is rightfully ours will be a hindrance to the gospel.

We have to seek spiritual discernment from God to know when that is (without swinging over to the extreme of legalism and people-pleasing) and how to deal with the sense of loss when we choose to limit our personal freedom.

Here's a prayer I wrote in my journal a while back when I was thinking about these things: "Dear Father, my heart wants to cling to all my rights, to drain every possible drop of satisfaction and pleasure they bring. Help me to be alert to those times when, for the sake of the gospel, I am to set the full glass of pleasure aside, untasted, and pick up the cup of kindness instead."

• HEART-DEEP IN THE WORD •

Matthew 5:7 says, "Blessed are the merciful, for they will be shown mercy." Someone has defined mercy as "not getting the punishment we deserve." In the light of *kindness by omission,* what can we draw from this verse that will fuel us for the times when we blow it and need mercy and kindness?

_____

_____

_____

_____

_____

In 1 Corinthians 9:9–18, Paul talks about some things he chose not to do for the sake of the gospel. He says in verse 12, "But we did not use this right. On the contrary, we put up with anything rather than hinder the gospel of Christ." Read through that section and then answer this: if you were making your own *kindness by omission* list, what things would be on it? Can you think of anything else Jesus did *not* do that shows the kindness of God?

_____

_____

_____

_____

Proverbs 11:17 says, "Those who are kind benefit themselves, but the cruel bring ruin on themselves." We know others are helped by our kindness but how do we benefit from being kind?

_____

_____

_____

_____

Speaking of the virtuous woman, Proverbs 31:26 says, "She opens her mouth with wisdom, and on her tongue is the law of kindness." What might our tongues' "law of kindness" require? What "law of kindness" do we break most often when it comes to our words?

_____

_____

_____

_____

chapter nine

THE GREEN ROOM

LEADERSHIP QUALITY: SOUL-CARE

· · · · · · · · · · ·

The oldest, shortest words, yes and no,
are those which require the most thought.
—PYTHAGORAS

A few years ago, Don and I had a chance to go to Israel, the trip of a lifetime. On this particular tour was a man with one of the oddest habits (or maybe conditions) I've ever seen. At stop after stop, our group would scramble off the air-conditioned bus to gape in amazement at some ancient archeological site or to view an astounding setting that seemed to have slid right off the pages of the Bible. As our guide explained the fascinating facts and stories behind these remarkable locations, we would all gather round and listen eagerly while taking in our surroundings. All of us except for this one guy, that is; he would fall sound asleep . . . standing up.

The first time it happened, the rest of us on the tour nudged each other, smiled, and nodded in his direction. Surely it was just a fluke; he would probably be fine after a quick catnap on the bus once we were back on the road. But it happened over and over. As he drifted off to sleep in his standing position, the guy would lean and lean and lean—just till you thought he was going to topple over, *for sure,* this time—and yet stay right at the tipping point. It got so extreme that the rest of us would station ourselves around him as catchers, just in case he finally went down. Sometimes we were almost more amazed by our friend, the incredible leaning man and his ability to defy gravity, than the site we were seeing!

Are you so tired that this is how you live life—as the "incredible leaning woman"? You go and go until you have no energy left to see the wonders all around you. Your life feels off kilter, and you have a secret fear that one of these days you just might pass that tipping point and actually crash. Do the people around you show concern that they might have to break your fall when that happens?

This seems to be a hazard for women in leadership, even the Jesus-hearted ones. We deny our physical limits by not getting enough sleep or exercise. We forget to leave any white space in our busy calendars just to *be:* be with our families and friends, be engaged in activities that replenish, be quiet and hear God's voice, be still enough to let His love refill our depleted souls . . . just *be.*

Peter Scazzero, a pastor and the author of great books like *Emotionally Healthy Spirituality* and *The Emotionally Healthy Church,* says, "When you are sustaining your activity for God with very little relationship with God, you will crash."[37] Been there; lived that—and I know I'm not alone. No one is immune from this propensity to wear ourselves down to a soul-aching weariness, but I think women who lead in ministry are especially susceptible. We've bought into the myth that we can be nonstop multi-taskers who, if we truly want to serve God and make a difference, respond to every need we see and continually add to our massive to-do list.

• I NEED A GREEN ROOM •

Stressed-out, burned-out, worn-out . . . those words describe too many women today who are on their *way out* when it comes to leadership. As I chatted with a new friend I met at a training event for coaches, she told me how beat she was from the pace she had been keeping. In fact, she explained, the night before our seminar she had taken a Tylenol for a stress headache before going to bed. When she woke up the next morning, the pill was still in her mouth. She had been too exhausted to swallow it! Extreme fatigue seems to sabotage our ability even to do the things that could move us toward health and comfort. We're too tired to take our own medicine!

Another good friend—a gifted minister, musician, educator, and leader—opened up her heart to a few of us at a retreat for leaders. "I need a green room" she said. My friend went on to describe how the relentless duties associated with her ministry roles, on top of other exceptionally stressful situations, had affected her physically to the point that she had cracked the dental crowns on her molars from grinding her teeth in her sleep. She longed for her own green room like the ones set aside for actors, performers, and presenters—a place offstage, that quiet room graciously appointed with deep cushions of privacy, thoughtfully stocked with personalized refreshments for mind, body, and spirit.

While there's no doubt the pace and complexities of twenty-first century life intensify our need for a green room, this longing is not new for women in ministry. In the early 1800s, Narcissa Whitman traveled with her physician husband, Marcus, to the Oregon territory to do missionary work among the Native American Cayuse people. (She and Eliza Spalding were the first European-American women to cross the Rocky Mountains.) The Whitmans set up a mission station near present-day Walla Walla, Washington and spent many years there bringing the gospel to tribal peoples in that region.

Not long ago, Don and I visited the old Whitman Mission, which is now a Historic Site in the National Park Service. Though the Whitmans could have benefitted from the cross-cultural training available today, my admiration for this educated, courageous woman grew as I browsed the museum and learned about her life and labors.

Narcissa taught in the mission school and assisted with the church services and religious ceremonies. She also ran the household, made soap and candles, and did all the daily cooking and laundry chores while serving as hostess to any visitors—and there were many—who came to the mission. The Whitman's only child, a little girl named Alice (the first Caucasian born in the Oregon territory) drowned in a nearby river when she was only two, but they raised many other children including seven orphans, all siblings from the Sager family, who considered Narcissa their second mother.

THESE FEELINGS MAY EVEN OCCUR AT THE SAME TIME—LONELINESS *AND* PEOPLE-FATIGUE.

I was touched to read this entry from Narcissa's journal (dated October 9, 1844): "Here we are, one family alone, a way mark, as it were, or center post, about which multitudes, will or must gather this winter. And these we must feed and warm to the extent of our powers. Blessed be God that He has given us so abundantly of the fruit of the earth that we may impart to those who are thus famishing."[38]

The placard on a display of their table settings at the Whitman Mission reads:

> She was lonely for a while but then overwhelmed by "helpers" and those seeking shelter. One visitor wrote, ". . . she has less help from the other ladies than she ought." Men crowded around the cooking fire for warmth while Narcissa and other "sisters" tried to cook. One man actually used the fireplace for a spittoon. Mrs. Whitman wrote, "Oh! I wish I had a little chamber where I could secrete myself."[39]

"A little chamber where I could secrete myself" . . . a green room. Even back then, this strong woman, devoted to serving God and others, longed for a place to care for her soul . . . a private chamber for solitude and rest. Like Narcissa, we sometimes feel we're a "center post about which multitudes gather." We swing from being lonely to people-weary, overwhelmed both by those seeking spiritual shelter as well as the "helpers" who work beside us. These feelings may even occur at the same time—loneliness *and* people-fatigue. *Oh! I wish I had a little chamber . . .*

While we may not have a little chamber or a green room, we can be sure our Shepherd intends to lead us to green pastures where we can lie down beside still waters. Psalm 23:2–3 describes a well-cared-for soul: "He makes me lie down in green pastures, he leads me beside quiet waters, he refreshes my soul." What a picture of peaceful provision, of a life soaked in serene, renewing grace!

Yet, there's tension in my neck and shoulders as I work on this chapter. It comes from long hours and many days of writing at the computer along with numerous other commitments and responsibilities. And to be honest, there's tension in my heart, too, because I know I don't fully adhere to the soul-care principles that I put on paper, even though God has been dealing with me about them for a while, now.

But my guess is that if we could only teach, preach, write, or talk about the values and principles we've fully mastered, we wouldn't have a whole lot to say. A highly accomplished friend, one of the most authentic Christ-followers I know, told me once, "Jodi, I feel like a fake every day. There are still so many ways I need to grow and things I aspire to in my spiritual walk. If I let myself focus only on my shortcomings, I would never walk out my front door or open my mouth again. But God works to grow us as we help others grow, even when we haven't arrived yet."

Yes, He does. This doesn't mean we're free to spout spiritual truths we don't intend to live—that's called hypocrisy. It does mean we can talk honestly about what God expects of us, and what He provides for us, even when we're still on the journey to live out both fully.

So just know that if what we're about to explore hits home with you, it does with me, too. I'm committed to being a leader who not only *endears* but who *endures*. And that simply won't happen without some serious soul-care along the way.

• SOUL-CARE •

I can't put my finger on when it began. All I knew was that life—the life I loved, the ministries and activities I thrived on—had become a thick, leaden cape on my shoulders. Everything felt burdensome. Even trivial matters seemed heavy and far more consequential than they were. That's one of the symptoms of a frayed soul: little things become big and big things become little. Somehow the laundry that has to be folded, the phone call you should return, the simple decisions you need to make to navigate the day—all loom large and feel disproportionately oppressive.

On the other hand, *big* things—God's faithful presence and provision of strength . . . the blessings of being able to breathe, and see, and walk, and talk . . . having people you care about who also love you . . . having a safe place to live and enough food to eat—these big things are minimized. Resources intended to sustain you feel scant, and you're sure you'll run out of what you need before the day ends. Such is weariness.

I was doing all the "right things" I knew how to do—things I had been doing pretty much all my life: spending daily time in the Word and prayer; fellowshipping with other believers; serving God with the gifts He had given me; pursuing life goals; working to maintain healthy relationships with my family and friends. But *doing* doesn't always equate to *being:* being healthy, being whole, being rested—just being *me* while being *His.* There's always one more thing we really *should* do; each of those "right things" can become just another item to check off the list of what a good Christian girl does.

It struck me one morning as my groggy mind registered that another day had begun: *I'll be glad when my first, coherent thoughts upon waking are more about who God is, and who I am in Him, than about all I have to get done before I crawl back into this bed again.* I knew the sense of dread that accompanied the start of each day wasn't what my Maker had in mind when He made me, redeemed me, and gave me a life He describes as "abundant."

About that time, I wrote this prayer in my journal: "God, give me, not an easy life, but a life with ease. Not a peaceful life, but a life with peace." I somehow knew the answer to this deep weariness (author Ruth Haley Barton calls it being "dangerously tired"[40]) wasn't about eliminating all the external demands and stresses of life. It wasn't about abandoning responsibilities and moving to an idyllic mountain cabin far from civilization—although visiting a place like that can be a refreshing.

On our trek towards heaven there are many battles worth fighting and plenty of struggles worth the effort. I see nothing in Scripture that indicates we can expect to avoid hardship and stress in this world—quite the contrary, and especially as leaders. Don't you think Paul sounded a wee bit weary when he wrote 2 Corinthians 11:27–29? "I have labored and toiled and have often gone without sleep; I have known hunger and thirst and have often gone without food; I have been cold and naked. Besides everything else, I face daily the pressure of my concern for all the churches. Who is weak, and I do not feel weak? Who is led into sin, and I do not inwardly burn?"

Yes, changing our externals can be part of the solution. But a life with ease starts on the *inside* as we answer Jesus' quiet, simple invitation to the weary and burdened—to those who have lost their enthusiasm and sense of peace about life. He says, "Come to me, all you who are weary and burdened, and I will give you rest. Take my yoke upon you and learn from me, for I am gentle and humble in heart, and you will find rest for your souls. For my yoke is easy and my burden is light" (Matt. 11:28–30).

From Jesus we learn how to rest—how to be kind to our souls. At the same time, He teaches us a different perspective on how to work—how to carry even heavy things in a lighter way. I'm still a student in these matters, but a serious one. As part of my soul-care education, occasionally I go away for a personal prayer and solitude retreat. While there, I try to follow this advice someone gave me: *rest well, listen closely, and produce nothing.* Taking time to be by myself in the presence of Jesus has been nothing less than life-changing. I'm due for another retreat soon, I assure you.

> **FROM JESUS WE LEARN HOW TO REST—HOW TO BE KIND TO OUR SOULS.**

It would be impossible to condense all the things I'm learning (much of it through these prayer and solitude retreats) into one short chapter, and there are plenty of excellent books on this topic. (I'll give you a list of my favorites at the chapter's end.) But if you, too, long for a life with ease, there are three crucial components of soul-care to consider: *limits, boundaries,* and *replenishment.*

Portion Control

Limits and *boundaries* may sound like the same thing but, from my perspective, they're actually a little different when it comes to soul-care. Your own hand can illustrate the distinction between the two. Hold your arm out in front of you—bent at the elbow—hand open, with your palm facing toward you. Think of this as a limit; it's self-imposed and deals with your actions and choices.

Now turn your palm (still open) away from you, like a traffic cop ordering a car to stop. That represents a boundary; it's something you impose on others (as you are able) and deals with their actions and choices that could affect you. We need both limits and boundaries to maintain a healthy soul. And, as with so many things in life, it's usually best if we start with what we have (or should have) the most control over—ourselves.

Establishing healthy personal limits is tied to perhaps the most overlooked fruit of the Spirit: self-control. While last on the list in Galatians 5:23, it is vitally important for those who want to lead with love and endure. Think about it. How many leaders come to mind when you consider those who've been disqualified because they lacked self-control and violated their personal limits in one of these areas: finances, sexuality, authority, relationships, or a healthy lifestyle (proper eating, enough rest, and exercise)?

In 1 Corinthians 9:24–27, Paul uses an athletic metaphor to show how the limits we impose on ourselves make us more effective in sharing the gospel. As I confessed earlier in this book, an athlete I am not. But I do know that serious, high-performing athletes limit themselves in certain ways (with what and how much they eat, and by avoiding activities that could harm them or displace training time, for example) in order to break limits in other ways. The same holds true with us. The right kinds of limits help us to be more unlimited in our influence for Jesus.

LIFE WITHOUT LIMITS IS NOT GOOD FOR US.

First Peter 1:13 says, "So think clearly and exercise self-control." It's encouraging to me that God's Spirit is always present to help us do both, especially in a world that scoffs at moderation and personal perimeters. Psalm 17:14 talks about people of the world "whose portion is in this life."

On a flight a few years back, I sat next to a psychiatrist who is the head of a large pain clinic in a major US city. As we conversed, the doctor told me his practice involves working with an elite clientele who are extremely wealthy and, in his words, "very messed up." He described them as being almost the same as homeless addicts in that they have no limits, no boundaries, no responsibilities, no drive, no coping skills, and no meaning in their lives, even though they're fabulously wealthy.

He went on to say that, in most of the cases, his patients had nothing to do with earning their enormous wealth. They had either inherited it or married into it. And because they had no personal limits, they dove head-long into excess, gratifying every possible desire and whim to the max. The result? Pleasure at first, yes. Then eventually pain—physical, emotional, psychological, and spiritual pain. Life without limits is not good for us.

Yet, even as believers, we sometimes live as if we have no limits, even though our violations may run in another direction that, on the surface, appears nobler. We act as if we have an endless supply of energy, emotional capacity, physical and spiritual stamina, and time. But deep inside, we know better. Having it all, doing it all, being it all—that's only something our infinite Creator can claim. We humans live life best when we live it in portions, honoring the God-designed limitations placed upon our existence.

So, what's on your plate? I can't tell you how many times I've said, "I really have a lot on my plate today." Guess what? Most of the time, I'm the one who put it there. And I'm the one who had the most say over the heft of those portions on that twenty-four-hour-sized plate. Far too often I have supersized activity and skimped on rest, reflection, and relationship—the things that truly feed my soul.

Learning how to practice portion-control is Successful Dieting 101, and crucial to anyone who wants to lose a few pounds or maintain a healthy weight. Too much of a good thing is still too much. And too much of a bad thing? Well, that's *really* bad. Lately I've been giving a lot of thought to the concept of portioning and how it affects much more than the numbers on the bathroom scale.

In the middle of that breathtaking passage about God's great faithfulness and how His mercies are new every morning (Lam. 3:21–26), Jeremiah says, "I say to myself, 'The LORD is my portion; therefore I will wait for him.'" The prophet wants us to know that, whatever else is on his plate (and if you read the earlier part of that book, you'll see he was dealing with *a lot),* he claimed God as his true allotment, his share, his slice of life. You can never feel cheated out of the best if you have a plateful of the Holy One!

When I have the Lord as my portion, He teaches me how to apply portion-control to the other things on my daily plate. I learn how to divide what is mine from what should go to someone else—what is for today and what should belong to tomorrow. As I listen to His Spirit, He coaches me on what is too much, or not enough, to take on. He nudges me when I choose a big helping of the trivial that leaves no room for the eternal. With His help, I've been learning to say these words: *What I've done is enough for now.*

Enough Is Enough

Here are just a few of the things I am learning to limit for the sake of my soul. You probably have your own list, but see if you can relate to any of these:

- **Limit the number of times I check my e-mail per day** (ditto for Facebook and Twitter). I went through my inbox recently and unsubscribed to a number of e-zines and updates I was getting but never had time to read. It's probably time to do it again. Time management experts say that choosing (and limiting) set times to be online each day vastly increases overall productivity. And, I would guess, peace.
- **Live with fewer luxuries.** I'm thankful to live in a land of plenty, and I know God is generous with gifts of all kinds. The trouble begins when occasional treats become regular indulgences— when excess often escalates to expectation, and I'm no longer grateful for what I have. For me, that means (among other things) that my favorite barista at Starbucks may not see my face quite so often—for you, it might mean something entirely different. It seems odd to the American mindset that having less may actually mean enjoying life more—that we appreciate what we don't take for granted! But I'm discovering that limiting luxuries creates more breathing room for my soul.

- **Limit speaking, writing, or coaching assignments each month.** While they are my passions, I've learned from experience that if I schedule too many "ministry exertions" back-to-back without down time to replenish my body and spirit, I become depleted and have little to offer that's worthwhile. Additionally, my primary relationships (with Jesus, my husband, our family, and my friends) start to suffer. *What I've done is enough for now.*

- **Limit personal expectations.** This is a tricky one, but I'm realizing that my own high-performance expectations and perfectionist tendencies cause me to pile things on my plate that don't need to be there. Here's one example: when I host people in my home for a meal and stay-over, I tend to "sweat the small stuff." My daughter Jana reminded me recently that while God is our perfecter, He's not a perfectionist. He seems to prefer a little messy imperfection with joyful-heartedness in His kids rather than flawlessness without joy. *Ouch!*

- **Take care with relational obligations.** Even for someone who's a people person, like me, this can be a delicate matter. With higher levels of leadership, especially those that put you in the public eye, relational obligations can become complicated. People feel like they know you (through your speaking or writing), and they may want to deepen that connection.

Sometimes that's appropriate, and I would never exclude that possibility. Without meaning to, however, you can raise expectations for a deeper relational connection with more people than you can possibly sustain. These are *great* people, not stalkers, and you would *love* to get to know them better. It's just that they have no idea about the demands on your schedule or that you're trying like crazy to find enough time to connect with even your closest friends and loved ones.

We'll look at this a little more when we explore the boundaries issue. But I'm learning that it's best *not* to say (even with good intentions), "Hey, let's get together sometime!" or "We should do coffee one of these days!" People may feel your offer was insincere when those meetings don't materialize, or rebuffed when they try to make it happen and you can't fit it in. If the Lord is leading you to deepen that connection, better to wait until you really *can* get together, and *then* call that person and make a definite plan to connect.

- **Replace worry with trust.** When I'm overly anxious, I'm like a toddler fiddling with her mommy's phone and speed dialing 9-1-1 again and again. I create a state of high alert where everything is an emergency, even when it's not. Yes, I would like to eliminate worry altogether. But for now, at the least, I can make efforts to limit its effects on my head and heart. That starts when I admit that I *am* worrying, and I remember how detrimental it is to my soul. From there, I can re-direct my thoughts to something more faith-filled and true.

Philippians 4:6–8 is my go-to scripture for redirecting worry-filled thoughts: "Do not be anxious about anything, but in every situation, by prayer and petition, with thanksgiving, present your requests to God. And the peace of God, which transcends all understanding, will guard your hearts and your minds in Christ Jesus. Finally, brothers and sisters, whatever is true, whatever is noble, whatever is right, whatever is pure, whatever is lovely, whatever is admirable—if anything is excellent or praiseworthy—think about such things."

I wish I had known Corrie ten Boom! Her words about worry still speak powerfully to me, even though she's in heaven: "Worry is a cycle of inefficient thoughts whirling around a center of fear," she said. "Worry does not empty tomorrow of its sorrow, it empties today of its strength."[41] How much better, richer, sweeter, and more Jesus-hearted my life is when I limit my worry time.

- **Limit the times I say yes.** I could write pages about this; others have. American animator and cartoonist, Walt Kelly, who's best known for the classic comic strip, *Pogo*, wrote "We are confronted with insurmountable opportunities."[42] Boy, did he nail it!

  For me, "insurmountable opportunities" means: too many books I should read, too many Web sites I should check out, too many classes I should take, too many seminars I should attend, too many committees I should serve on, too many places I should send my dollars, too many invitations I should accept, too many needs I should meet—too many yes's I should say. Or should I?

I used to live by the motto, "God's will is the closest thing that needs to be done that you can do." While there's some truth to that (we often start right where we are in pursing God's will), I can tell you there are a zillion things that need to be done that you can do! But *should* you? "Insurmountable opportunities."

Because neither you nor I are omnipotent or omnipresent, a yes here, always means a no somewhere else, and vice-versa. How we need God's help to sort out which goes where! It's been a painfully slow lesson, but I am learning not to rush to yes. My good friend, Pastor Bob Stone once said, "Don't let others, or even needs, set your priorities. Needs and opportunities are not necessarily true indicators of God's will."

Earlier I mentioned Alicia Britt Chole's wonderful booklet, *Ready, Set . . . Rest*. In it, she writes, "There is a great deal of difference between saying, 'I volunteer because there is a need' and 'I volunteer because there is a God.' The greatest gift I can give those whom I need to say 'no' to, is being faithful to those whom God calls me to say 'yes' to."[43]

Yes. And that just might be my limit for today.

Brilliant Bridesmaids

Now about those boundaries—they have to do with the restrictions we place on others, as far as their choices and actions affect us. (Hand up, palm out, like a traffic cop, remember?) In chapter seven, we looked at the dangers of defensiveness and unbridled self-protectionism. But there's another side to that coin and, if we're serious about caring for our souls, we need to examine it, as well.

What can you learn from a bridesmaid? My best guess would be how long an ugly dress should stay on its plastic-draped hanger in the back of a closet before it gets thrown out. Jesus, however, found a little more there, which is so like Him. When He told stories with a point (we call them parables), He used a variety of interesting subjects in the starring role . . . pigs, pearls, and prodigals . . . seeds, salt, and sheep . . . just to name a few.

But when Jesus tells a story about "brilliant bridesmaids" I have to take notice. (Okay, so those familiar with the Gospels would probably think of this as the parable of the ten virgins . . . I still like my title better.) It's found in Matthew 25:1–13 and it goes like this in the *New Living Translation:*

> The Kingdom of Heaven can be illustrated by the story of ten bridesmaids who took their lamps and went to meet the bridegroom. Five of them were foolish, and five were wise. The five who were foolish took no oil for their lamps, but the other five were wise enough to take along extra oil. When the bridegroom was delayed, they all lay down and slept. At midnight they were roused by the shout, "Look, the bridegroom is coming! Come

out and welcome him!" All the bridesmaids got up and prepared their lamps. Then the five foolish ones asked the others, "please give us some of your oil because our lamps are going out." But the others replied, "We don't have enough for all of us. Go to a shop and buy some for yourselves." But while they were gone to buy oil, the bridegroom came, and those who were ready went in with him to the marriage feast, and the door was locked. Later, when the other five bridesmaids returned, they stood outside, calling, "Sir, open the door for us!" But he called back, "I don't know you!" So stay awake and be prepared, because you do not know the day or hour of my return.

As a woman who has invested her life in ministry and, by God's grace, been given the opportunity to serve in varying leadership roles, this little story by Jesus captivates my attention. First of all, there's the whole wedding thing. What is it about a wedding that just gets to a girl's heart, whether she's eight or eighty, married or single? I think it's the combination of so many things we love—relationship, romance, commitment, and celebration—all wrapped together in an unforgettable event. I like it that Jesus talked about weddings and performed His first miracle there—and that He included unmarried people in starring roles.

I'M MORE THAN HAPPY TO BORROW MY BRILLIANCE FROM SOMEONE LIKE JESUS, SINCE I'M NOT VERY GOOD AT CREATING MY OWN.

Then there's the whole wisdom theme running through these thirteen verses. Five of the bridesmaids were smart and five were foolish. As a woman in ministry leadership, I prefer being the former, although I've definitely been the latter. And I'm more than happy to borrow my brilliance from someone like Jesus, since I'm not very good at creating my own.

Like other parables, there can be many implications and applications to this one. But within the framework of examining Jesus-hearted leadership, here is my take-away from this story: since God plans for us to live as a light source for others while we're on our way to see Him face to face, we had better make sure we have, and keep, enough lamp oil to burn brightly through an extremely long and dark night.

It's like this. In the story, all ten bridesmaids required a certain amount of lamp oil to perform their roles as attendants at the wedding ceremony. They had a leading role to play and needed to be ready for their part. But five ran out of fuel and tried to borrow from the others.

Now at this point in the story, since Jesus was so generous and always encouraged sacrificial giving ("It is more blessed to give than to receive"), you would expect that He would have had the five wise virgins say: "Of *course* we'll share our lamp oil with you. Help yourself! What's ours is yours."

But He didn't. As a woman in leadership, here's where the story hits home. God doesn't ask me to solve everyone's problems for them, even in my area of experience or expertise. I require a certain amount of "fuel" (spiritual verve—what sustains, empowers, and enlightens me) to perform my role in uniting those in a waiting world with the Bridegroom who longs for them. I can shine my light for anyone and everyone without hesitation. But if I'm going to have any light left to give throughout the long night ahead, I have to understand my limitations and establish boundaries with those who would drain me dry. Otherwise, I might be able to show up, but I will never shine.

If you're a woman who leads others, especially in a spiritual sense, you know what I'm talking about. It is daunting to know what to take on and what to pass on—the needs and the projects are endless. In our desire to serve as God's attendants who literally breathe to make a difference in the darkness of others, we can unwittingly give away our fuel, drop-by-drop, until our own light sputters and dies.

Rather than deceive ourselves that we're the unlimited supply for every need around us, we should take a lesson from the brilliant bridesmaids. They sent their friends to the source so they could get their own fuel ("Go to a shop and buy some for yourselves" v. 9). There is no "special reserve" for ministry leaders. Everyone can, and must, get their own. While I give my light freely, I guard my fuel fiercely so I can burn brightly in a grace-deprived world that has lost its shine. Good boundaries help me do that, but I have sometimes learned that the hard way. Earlier we considered how Jesus made Himself vulnerable, even to fallible and evil people, but we can also follow His example when it comes to setting boundaries. Jesus didn't answer every request with a yes. He actually said no fairly often, both by His words and His actions.

Jesus refused to be the arbitrator between two brothers feuding over an inheritance (Luke 12:13–15). He didn't obligate himself to the mother of James and John who wanted her boys to have prime spots of authority (Matt. 20:20–23). There was even a time while He was talking to the crowd that He was inaccessible to His own mother and brothers, who wanted an immediate audience with Him (Matt. 12:46–50).

We can spend our lives serving on a parallel plane to God's best for our lives—doing things *close to* or *almost like* what we should really be doing. Often, this happens because we try to meet everyone's expectations. Our time, energy, and resources are limited, so it's crucial to know the difference between holy generosity and an unhealthy waste of the precious gifts we steward.

Jesus' words in Matthew 7:6 are perhaps the most direct statement about the need for boundaries: "Do not give dogs what is sacred; do not throw your pearls to pigs. If you do, they may trample them under their feet, and turn and tear you to pieces." It is pointless, He tells us, to give what is holy and valuable—the best we have—to those who will waste it and likely wound us in the process.

The Old Testament book of Nehemiah gives a great picture of someone who put new boundaries in place while building old walls. In chapter six, the scoundrel Sanballat tried to distract Nehemiah from fulfilling God's mission for his life under the ruse of getting together for a friendly chat. Sanballat was the kind of guy who put the "lie" in "reliable," even when issuing a neighborly invitation! Nehemiah didn't buy it:

> "Come, let us meet together in one of the villages on the plain of Ono." But they were scheming to harm me; so I sent messengers to them with this reply: "I am carrying on a great project and cannot go down. Why should the work stop while I leave it and go down to you?" Four times they sent me the same message, and each time I gave them the same answer." (Neh. 6:2–4)

Nehemiah had the whole boundary thing figured out long before people were writing books about it! He put up his "traffic cop hand" towards Sanballat because he understood the importance and potential of his "great project," a project that would affect a nation for generations. Knowing we're called to do greater things weakens the power of big threats from small people.

But the "people-boundaries" required to be Jesus-hearted leaders are not just a question of "who" or "what kind" but often "how many." It's not always about the person who's extra needy or extra evil (like Sanballat). Sometimes it's more a matter of volume. We feel a vague sense of responsibility for multiple needs; we know too much about too many people—their hidden hurts and secret struggles—that others don't know. We want to help as many as possible, as much as possible. So we try to do the *im*possible by taking on more and more.

Here's a familiar scenario from my days as a pastor's wife, although it happens in other settings, too. I walk into the church foyer on a Sunday morning, eager to greet newcomers and chat with friends. Then I notice two women walking towards me from different parts of the room and neither of them sees the other. As I glance around, both make eye contact with me and I know each one has different but similarly crushing things going on in her life that she wants to talk about in the ten minutes before service begins.

The one on the right recently found out her husband is having an affair. The one coming from the left lost her job and is about to lose her home. Neither woman knows what the other is going through—not many people do.

In a split second, I gauge that they're going to reach me at almost the same time. No big deal, right? It is to me. In my mind I'm thinking, *Who do I turn to first . . . who do I make wait?*

Whoever I speak with first may require all the time that's left before I need to go into the service. Will the other person feel slighted, even though I offer to meet with her later? And what about that new couple who just walked in the door looking bewildered about where to go—why isn't someone talking to them and making them feel welcome?

No, I don't have a messiah complex. Okay, maybe just a small one. But while I'm often overwhelmed by the quantity of human need, the real Messiah was not. Jesus walked . . . a lot. And He simply ministered to the people in His daily path—He didn't have a scattered urgency that He would "miss somebody." He didn't look past the face and over the shoulder of the person He was conversing with, to see who might need Him more. He gave attention to the one He was with, in the moment.

> **[JESUS] GAVE ATTENTION TO THE ONE HE WAS WITH, IN THE MOMENT.**

When it came to crowds, Jesus wasn't intimidated. Yet He put space between Himself and the throngs at times, even for His personal safety. Mark 3:9 says, "Because of the crowd he told his disciples to have a small boat ready for him, to keep the people from crowding him." Also He didn't hesitate to withdraw from the multitudes for prayer and solitude, even when He had not met all the needs of every person (Luke 5:15–16). Jesus was available, approachable, even interruptible, yet He still had boundaries.

Rather than be overwhelmed into ineffectiveness by the needs around me, I'm learning to ask myself some questions:

- What person has God put in my path today? How can I be fully present with him or her?
- What are the needs that come to mind when I pray, watch the news, hear a siren, or get a call or e-mail from a friend? Are those assignments to act upon, or prompts for more prayer?
- Can I do what I sense God wants me to do and still be okay when it looks like "not enough," knowing I'm not the only one He's speaking to about the needs around me?

Those wise virgins in Jesus' parable had a good grasp of both limits and boundaries. These days I'm trying to take my cues from them more often. Share my light? Sure! But when it comes to lamp oil, you'll have to get your own. Though I'll be happy to point you to the greatest Source of all—the "oil" of God's Holy Spirit within, which is ample provision for us all. Together, we can shine as brilliant bridesmaids on our way to the wedding that's about to unfold!

• "TRAVELATORS" •

Even with appropriate limits and boundaries in place, simply living uses up life. Sure, there are times when we feel like we're on a people-mover—one of those moving sidewalks at airports, also called *travelators*. Each time I'm on one, I have to resist the urge to lean forward, put one hand behind my back, and take gliding steps like an Olympic speed skater heading for the finish line. (That's not easy to do when you're pulling a carry-on suitcase, so I can usually suppress the urge.)

The wonderful thing about people-movers is this: for every small step you take, you're propelled along at about double the normal rate of walking. For the same effort, you cover more than twice the ground. In fact, you can even stand still and you'll *still* get to your destination. Now that's a great thing! If they would replace the sidewalks in my town with *travelators,* I would get back into a daily walking routine, for sure. But no! In North Bend, Washington, where I live, if you want to get somewhere by foot you have to walk on ground that doesn't move. It's a shame.

I love, and actually pray for, what I have come to call *accelerated accomplishment* days, when every step takes me farther than I would go on my own. On those days, the wind of the Spirit is behind me. Everything I put my hand to is blessed. I achieve more than I expect, and there's even time to connect with those I love.

Then there are those *other* days. It would be helpful if life provided the same automated announcements that people hear on the moving walkways: "Caution. Moving walkway is nearing its end. Please watch your step!" What that *really* means is, if you don't recalibrate your pace and pay extra attention to your footing, you'll do a face plant. I say this as someone who has extracted industrial-strength carpet fibers from my face from time to time. If we're not careful, we can stumble badly when life moves, almost without warning, from a period of accelerated accomplishment to a season that is just the opposite.

I have this Jodi-ism about those *other* days: Everything takes longer than it does. (I say it in my best "Eeyore" voice.) Maybe you're scratching your head over that phrase. Or maybe you know *exactly* what I mean. Things that look fairly simple on paper, the project that should just take a few minutes, the day that seems sensibly planned—these can go so wrong, become so complicated, and take so long.

You wash and dry a load of jeans with a Kleenex in the pocket. (Don't you just love picking a snowstorm of finely-shredded white tissue off your clean clothes?) Your son forgets to take his homework assignment to school and even though you're already running late you agree to drop it by—only to run out of gas three blocks from the school. (It's raining, of course, and naturally, your umbrella is still propped by the front door

· · · · · · · · ·

IF WE'RE TO BE JESUS-HEARTED WOMEN WITH ENDURING INFLUENCE, WE SIMPLY *MUST* BE REPLENISHED, BECAUSE LIFE DRAINS US.

· · · · · · · · ·

at home.) Or you've just spent all morning working on a big project at the office, taking great pains to make sure the wording is just right—then your computer freezes up. (And yes, the last time you saved it was three hours ago.) That's just the ordinary stuff of life. Then, occasionally, there are those bigger crises—the cancer diagnosis, the marriage struggle, the unexpected pay cut— that can *really* send us reeling.

If we're to be Jesus-hearted women with enduring influence, we simply *must* be replenished, because life drains us. When I'm drained . . . when my soul is depleted by dealing with the stress of living or because I lack regular times of refilling in the presence of Jesus, my source of Living Water, then I, too, begin to sink and tilt. I become the "incredible leaning woman" with a cracked foundation and a sense of vertigo about life.

Jesus knew our strength and stamina would dwindle with use and that we would need to be replenished—often. What a refreshing invitation He gives to us who are bone dry and bone weary: "On the last and greatest day of the festival, Jesus stood and said in a loud voice, 'Let anyone who is thirsty come to me and drink. Whoever believes in me, as Scripture has said, rivers of living water will flow from within them'" (John 7:37–38). As He rehydrates our souls we go from staggering to standing to striding once again.

More and more I'm discovering the replenishing power of something I call the *prayer of immediacy*. Romans 12:12 (KJV) says that we are to be "instant in prayer" and 1 Thessalonians 5:17 tells us to "pray without ceasing." For me, one application of those scriptural instructions is on-the-spot prayer. That means when I'm talking with someone about a matter that's disconcerting to one or both of us, or discussing something we long to see happen, I suggest we pray about it right then. It's not a long or flowery prayer. But in some mysterious way, bringing our concerns to God at the moment they come to our attention replenishes our spirits with hope.

Talking *with* God while we talk to others should be as natural as talking *about* God while we talk to others. Including Him as our real but unseen conversation partner transforms where we land on so many subjects.

While it's true that talking things out with those we trust can be therapeutic, the opposite can also be true. The more we discuss our problems and fears and the more we focus on what we *don't* have without the counterbalance of remembering the mighty God who loves us, the more daunting and impossible those things seem. We've probably all met with friends over a meal, expecting a time of heart-sharing and encouragement, only to experience a two-hour gripe or worry session that made everyone feel discouraged and on edge.

When this happens to me, I'm learning to speak up with, "Could we pray about this together right now?" This is important not only for others but for me. Sure I can, and often do, pray about those things later. But have you ever noticed, we often pray differently when we pray with someone else . . . more thoughtfully, more intentionally. We choose our words more carefully and sometimes say them with greater passion in our voices and deeper feelings in our hearts.

Maybe that's why we're encouraged not to forsake coming together (Heb. 10:25) and we're told that wherever two or three of us are gathered, Jesus is there in a special way (Matt. 18:20). And maybe that's why we're told to pray for one another that we may be healed (James 5:16). "Together prayer" is healing prayer.

I've prayed the prayer of immediacy about all kinds of things in all kinds of places: in stores, in restaurants, on airplanes, and in hotel lobbies—sometimes even with people who are not believers in Jesus, as they give me permission. I know many of you do the same.

As a leader, when I begin the meetings I chair these days, I often explain the prayer of immediacy. Even though we begin and frequently end our meetings with prayer, I let those around the table know that anyone, at any time during the meeting, can call for on-the-spot prayer. I love it when someone speaks up and says, "It seems like we're stumped on this issue. Can we just stop and pray about it?" Then we pause and ask God what *He* thinks about the direction our discussion is taking us.

Though a brilliant shaft of light doesn't pierce the ceiling and give us easy answers, the atmosphere changes and our spirits are more receptive to divine guidance and, oddly enough, to each other. As we continue with our discussion, batting around ideas and hammering out plans, there's a greater sense that we're carrying our leadership load *with* Jesus, and it doesn't feel quite as heavy. As Matthew 11:28–30 promises, when we come to Him often and are yoked with Him, He lightens the burden and brings right-in-the-middle-of-the-muddle rest to our souls.

Before we go any farther, I want to point out that you're a multifaceted creation, and it's not just your spirit that needs rejuvenation. Jesus-hearted women have bodies, minds, and emotions. Those parts that make up the whole you are designed by God and require regular refreshing.

What replenishes you? A walk? Working out at the gym? Meeting a friend for coffee and conversation? Watching an old movie on TV with your husband? Reading a good book by the fire? When I was a young pastor's wife, an older, wiser mentor whom I greatly admired told me, "Jodi, sometimes the most spiritual thing you can do is take a nap."

Interestingly, the way I'm replenished is not static. I'm renewed by different things at different times. Sometimes I need to be with people, and sometimes I need to be alone. Kicking back on the deck with my Kindle and a large glass of iced tea might be just the ticket on some days. And as strange as it may sound, I might be completely reinvigorated by spending another Saturday in my sweats, cleaning out closets and drawers. (Okay, that *is* strange, but it's true for me.) In fact, changing things up a bit can be one of the best forms of renewal. Doing something different is sometimes as restful as doing nothing.

Start to notice the things that replenish you. When you find ways to be refilled on a regular basis, you'll have more endurance and you'll be more endearing. It's no fun to be with grumpy women, even if they are great leaders!

• A DEEPER KIND OF REST •

While attending to our physical and emotional well-being can't be separated from true soul-care, there's another, deeper kind of rest and replenishment that Jesus-hearted women desperately need but often are not sure how to find.

When I was a young wife and mom learning the first lessons about what it means to lead, I spent a frustrating day trying to cross off every item on a very long list. At the end of the day, I hadn't even made it a third of the way through my precious list. Furthermore, I was tired, irritable, and short with my family—the ones I love most of all.

I felt thoroughly defeated when I opened my Bible late that night and read again the story of Mary and Martha in Luke 10:38–42. Jesus could easily have substituted my name when He addressed the older sister in this story: "Martha, Martha," the Lord answered, "you are worried and upset about many things, but few things are needed—or indeed only one. Mary has chosen what is better, and it will not be taken away from her."

This was a couple of decades before my dear friend Joanna Weaver wrote one of my all-time favorite books, *Having a Mary Heart in a Martha World: Finding Intimacy with God in the Busyness of Life,* but I sure could have used it back then. (Joanna's book and the sequel, *Having a Mary Spirit,* have sold over a million copies and have been translated into many languages. If you haven't read this outstanding book yet, do yourself a big favor: put it on your *must-read-soon* list.)

The next day, still feeling the sting of all I had chosen instead of that "one thing," I sat down at the piano and wrote these lyrics to remind myself what really matters in the span of a day:

One Thing is Needful

This day is now dawning; I have so much to do.
Yet I hear a soft whisper, as You call me to You.
Will I hurry along now, living life incomplete?
Forgetting one thing is needful, to sit at Your feet.
Chorus
One thing is needful, to sit at your feet,
To wait in Your presence, to feel Your heartbeat.
Other needs beckon, for time they compete,
But one thing is needful, to sit at Your feet.

Handel's Messiah, it isn't, but it's often been the background music playing in my heart on my busiest days since I wrote those lyrics as an overwhelmed twenty-something. Life keeps reinforcing its truth: There are many ways to be replenished, but only *one thing* will seep down into the deepest, driest places of our spirit and, like liquid-grace, restore our parched souls.

• A PORTABLE SANCTUARY •

My wonderful friend Gail Johnsen has a sparkling personality, a sharp mind, and a contagious passion about being on an odyssey with Jesus. She serves as the pastor of spiritual formation at her church. We've dubbed ours an iron-sharpening-iron friendship because every time we manage to steal away for coffee and conversation, we each leave feeling that our spirits have been honed and our hearts enhanced.

Gail and I have been on similar journeys in many ways, but especially in this quest to create more space in our souls for knowing Jesus—for replenishment through spiritual disciplines like solitude, quietness, prayer, and the true rest that comes from trust. She's pulled ahead of me on this expedition and keeps beating down the dense brush of frantic activity to clear a path that others, like me, can follow.

It wasn't always so. As a busy pastor's wife and devoted mom, (not to mention a gifted speaker, writer, and teacher) Gail lived a high-demand, high-output life. But somewhere along the way, she found herself saying, "There's *got* to be something more. I'm dying on the inside. What am I missing?"

As she dared to ask the questions many of us feel deep in our gut but try to subdue with even more doing, Gail's journey into the adventure of knowing Jesus on a whole new level—one that places *being* above *doing*—began. She discovered a new (yet old) approach to living that gives her whole being a rhythm of work and rest that's both biblical and sane.

A big brown, comfy chair where she meets with Jesus and prays, "O LORD, let my soul rise to meet you as the sun rises to meet the day," is a piece of the equation. Gail had no idea the part that chair would play in the harrowing experience she would face. With her permission (and in her own beautiful words taken from her blog at www.gailjohnsen.com), here is Gail's "chair story."

> In solitude, where we create space to attune our hearts
> to the voice of God, where we confront our driven souls
> and stay present to the work of the Holy Spirit in our

lives, what we soon discover is our hearts have become a portable sanctuary which enables us to be present to Christ throughout our day.

In order to maintain this inner quality, however, it will always be necessary to maintain the "place" where solitude can be nurtured. My "place" is an overstuffed, brown leather chair next to an open window with a strategically-placed fountain outside. Unknowingly, my heart is transformed in ways I have yet to understand and fully appreciate. In fact, only through a crisis did I come to realize the fullest extent of that shaping and the absolute necessity of this ongoing process in my life.

"Mom! He's in our lane!"

Even before my daughter screamed the words, I saw him coming, crossing over into my lane of traffic. We were traveling the 60 miles-per-hour speed limit on a two-lane country road.

"I know, I see him," were all the words I could get out. The mind is an amazing thing. In the few seconds I had left before impact, I assessed all the options. I thought about hitting my brakes but knew there was a semi-truck following too close. We would be fatally smashed from behind, for sure. I couldn't swerve right because there was a long, rapidly moving line of oncoming traffic. That didn't seem like a great option either. We were going too fast, he was too close, and we had nowhere to go. Collision was inevitable.

Out of options, I turned my wheels hard left in the direction of the oncoming car. Collision was still eminent but perhaps I could lessen the blow. I remember thinking, *I don't know how this is going to turn out.* Honestly, I didn't think it would end well.

I watched our vehicles speed straight for each other; then just before impact, I closed my eyes. It wasn't how I always thought I would close my eyes in such a situation. I didn't squeeze them tightly shut, covering them with my hands, and grimacing my face, like I do at a terrifying scene in a violent movie. Instead, when I closed my eyes, I was immediately taken back to my big brown, overstuffed, leather chair. It's the chair in the den I sit in every morning to meet with Jesus.

I closed my eyes in the car that day the same way I close my eyes every morning when I shut out all the outer distractions and allow my soul to commune with God: slowly, worshipfully, peacefully, hopefully. I experienced the same Presence in that moment that meets with me daily in the quiet place.

The truth of Isaiah 26:3, "You will keep in perfect peace those whose minds are steadfast, because they trust in you" became a reality. In those daily encounters with Jesus, solitude had become a training ground where my heart had become not only aware of God's presence in the place of quiet, but had, imperceptibly, produced a quality of "steadfastness" in the storm. There was a divine formation and activity going on beneath my consciousness that formed in me a well-trained heart—a grounded, God-centered heart that gave me the ability to be kept in perfect peace in the most dire of circumstances. And more.

I don't remember hearing shattering glass or the sound of crushing metal. I don't remember an impact or coming to a stop. In fact, when I slowly opened my eyes, I expected to see my den, stacks of books, and the pictures of my family. What I saw was our completely demolished van. Every window was shattered, the front end appeared gone. Cars had stopped; people were yelling to see if we were okay. Not only were we miraculously alive, other than some deep bruises, we were fine.

Jesus, literally, saved our lives that day. Yet in a similar fashion, he has saved my soul . . . through solitude in my big brown chair.[44]

I absolutely love Gail's story and how she tells it. It reminds me that, although most of us will never have a green room devoted exclusively for soul-care, we can all have our own "big brown chair" (which comes in many colors, by the way) where we develop a portable sanctuary that goes with us on the fast-moving, sometimes hazardous, freeway of life.

So, my Jesus-hearted friend, take a seat. Someone is waiting.

• JODI'S COACHING QUESTIONS •

- The three main components of soul-care discussed in this chapter are limits, boundaries, and replenishment. What limits have you set for yourself to keep your soul healthy? What other limits *should* you set for yourself to have a more cared-for soul? What one next step could you take in that direction?

- "What I've done is enough for now." Is it easy or hard for you to say (and mean) those words? Why?

- Boundaries—the restrictions we place on the actions and behaviors of others—now that's a tricky issue. What are some of the signs to watch for that might indicate a boundary is in order? How can you keep from swinging the pendulum too far into an overly-guarded life of self-protectionism?

- Without using names or betraying confidential details, tell about a time when you had to put up a boundary in order to keep someone from doing you harm or wasting your resources? What was the result? Is there anything you would do differently if you had it to do over again?

- Have you ever felt like the "incredible leaning woman"? What are the things that drain you most as you lead others? What are the things about ordinary living that sap your energy and joy?

- How are you replenished? How often do you incorporate those replenishing things into your routine? What is the next thing you will do to be rejuvenated?

- Most of us don't have our own green room or Narcissa Whitman's longed for "little chamber" devoted exclusively to the care and feeding of our souls. If you could have a room like that, describe, in as much detail as possible, what it would be like. If you do have a room like that, tell about it.

- I love how Gail says that solitude helps turn our hearts into a "portable sanctuary" where we stay present to Christ wherever we go throughout the day. Are you comfortable with solitude and silence? Why or why not?

- What is your own equivalent to Gail's big brown chair where you meet with Jesus? If you're not satisfied with how you're making the "one thing"—being with Him, unhurried and fully attentive to His presence—the center of your life and your source of soul-care, what is the next "one thing" that might move you in that direction?

• A LITTLE LESSON FOR NEW LEADERS •

As promised, here is a list of my favorite books on the subject of soul-care, although I'm sure there are many more out there. This topic is much bigger than one chapter so I urge you, no matter where you are on the leadership journey, to invest in learning all you can about this issue. Caring for your spirit (as well as your body, mind, and emotions) can keep you from ending up with no lamp oil and a flame that fades away to darkness.

Now for that list:
- *Margin* by Richard A. Swenson, MD
- *Having a Mary Heart in a Martha World* by Joanna Weaver
- *Strengthening the Soul of Your Leadership* by Ruth Haley Barton
- *Invitation to Solitude and Silence* by Ruth Haley Barton
- *The Life You've Always Wanted* by John Ortberg
- *The Worn Out Woman* by Dr. Steve Stephens and Alice Gray
- *Boundaries* by Henry Cloud and John Townsend

• HEART-DEEP IN THE WORD •

Sabbath helps us place a reasonable limit on the *doing* part of our lives—it teaches us to exercise portion control with the heaps of activity we slap onto our daily and weekly plates. Read Exodus 23: 11–12. What does Sabbath look like in your life? What do you want it to look like?

_____

_____

_____

_____

_____

_____

Read 1 Corinthians 6:19–20. How might healthy boundaries and soul-care help us glorify God with our bodies?

_____

_____

_____

_____

_____

_____

_____

Psalm 46:10 says, "Be still and know that I am God." How is stillness related to knowing God? What is your biggest obstacle to finding times of stillness?

_____

_____

_____

_____

_____

_____

_____

_____

chapter ten

DANCING ON PRAYERS

LEADERSHIP QUALITY: VISION

· · · · · · · · · · ·

*If there's a book you want to read,
and it hasn't been written yet, then you must write it.*
— TONI MORRISON

Teresa, with her gorgeous red hair, saucy attitude, and fog-horn laugh was one of my best buddies in high school. Along with the other third of our friendship triad, Kim, a tall willowy beauty, we considered ourselves girl versions of the three musketeers as we adventured our way through the teen years toward adulthood. I'm not sure which of us came up with the idea, but Teresa and I prided ourselves on our micro-penmanship. We competed to see who could write in the most infinitesimal yet legible script possible—to someone with the vision of an eagle that is. Sharpening a pencil to its very finest point, we composed notes to one another in lettering so tiny that, had they been confiscated by our teachers, we figured they wouldn't be able to read them.

285

Long before cell phones and texting we devised our own means of private messaging. Our secrets were contained in smallness.

I smile when I remember those miniature notes. I couldn't possibly write anything nearly that teeny these days. In fact, even my regular-sized penmanship is getting harder to read, probably because I rarely write by hand anymore, except to dash off a short personal note or a thank-you. And to actually *read* tiny text? Forget about it!

I had always heard that vision starts to decline in your forties. They didn't tell me it would be over a weekend at age forty-two, but that's pretty much what happened with me. *So,* I said to myself, *it's true. Outside every young girl, there's an old woman just waiting to get in.* And the reading glasses stashed all over our house prove she's making steady progress.

What a remarkable gift is this thing called vision! Even now, as I glance around my little office-guestroom-writer's lair, I see shapes, textures, patterns, hues, and colors by the hundreds—maybe thousands—within this small space. Looking out the window to my right, I detect movement just over our weathered fence as a breeze gently strums the branches of an enormous alder tree, rippling its rich green leaves into undulating waves against the backdrop of a sea-blue summer sky. I take all this in with one quick, sweeping glance.

In a way that's a complete mystery to me, my eye captures the things "out there" as images and transmits them to my brain, which, in turn, makes sense—and creates pictures—of all that data. To take that phenomenon a step further, with the power of descriptive words I convey these images to you, so that you see a similar picture in your mind's eye. I don't get how it works;

even scientific explanations don't adequately capture the wonder of vision. But I'm so glad I can see!

Like many things, we often take sight for granted. We don't fully appreciate it until it begins to diminish or we're in danger of losing it. And even with this marvelous God-gift of eye-sight we tend to overlook true beauty in the quest for gaudy trinkets.

As I strode through a busy shopping mall one day on a mission to find just the right birthday present, I started to feel annoyed by the throngs of shoppers around me. After all, I was on a buying mission and others, apparently on their own missions, were impeding my plan to find the item quickly, purchase it, and get home. *It would be so much easier to find what I want if it weren't for all these people,* I brooded.

But I slowed my brisk pace as another thought elbowed its way past my selfishness. The most valuable assets in this large retail space were not the pricey clothes, pieces of sparkling jewelry, or selections of expensive merchandise on display—they were the thousands of fellow shoppers walking past me. Each of them—the wan-faced teenager with stringy hair, a holey T-shirt, and vacant eyes . . . the elderly, balding man shuffling along behind his plump, gray-haired wife . . . the pretty young mom in a yellow blouse, skinny jeans, and high-heeled boots, herding three rambunctious kids from store to store—is an eternal soul with a unique story. Each one has an amazing capacity for joy and pain, hope and despair, doing great good or causing deep harm.

NO MATTER WHAT COMES INTO YOUR FIELD OF VISION TODAY, THE MOST PRICELESS THING YOU WILL SEE IS ALWAYS THE NEXT FACE BEFORE YOU.

No matter what comes into your field of vision today, the most priceless thing you will see is always the next face before you. Even as Jesus-hearted leaders, we often need spiritual corrective lenses to read the fine-print of how God is at work in the circumstances around us and how we fit into His plan to transform lives. It's not always obvious. Like the miniature script from my high school days, God sometimes conceals, and also reveals, secrets in smallness—if only we have the vision to see.

Not far from where I live, a little girl named Rachel wanted to do something big for her birthday—something she had learned about at her church. She was turning nine and instead of birthday presents, she set up a donation page asking friends and family to donate nine dollars each to an organization called *charity: water* that helps to provide safe drinking water around the globe. Her goal was to raise $300, which would give fifteen people clean water to drink. She came close—only $80 short, which was no small thing. How many other nine-year-olds not only forego presents but give away $220 on their birthdays?

Then, the unthinkable happened. About a month after her birthday, Rachel Beckwith was riding in a car with her mom and sister on Interstate 90 (just about twenty minutes from my house) when a horrible accident occurred that involved more than a dozen cars. Rachel was the only one seriously injured and three days later, on July 23, 2011, she was taken off life support. The huge outpouring of sympathy in the Seattle area turned to admiration as more and more people found out about the birthday fundraiser Rachel had set up only a month earlier. Then the real groundswell began.

As major news sources around the world picked up Rachel's story and the *charity: water* cause she raised money for, the small seed of compassion that had sprouted in a young girl's heart flourished into a mighty tree of generosity, and donations started pouring in. Within one month, more than 30,000 people from all over the globe had given more than 1.2 million (yes, *million*) dollars!

The small script of a birthday wish contained a divine secret, and I think Rachel saw it first. She had a vision to help fifteen thirsty people. Instead, this small girl with a huge heart gave more than 63,000 people in 149 communities the gift of clean drinking water and the chance at a healthier life.

I don't believe God caused the terrible pile-up on I-90 that took Rachel's life, and I'm sure He wept with Rachel's parents and all who were brokenhearted to lose her. But then God did what He's so good at—He took the sweetness of little dreams along with the bitterness of a big loss and transformed the whole thing into the gush of hope for thousands. All of this happened because a young girl had a vision for others to have clean water.[45]

• FINDING YOUR FOCUS •

You can find many vision references in both the Old and New Testaments. Some of the visions were extraordinary, divine revelations God gave (frequently through dreams) to those who represented Him to others. Often they had to do with the meaning behind circumstances occurring in that time and setting (Amos 3:7; Rev. 1:19; Dan. 2:36–45). Many times they unveiled things about the future that were impossible to know otherwise (Gen. 37:5–10; 41:25; Jer. 31:38–40; Joel 2:28–32). On other occasions, the visions disclosed more about God—His nature, character, and acts (Isa. 6:1–5). Numbers 12:6 says, "He said, 'Listen to my words:

When there is a prophet among you, I, the LORD, reveal myself to them in visions, I speak to them in dreams.'"

But there is another kind of vision implied in Scripture that's less about supernatural revelation and more about catching sight of what God might want to do through our lives. This kind of vision can happen suddenly or develop gradually . . . usually the latter, in my experience.

We catch that vision in different ways: through the inner desires God places in our hearts, by outer circumstances that stir us, and because of the gifts—those God-given talents, abilities, and interests—that beg to be used as an expression of our faith and love. Vision can also grow directly out of God's call on our lives. Usually it's a combination of all the above.

Think about the different visions of people in the Bible. Abraham had a vision to travel to a new place and call it home (Gen. 12:1–9). Joseph had a vision to become a leader worth his family's respect—and another vision to create a massive civic plan to sustain Egypt during famine (Gen. 37:1–11; chapter 41). Moses had a vision to lead his people out of slavery into a land of freedom and promise (Exod. chapters 3–40). David had a vision to build a magnificent temple for the Lord (2 Sam. 7; 1 Chron. 28). Hannah had a vision to bear a child who would be dedicated to God (1 Sam. 1:11–16). Esther had a vision to prevent the genocide of her people (Est. 4:15–9:32). Nehemiah had a vision to rebuild

> THERE'S ONE THING ABOUT A VISION— ONCE IT CAPTURES YOUR HEART AND STIRS YOUR PASSION, IT BECOMES A RUDDER THAT STEERS THE COURSE OF YOUR LIFE.

the broken walls of Jerusalem (Neh. 2:11–20). Paul had a vision to bring the good news to the Gentiles (Acts 22:21; Rom. 11:13). Jesus had a vision to become human, live as God among us, give His life as payment for our sins, conquer death once-and-for-all, secure humanity's redemption, and offer eternal life for all who believe (John 3:13–17).

There's one thing about a vision—once it captures your heart and stirs your passion, it becomes a rudder that steers the course of your life . . . if you pull up the anchor of hesitation and go with it. Some visions are for a season—we follow them until they become a reality and then entrust them to God as He places a new vision with new goals before us.

So, what is *your* vision? Maybe that word seems too daunting—or too ethereal, like a wispy dream that has no tangible connection to the real world. Let me put it another way. In Matthew 6:19, Jesus prayed the Father's will would be done on earth just as it is in heaven. With that as the backdrop, how would you answer these questions?

- If you could do anything you wanted (no limitations) to make this world a better place for people and more in line with God's will, what would you do? (Don't just think about what you *should* do; think about what you would actually *want* to do if you were equipped to do it.)
- When you consider all the injustices, brokenness, pain, and evil associated with humanity, what are the top three things that break your heart? If you could help change any of those, what would be your top priority?

- Make a list of all your gifts—your God-given talents, abilities, and interests. Spend some time prayerfully brainstorming possibilities (as many as you can come up with) as to how you could use those gifts to make a difference.
- Consider carefully any specific sense of God's call upon your life. Revisit when and how that came about. How are you letting that call define the vision for your life? What is the next thing you can do to align your actions to that vision?

Praying through these things will bring your vision into sharper focus. It's like the inquiries your optometrist makes during an eye exam to determine the correct strength of your glasses or contact lenses: *is this better . . . or this? This one . . . or this one?* Even slight adjustments in our vision can shed light on how best to spend our days on this earth.

If you're still stumped after seriously considering those vision-clarifying questions, here's a suggestion: Find someone who has a Jesus-hearted vision you can support and help her out! I believe that some people's vision is to help others achieve *their* visions—and that's a grand aspiration! Our visions usually have permeable borders. It might be *my* vision but I need you to achieve it and vice-versa. Often in that give and take, we begin to share each other's visions—a delightful prospect! God-given vision is contagious—you can catch it and you can spread it.

• THE MIDWIFE MINISTRY •

Years ago I developed a Bible study for women called "The Midwife Ministry." It's based on the story of Shiphrah and Puah, the midwives in Exodus chapter one. Without going into all the details, as I studied these brave women who defied Pharaoh's order to kill all the newborn Hebrew baby boys, I discovered some fascinating things.

A number of biblical scholars and commentators believe that Exodus 1:15, which calls Shiphrah and Puah "Hebrew midwives," should be translated, "midwives to the Hebrews."[46] Part of their reasoning is that their names (Shiphrah and Puah) are Egyptian, not Hebrew, and it's unlikely Pharaoh would have trusted the assignment of infanticide to those who would likely disobey it.[47] Further, these women had intimate knowledge about the Egyptian birthing process and could compare it to the way Hebrew women gave birth (Exod. 1:19). Also, verse 22 says Pharaoh gave the order (to throw all the Hebrew baby boys into the Nile) to "his people."

So, if it's likely that Shiphrah and Puah were Egyptians, Exodus 1:20–21 takes on a deeper poignancy. It says, "So God was kind to the midwives and the people increased and became even more numerous. And because the midwives feared God, he gave them families of their own." That would suggest these two Egyptian women (perhaps previously single or possibly barren) were included in the Exodus, since it's unlikely God would give them families and then leave them in a land decimated by plagues and death.

I learned some valuable Jesus-hearted lessons from that Midwife Ministry study. When we help to birth the dreams of others, God gives us our own dreams. When we protect the

. . . .

**I CAN'T MAKE GOD
ANY BIGGER THAN
HE ALREADY IS, BUT
THE RIGHT VISION,
COUPLED WITH MY
TRANSPARENCY, CAN
HELP OTHERS SEE HIM
MORE CLEARLY AND
IN GREATER DETAIL.**

. . . .

brand-new, fragile ministry efforts of others, God protects our serving endeavors. When we invest in the fruitfulness of others, we become fruitful.

One of the women in that original Bible study was even younger than me—and she never lets me forget it! Cheryl Werth decided to become one of my "ministry midwives" for life—like praying for me when I speak for an event—ever since. This dear friend was one of the few who knew about my dream to be a writer back in those days.

After we both moved and lived several hours apart, we talked by phone occasionally and Cheryl would slip in comments like, "How's your writing going?" or "When are you going to write that book?" She did this gently, but insistently, year after year when I had absolutely nothing positive to report. She'll probably never know how her consistent reminders helped bring my embryonic dream to full term. Hopefully, when she holds this living "baby" in her hands, she will have some idea. *Thank you, dear midwife friend!*

As for her own ministry, I've watched Cheryl blossom through the years. She was always the quietest one in our Bible study, although incredibly insightful when we talked one-on-one. These days this soft-spoken woman is roaring with courage as she ministers to victims of domestic violence and serves in leadership roles at camps for foster kids who've been abused. My "ministry midwife" has birthed some remarkable "babies" of her own, *thank you very much!* And I couldn't be prouder as I get to pray for her and cheer *her* on.

• EYE EXAM •

Once you've identified a Jesus-hearted vision you can get behind (yours or someone else's), there are a number of things to keep in mind if you want to see it endure and flourish.

1. The right vision starts and ends with seeing God more clearly.

My husband once preached a sermon titled "20/20 Vision" and used as his text John 20:20, which says in part, "The disciples were overjoyed when they saw the LORD." Hebrews 12:2 tells us to keep our eyes fixed on Jesus—that's where our faith begins and finishes.

A couple of good questions to test the validity of our visions are: What can I see of Jesus when I step back and view this vision objectively? Will achieving this vision help others to see God more clearly—does it help me to see Him more clearly? If the answer is "not so much" then perhaps you have a goal—maybe even a noble one—but no true vision.

Psalm 34:3 (ESV) says, "Oh, magnify the LORD with me, and let us exalt his name together." A magnifying glass doesn't make an object bigger, but it helps us see the object more clearly and in greater detail. I can't make God any bigger than He already is, but the right vision, coupled with my transparency, can help others see Him more clearly and in greater detail.

2. Don't let others define or limit your God-given vision.

John 6:15 says, "Jesus, knowing that they intended to come and make him king by force, withdrew again to a mountain by himself." Jesus would not settle for being king when He knew He was meant to be King of kings.

When Jana, my daughter, started her ministry with women who were addicts or in jail, someone pulled her aside and advised that she shouldn't get involved with those kinds of ministries. The reason? Since she was raised a "church girl" who had never experienced those kinds of life-controlling problems or extreme situations, she wouldn't be able to relate to those women—and they certainly wouldn't be able to relate to her! As it turned out, nothing was farther from the truth. The women in the treatment centers and jails adored and trusted Jana right away, probably because they could see how much she loved them.

Of course it can be an advantage to have things in common with those we minister to. But if we applied that reasoning to every vision, we would have to tell people like David Wilkerson (who founded Teen Challenge centers for those with addictions) and Mother Teresa (who cared for the destitute and dying in Calcutta, India) they had the wrong vision. And, now that I think about it, that reasoning would pretty much exclude Jesus, too!

Input from wise spiritual advisors about our vision can be good. But please don't let others define or limit a vision you know is from God.

3. Vision requires feet.

Henry David Thoreau said, "If you have built castles in the air, your work need not be lost; that is where they should be. Now put the foundations under them."[48] God doesn't give us glimpses of possibilities so we can sit around years later and think what could have been. Vision requires us to act on what we see.

I've seen this principle so clearly in my best friend and fellow ministry leader, Vicki Judd (who also happens to be my "co-mother-in-law" since her son married my daughter!). David and Vicki are extremely talented musicians (he's been a high-school choir and band teacher for many decades) and as young parents they had a vision that each of their children would also know and appreciate music. They could've seen that dream in their minds' eyes for years without letting it affect their kids. But today, all four of the adult Judd offspring are gifted musicians because their parents put feet to their shared vision: they paid for years of music lessons, insisted on daily practice, and regularly exposed their children to all things musical. No doubt these efforts were costly, time-consuming, and even painfully mundane, at times. But anyone who has experienced a Judd family concert knows the slow march toward their vision has led to magnificent music.

Vicki is a woman of "vision with feet" in other ways, as well. She was part of the staff at the church where my husband was pastor for thirteen years, and she continued to serve there several years after he left. Countless times I've watched her catch a vision for some way to make an eternal difference in her church or community—and then do the hard, unglamorous things to see the vision realized. She's known as "Momma Vicki" to a large number of people, especially the flock of young women (like Tiffany, whom I mentioned earlier in this book) who look to her as a mentor. Vicki is an enduring, endearing, Jesus-hearted woman. It's because she puts feet beneath her vision and walks her way right into people's hearts.

4. Jesus-hearted leaders keep their vision open to course correction.

There's an interesting section of scripture in Acts 16:6–10 that's worth another look:

> Paul and his companions traveled throughout the region of Phrygia and Galatia, having been kept by the Holy Spirit from preaching the word in the province of Asia. When they came to the border of Mysia, they tried to enter Bithynia, but the Spirit of Jesus would not allow them to. So they passed by Mysia and went down to Troas. During the night Paul had a vision of a man of Macedonia standing and begging him, "Come over to Macedonia and help us." After Paul had seen the vision, we got ready at once to leave for Macedonia, concluding that God had called us to preach the gospel to them.

Wow, that's a whole lot of course correction—some significant no's to a group of people with a noble vision: to preach the gospel to those who need to hear. But here's the thing. In order to go where you're supposed to go, you have to *not* go where you're *not* supposed to go. In order to marry the one you're supposed to marry, you have to *not* marry the one you *shouldn't* marry. In order to serve where you're supposed to serve, you have to be unencumbered from serving in the place that's not right for you. And no one knows more about all these things than God, so trust your vision to His course correction.

Kerry Clarensau is a gifted author (check out her wonderful books *Love Revealed* and *Redeemed!)* and an exceptional national leader of women. She's also a dear friend who hosted me a few years back when I spoke for her church in Wichita, Kansas, where she lived at the time. During my visit, Kerry took me for a leisurely afternoon stroll through the city's beautiful Botanical Gardens. As we walked and talked our way through the many acres of that lovely garden, we came upon the butterfly house—a 2,880 square foot, net-covered exhibit. The fifty species of native and exotic butterflies fluttering all around us looked like a colorful garden of flying flowers that had somehow learned the secret of release from their earth-bound roots.

GOD KNOWS THAT IF WE DON'T CLOSE THE DOOR TO THE PAST, WE'LL LOSE THE BEAUTY AND WONDER HE'S PREPARED IN THE SPACE AHEAD.

Before we could enter that magical space, though, we had to walk through a little ante room with a sign that read something like this, "Be sure to close the door behind you before opening the door in front of you so the butterflies don't get out."

I've thought about that little sign many times since. Not only do our visions require a healthy dose of course correction, sometimes God waits for us to close the door behind us before He opens the door of opportunity in front of us. He knows that if we don't close the door to the past, we'll lose the beauty and wonder He's prepared in the space ahead.

I think that's, in part, what Paul was referring to when he discussed his vision and goal in Philippians 3:12–16. In verses 13 and 14, he talked about "forgetting what is behind" in order to press on towards what is ahead.

Are you willing to let God course-correct your current vision? What doors do you need to close firmly behind you so that no butterflies of blessing escape?

5. Jesus-hearted vision shows us the unseen, the things that others miss.

Second Corinthians 4:16–18 says, "So we fix our eyes not on what is seen, but on what is unseen, since what is seen is temporary, but what is unseen is eternal." This is *so* important, since most of us will live for a long time without really knowing whether our best efforts are paying off or not. There's an ambiguity to our fruitfulness, at least for a season. Once in a while we catch a glimpse that what we're doing is making a difference; most of the time, however, we're in the dark. But that's where seeds are supposed to live.

Dr. Peter Kuzmic, a Slovenian-born theologian, said "Hope is the ability to hear the music of the future. Faith is having the courage to dance to it today." If anyone needs to hear music of the future and learn to dance to it today, it would be church planters. My friend Stacy Newell is a Jesus-hearted woman who, along with her husband, Mark, and their two darling daughters, planted a church in Vancouver, Washington.

In the course of working on the building where their church plant would meet, Stacy found out just how significant the unseen can be, especially in sustaining the enduring vision needed to start a new church. She allowed me to share this powerful story (in her own words) from her blog at www.stacynewell.com:

I feel like my eyes were opened to a bigger plan on Monday. A plan that has been in the making for literally generations.

First of all, let me give you some background. It all began three years ago this week when we first looked at the bar to move our church into. We felt like God gave us a gift in our landlord, and he helped us by cutting the rent to pennies on the dollar in order for us to get into the building at all. We had very little money left for any fixing up of the place, so we did what we could with a massive effort of volunteers and donations. It was devastatingly exhausting.

It was on one of those work days that a man named Jerry came into the building to ask what we were doing. When we told him we were launching a church, he began to cry. For months he had been coming here to pray because he felt like God had a plan for this corner of our community. We were the fulfillment of those prayers. I still remember thinking how humbling it was to be a part of the story.

And this Monday, standing in the exact same place I was standing when Jerry walked in years ago, I looked down at the now, finally-bare concrete floor due to our renovations, and began to cry.

There, at my feet, written all over our floor were scriptures, prayers, and messages to Jesus. Decades ago there was another church in our building, and they had consecrated this space by writing what was on their heart for this place. They had dedicated our auditorium before most of our congregation was out of diapers.

I thought to myself about the irony of the many times we had all stood there worshipping Jesus with His Word literally under our feet. I thought about the nightclubs that had moved in before us, and how so many people so far from God had danced with scriptures surrounding them. I thought about the fact that God has been fighting for this corner for decades. And for this season, He chose us to be His placeholders.

It was one of those times when I felt very small in the enormity of an almighty God. I once believed our church plant was the beginning of something. No, no. It's the continuation of a plan that has many players, many beginnings, and many endings. It's all very purposeful and it's all ordered. And I'm humbled, moved, and completely willing to allow God to use us however He wants to accomplish His ultimate plan.

Your move, God. Your move.

Stacy's beautiful blog (which always makes me cry, no matter how many times I read it) reminds me to have the kind of vision that looks for the invisible God underneath, below the surface of life's more obvious layers. Often, without even realizing it, we're walking on mystery. And just when I think my prayers are being trampled on by careless feet, perhaps they're being danced upon instead, by those who hear the music of the future.

• JODI'S COACHING QUESTIONS •

- Have you ever discovered a secret of God in something that seemed small and insignificant at first glance? If so, tell about it.

- Use the list on pages 291 and 292 to define or further refine your vision. If you're with others, share as much as you feel comfortable with those in your group.

- What do you think it means to put feet to a vision? Give any specific examples you can think of from real situations.

- Have you ever had to close a "door" behind you in order to open one in front of you? Was that easy or hard? What did you learn from that experience?

• A LITTLE LESSON FOR NEW LEADERS •

It's easy to overlook the unseen, to miss the music of the future, to forget that we might be "dancing on prayers" as we go about our seemingly feeble attempts to serve God and to worship Him as He deserves. Stacy wisely recognized that their church planting vision and efforts were just the continuation of something God had been doing for a long time and through many people. This realization renewed her determination to trust Him for what He was up to on their watch.

Sometimes we mistakenly believe that when it comes to fulfilling a certain God-given vision everything rises or falls solely on our efforts. We can take comfort from Stacy's words: *No, no. It's the continuation of a plan that has many players, many beginnings, and many endings. It's all very purposeful and it's all ordered.*

Rest in knowing that your vision is just one part of the bigger picture God sees, and *oversees,* with great precision. Rest, my Jesus-hearted friend . . . then put on your dancing shoes!

• HEART-DEEP IN THE WORD •

Read Exodus 1:8–21. Has someone served as a "midwife" to your ministry vision? Tell what things she (or he) did to help birth your dreams. How can you be a "ministry midwife" for someone else?

_____

_____

_____

_____

_____

_____

_____

_____

_____

Second Corinthians 4:18 says, "So we fix our eyes not on what is seen, but on what is unseen, since what is seen is temporary, but what is unseen is eternal." With so many sights all around us, how can we gaze steadily at the unseen, eternal things?

_____

_____

_____

_____

_____

_____

Read 2 Kings 6:15–17. What can we learn from this story about having our eyes opened to spiritual realities that exist beyond our five senses? How important is that to leadership? In what area do you most need God to increase your vision?

_____

_____

_____

_____

_____

_____

EPILOGUE

. . . .

S tarting to write a book is a little like setting off on an extended journey to a destination that's mostly unclear, using a map that could be mistaken for a crazy person's midnight attempt at artwork. Some days, on this long trek, the path is obscured by a thick, mind-numbing fog and you're not quite sure which twists and turns will actually get you there—wherever "there" might be.

Once in a while, though, when you round a bend in the road, the mists part and you come upon something surprising because of its utter clarity—something that takes your breath away due to its profound significance to life and faith. And suddenly the odyssey is worth every grueling step.

That's been the case with me as I've written *The Jesus-Hearted Woman.* Many times while laboring to write about one of the ten qualities so crucial to being an enduring and endearing leader, I've discovered something remarkably fresh . . . something that startled my predictable way of thinking, encouraged the deeper places in my heart, or inspired my sagging hopes.

At the same time—if I'm being completely honest—there were also many times when the bigger revelation was just how *Jodi-hearted* I am, instead of how *Jesus-hearted.* I still have miles to go before I fully bear the image of the Holy One living in me.

Perhaps you feel that way, too. And we both know there are other leadership qualities I could have added to this book—other paths of growing, and learning, and becoming. This journey towards enduring and endearing influence can seem pretty daunting.

Yet I take heart in this: all these leadership qualities (and infinitely more) are personified in Jesus. Colossians 2:9–10 gives me great hope: "For in Christ all the fullness of the Deity lives in bodily form, and in Christ you have been brought to fullness."

As we make more and more room for Jesus in our souls, He transforms our hearts, develops the qualities we need to serve Him best, and ultimately brings us to fullness. This, too, is a long journey with many twists and turns along the way. But His Spirit is navigating our steps, and He knows just how to get us there on time.

And as we go, it's life-giving to know that He has significant things for us to do along the way—things that make a difference now and impact eternity. Les Welk, a good friend and Team Leader at the Northwest Ministry Network, shared something with our staff after he had been on a mission trip to Haiti a few years ago.

While there, Les was moved by the gatherings of believers who were among the poorest of the poor. Many had witnessed the early deaths of close friends and family due to extreme malnutrition, disease, or natural disasters. Yet, amazingly, they were exceptionally joyful and lived with a strong sense of destiny.

Les brought a little booklet home from his trip entitled *God Is No Stranger,* a compilation of the unvarnished, yet powerful prayers of those Haitian believers. That morning in our staff meeting, our eyes and our hearts welled up as he read one of these prayers to us: "Lord, if we are alive today in spite of hurricanes, hunger, and sickness, we should say *Thank You, Lord. We must be here for a purpose.*" [49]

That's true of you, too, my friend. God would have no trouble calling you home if He were finished with you. Despite all you've been through and all the challenges ahead, you are *alive*—and

Christ, Himself, lives in you! You must be here for a purpose. The possibilities are stunning!

My prayer for you, as you close the pages of this book and take the next steps on your journey towards enduring and endearing, Jesus-hearted influence, is from Ephesians 3:16–21 (NLT):

> I pray that from his glorious, unlimited resources he will empower you with inner strength through his Spirit. Then Christ will make his home in your hearts as you trust in him. Your roots will grow down into God's love and keep you strong.
>
> And may you have the power to understand, as all God's people should, how wide, how long, how high, and how deep his love is. May you experience the love of Christ, though it is too great to understand fully. Then you will be made complete with all the fullness of life and power that comes from God.
>
> Now all glory to God, who is able, through his mighty power at work within us, to accomplish infinitely more than we might ask or think. Glory to him in the church and in Christ Jesus through all generations forever and ever! Amen.

ENDNOTES

. . . .

1. Robert Frost, *The Poetry of Robert Frost: The Collected Poems, Complete and Unabridged* (New York: Henry Holt and Co., 1969), 105.
2. Corrie ten Boom, *The Hiding Place* (Grand Rapids, MI: Chosen Books, 2006), 12.
3. http://abcnews.go.com/search?searchtext=whatwouldyoudo#30_
4. Jeff Iorg, *The Painful Side of Leadership: Moving Forward Even When it Hurts* (Nashville: B & H Publishing Group, 2009), 104.
5. Anne Morrow Lindbergh, *Gift from the Sea* (New York: Pantheon, 1991), 26.
6. Maureen O'Hagan, "When You Discover Your Husband Robs Banks," *The Seattle Times,* July 24, 2010.
7. Tony Stoltzfus, *Coaching Questions: A Coach's Guide to Powerful Asking* (Virginia Beach, VA: Tony Stoltzfus, 2008).
8. Charles Dickens, *David Copperfield* (New York: Vintage Press, 2012).
9. Wayne Booth, "Individualism and the Mystery of the Social Self" in *Freedom and Interpretation,* ed. Barbara Johnson (New York: BasicBooks, 1993), 81.
10. Joanna Barsh, Susie Cranston, and Geoffrey Lewis, *How Remarkable Women Lead: The Breakthrough Model for Life and Work* (New York: Crown Business, 2009), 125.
11. Ibid., 130.
12. Ann Voscamp, *One Thousand Gifts: A Dare to Live Fully Right Where You Are* (Grand Rapids: Zondervan, 2010), 164–165.
13. David Wilkerson, *The Cross and the Switchblade* (New York: Jove Publishing, 1986).
14. www.brainyquote.com/quotes/authors/c/charles_kingsley.html
15. Marsha Blackburn, *Life Equity* (Nashville: Thomas Nelson, 2008), 5.
16. Alicia Britt Chole, *Ready, Set . . . Rest: On Rest and Establishing the Discipline of Regular Prayer Retreats* (c. Alicia Britt Chole, 2010), 2.

17. Alicia Britt Chole, *Anonymous: Jesus' Hidden Years . . . and Yours* (Nashville: Thomas Nelson, 2006), 5.
18. Jon Acuff. From Michael Hyatt's Intentional Leadership blog: http://michaelhyatt.com/avoiding-one-great-temptation-every-new-dream-faces.html
19. A special thanks to Dr. Ava Oleson and all the amazing Jesus-hearted women who gave me permission to share their stories in this book!
20. Special thanks to my dear friend "Cindy" for letting me share her story.
21. A. A. Milne, *The Complete Tales of Winnie-the-Pooh* (New York: Dutton/Penquin, 1996), 266.
22. Andrew Murray, *Abide in Christ* (Kensington, PA: Whitaker House, 1979), 219–220.
23. Henry Cloud, *Necessary Endings* (New York: HarperCollins Publishers, 2010), 120.
24. Lettie Cowman, *Streams in the Desert,* ed. J. Reiman, (Grand Rapids: Zondervan, 1997), 69.
25. http://www.msnbc.msn.com/id/40674270/ns/us_news-crime_and_courts/t/woman-describes-hitting-school-board-gunman/
26. Corrie ten Boom, *The Hiding Place* (Grand Rapids: Chosen Books, 1971).
27. Information from Barnes' Notes on the Bible http://www.sacred-texts.com/bib/cmt/barnes/index.htm, which is part of the Biblos website commentaries: http://bible.cc/isaiah/41–10.htm
28. J. R. R. Tolkien, *Lord of the Rings* (Boston, MA: Mariner Books, 2012).
29. Special thanks to Ginger for letting me share her story.
30. http://science.nationalgeographic.com/science/archaeology/emperor-qin/
31. Daniel Goleman, *Emotional Intelligence: Why It Can Matter More Than IQ* (New York: Bantam, 2006).
32. Barsh, Cranston, and Lewis, *Remarkable Women,* 232.
33. Doris Kearns Goodwin, *Team of Rivals: The Political Genius of Abraham Lincoln* (New York: Simon & Schuster, 2006).
34. http://www.notable-quotes.com/k/korns_lewis_f.html
35. http://newyork.cbslocal.com/2011/04/12/emergency-recordings-of-airbus-superjumbo-jet-clipping-commerce-flight-at-jfk-released/

36. Richard Alleyne, "English Language Has Doubled in Size in the Last Century," *The Telegraph,* December 16, 2010, http://www.telegraph. co.uk/technology/internet/8207621/English-language-has-doubled-in-size-in-the-last-century.html, accessed June 22, 2012.

37. Peter Scazzero, *Emotionally Healthy Spirituality* (Nashville, TN: Thomas Nelson, Inc., 2011).

38. Whitman Mission National Historic Site Web site: http://www.nps. gov/whmi/index.htm

39. Ibid.

40. Ruth Haley Barton, *Invitation to Solitude and Silence: Experiencing God's Transforming Presence* (Downer's Grove, IL: InterVarsity Press, 2004), 55.

41. http://www.goodreads.com/author/quotes/102203.Corrie_Ten_Boom

42. http://www.brainyquote.com/quotes/authors/w/walt_kelly.html

43. Chole, *Ready, Set . . . Rest,* 3.

44. Big thanks to Gail Johnsen for the use of her story. Check out her blog at: http://gailjohnsen.com

45. See http://www.charitywater.org/blog/rachels-gift/ for more about Rachel's touching story.

46. Albert Barnes, *Notes on the New Testament: Exodus-Ruth* (1973; repr., Grand Rapids, MI: Baker, 1970), 8.

47. E. M. Zerr, *Bible Commentary* (Bowling Green, KY: Guardian of Truth Publications, 1954), 104.

48. http://www.brainyquote.com/quotes/authors/h/henry_david_ thoreau.html

49. Eleanor Turnbull and Sandra Burdick, *God Is No Stranger* (Grand Rapids: Baker Book House, 1970), 5.

ABOUT THE AUTHOR

. . . .

Jodi Detrick is an author and religion columnist for *The Seattle Times*. As a certified personal coach and much-in-demand speaker for many groups across America, Jodi talks to people at heart-level about things that matter most. She has a Doctor of Ministry degree in Leadership from the Assemblies of God Theological Seminary and is an adjunct professor at Northwest University in Kirkland, Washington. Jodi is currently the Chairperson for the national Network for Women in Ministry, having served alongside her pastor-husband, Don, in ministry for many years. Together they live in the rainy Pacific Northwest where lattes are always a good idea.

You can find more information about Jodi at www.jodidetrick.com. Learn more about being a Jesus-hearted woman at www.jesusheartedwoman.com.

TO ORDER MORE COPIES OF THIS BOOK

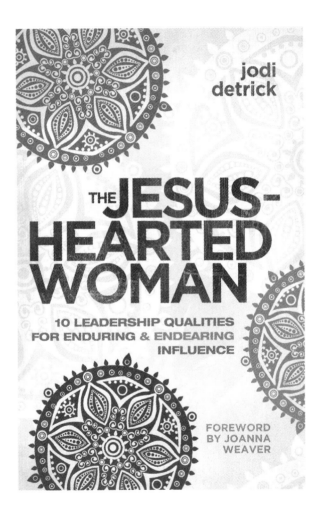

To order additional copies of this book visit
www.influenceresources.com